The Brothers Grimm and Folktale

The Brothers Grimm and Folktale

Edited by

James M. McGlathery

with

Larry W. Danielson, Ruth E. Lorbe,
and Selma K. Richardson

University of Illinois Press
Urbana and Chicago

FIRST PAPERBACK EDITION, 1991

©1988 by the Board of Trustees of the University of Illinois
Manufactured in the United States of America
1 2 3 4 5 C P 5 4 3 2 1
This book is printed on acid-free paper.

Library of Congress Cataloging-in-Publication Data

The Brothers Grimm and folktale / edited by James M. McGlathery, with
Larry W. Danielson, Ruth E. Lorbe, and Selma K. Richardson.
   p. cm.
   Includes index.
   ISBN 0-252-01549-5 (cloth : alk. paper).
   ISBN 0-252-06191-8 (paper : alk. paper)
   1. Kinder- und Hausmärchen. 2. Grimm, Jacob, 1785–1863—Criticism
and interpretation. 3. Grimm, Wilhelm, 1786–1859—Criticism and
interpretation. 4. Fairy tales—Germany—History and criticism.
5. Folk literature—History and criticism. I. McGlathery, James
M., 1936–
PT921.B76 1988
398.2′0943—dc19   88-3765
                                                          CIP

Digitally reprinted from the first paperback printing

UNIVERSITY OF ILLINOIS PRESS
1325 SOUTH OAK STREET
CHAMPAIGN, ILLINOIS 61820-6903
WWW.PRESS.UILLINOIS.EDU

Contents

Preface

Grimms' Fairy Tales are as much in the public consciousness today as ever. Within a few decades of its first publication, in two volumes (1812 and 1815), and long before the deaths of the Brothers Grimm (Wilhelm in 1859 and Jacob in 1863), their collection of folktales became known throughout Europe and beyond. In this century, Walt Disney's film versions of fairy tales, beginning with *Snow White* in 1937, helped add to familiarity with the stories. In recent years, widespread enthusiasm for every sort of fantasy, from science fiction to horror movies, has included a strong upswing of interest in fairy tale.

Like popular enthusiasm for fairy tale, scholarly study of folktale has persisted since the time of the Grimm brothers, and beginning in the late 1960s and early 1970s has experienced a tremendous increase. The two-hundredth anniversary of the brothers' births—Jacob in 1785, Wilhelm the following year—provided occasion for scholars and interested members of the public to come together at festive gatherings at a number of places around the world.

To our knowledge, the largest of these celebrations was held 10–12 April 1986 at the University of Illinois at Urbana-Champaign. This International Bicentenary Symposium on the Brothers Grimm gave rise to the present volume of essays, most of which were presented as papers there. This volume's aim is to offer a broad picture of the current state of scholarly research and critical thought on *Grimms' Fairy Tales*. The speakers at the symposium were asked to address their remarks as much as possible to the general educated public, not to other scholars alone; and the same principle has been observed in collecting the essays. It is hoped that this book will prove interesting and informative to a wide English-speaking audience.

Concern was taken to include as many of the currently prominent critics of folktale as possible, and particularly to improve English-speakers' acquaintance with research being done by scholars writing in German. To this end, I have translated the essays by Fink, Rölleke, and Scherf. In addition, Nitschke and Röhrich, who usually publish in German, have offered their essays here in English. Five of the fourteen contributions—those by Hearne, Röhrich, Rölleke, Scherf, and Mieder—have appeared earlier, but only Hearne's and Röhrich's are available in English.

The Introduction was written by the editor of this volume, assisted by the coeditors, who also helped organize and conduct the symposium. I would like to take this opportunity to thank Dr. Walter Breuer, director of the Goethe Institute, Chicago, for his support of the idea of the symposium and for the important funding he provided when the plan became a reality. Gratitude is due also to the Deutsche Forschungsgemeinschaft for additional help in making attendance by West German scholars possible. The principal funding for the symposium came from the Chancellor of the University of Illinois at Urbana-Champaign and the Department of Germanic Languages and Literatures, with cosponsorship from a dozen other units on the campus. I wish also to thank Judith McCulloh, executive editor of the University of Illinois Press, for her interest and encouragement in the preparation of the volume, and Patricia Hollahan of the Press for her many suggestions at the copyediting stage. Finally, I owe a huge debt of gratitude to Sheila Auer for typing the manuscript, not to mention her patience in seeing to so many details that helped make the symposium successful.

JAMES M. MCGLATHERY

Introduction

Grimms' Fairy Tales is a classic of world literature and will remain so. That is beyond dispute. Little else about this amazing work, however, is certain or uncontested. The essays here attempt to address some of the most important questions concerning this collection of stories that the brothers Jacob and Wilhelm Grimm published as young men and then revised throughout the course of their lives.

As the considerable stir occasioned by the publication of *The Uses of Enchantment: The Meaning and Importance of Fairy Tales* (1976) by the noted child psychologist Bruno Bettelheim demonstrated, the ultimate question is the point or meaning of these stories, individually and taken together. In the case of tales that are essentially the invention of a known author, such as those by Hans Christian Andersen, answers to this question may be sought with the help of biographical research and comparison of the stories with one another. With the Grimms' tales, however, the situation is the reverse. The style and manner of the telling of the stories is often the Grimms' own, but this is almost never the case with the tales themselves. The Grimms functioned as transmitters, retellers, or adapters of existing narrative material, and indeed saw this as their role. For *Grimms' Fairy Tales,* there are many authors and transmitters. It cannot be known with certainty just who the inventor of a given tale was. Biographical research on the Grimms, therefore, can tell us much about the meaning that the Grimms may have lent to the stories in transmitting them, but not about a given tale's prior meaning or significance. For answers to that question, scholars must necessarily look beyond the Grimms.

This problem of studying the meaning of folk narrative in general is addressed in the opening essay, by Lutz Röhrich. As he notes, folklorists have tended to avoid the question of meaning, preferring descriptive, structural, historical, geographical, and other approaches where folkloristic scholars can feel themselves on firm and familiar ground. He argues for a reversal of this tendency to avoidance. Folklorists must dare to interpret the tales. In doing so, they will be able to bring to bear their knowledge of the time and place of the given version of the story. Each version, that is to say, has its own meaning, within a given cultural context. There are, moreover, the questions of the individuality of the teller and the conventions of the narrative genre within which—consciously or unconsciously—the inventor or transmitter is operating. As Röhrich points out, though, to inquire about a tale's meaning is to ask, too, why the story was passed on, and ultimately why folktales, generally, have survived.

Following Röhrich, Alan Dundes attempts to shed light on the meaning of one of the most famous folktales, Little Red Riding Hood. He applies the folklorist's method of taking into consideration all known versions of the story, to arrive at an idea of the tale's original or authentic form. His aim in this is to avoid the pitfall, common among nonfolklorists, of claiming to discuss a well-known tale when they actually concern themselves with only one text, or several, instead of the many versions that folklorists have uncovered. Since Dundes aims, at the same time, to discover the story's meaning, he surveys interpretations, going back to the beginnings of folktale research in the Grimms' century, and then offers his own, psychoanalytically oriented answer. His argument with other psychoanalytical interpretations is that they have been made in ignorance of the way the story has been transmitted in oral tradition. Dundes thus provides an example for other folklorists of how to venture into the area of interpretation without abandoning their insistence on taking into account all known versions and attempting to establish which are authentic with regard to oral tradition and which are not.

While Dundes concerns himself with discovering the basic features of an often-told tale as they may have been preserved through oral transmission, Kay Stone delves into the question of what happens to a famous story at the other end, when a folktale that has become a literary classic is then adapted by the modern commercial media. Her example is the Disneys' version of the Grimms' "Snow White." Just as the Grimms' tale was not a version that existed exactly as such in oral tradition, the Disneys' *Snow White and the Seven Dwarfs* fundamentally altered the sense of the Grimm version. Stone examines the extent to which these variations between the oral versions, the Grimms' printed text, and the Disneys' film reflect differences in the medium itself. A fundamental distinction is that both in print and in film a story is fixed, and in that sense authoritative, while in oral tradition tales may be narrated many ways without ceasing therefore to be thought of as genuinely and authentically the same story. As Stone demonstrates, however, the fixing of a tale in print or film nevertheless does not prevent the audience from receiving the story in diverse ways and re-creating it differently in their own imaginations, just as more obviously happens in oral tradition.

The Grimms' role in this sort of mediation between fixed versions and oral tradition is the subject of Linda Dégh's investigation, specifically the interdependence of oral and literary tradition, and especially the influence of the Grimm collection on oral storytelling. Instead of looking for signs of the Grimms' influence merely in order to reject such tales as not authentic, Dégh argues that these stories should be studied for what they can show about how a given storyteller, at a particular time and in a particular place, changed the tale, and why these deviations from the Grimm version are significant. Dégh's own fieldwork in a village in post–World War II Hungary showed that the influence of the stories from books on oral storytelling was very considerable, and—directly or indirectly—was chiefly from the Grimms' collection. She is able, also, to point to other similar findings. She argues that when folklorists neglect to study the way booktales are adapted by oral storytellers, they are missing a prime opportunity for gaining insight into folk narrative processes. Dégh points, too, to the importance of studying the intriguing subject of the Grimms' tales' persistent influence on the modern media and popular commercial culture generally.

As has become more widely known, the Grimms' collection of tales was itself heavily influenced by literary versions of the stories, both directly and indirectly. Moreover, the Grimms and their collaborators, in most instances, tailored their stories to fit their ideas of what folktales should be like. A recent book, *One Fairy Story Too Many: The Brothers Grimm and Their Tales* (1983), by John M. Ellis has gone so far as to charge the Grimms with literary fraud, arguing that they passed off their stories as authentic tales from the folk when they knew they were not. Donald Ward, in his essay, undertakes a rebuttal to Ellis's indictment. Ward examines the wording of the Grimms' prefaces to the editions of their collection and concludes that they were more candid about their sources and their treatment of them than Ellis, who examined the same material, was willing to grant. Ward finds no evidence of bad faith on the Grimms' part. As he observes, they did clearly indicate that they were retelling stories in their own way, while trying at the same time to remain faithful to the originals; and they did not hide from their readers that their folktales were part of an Indo-European heritage and were thus, in that sense, not exclusively or necessarily of German provenience.

Precisely the complicated history of the texts that make up the Grimms' collection, and the question of how to approach this problem, is the subject of Heinz Rölleke's essay. Like Dundes, Rölleke emphasizes the importance of arriving at an authentic, original version of a given tale, to the extent that this is possible in an individual case. But here the concern is with establishing the Grimms' original or ultimate sources, not necessarily with the very first, or most typical, version of the story as it may have existed in oral tradition. Rölleke's approach, in other words, is philological rather than folkloristic. Similarly, while Rölleke shares Röhrich's and Dégh's appreciation of the artistic individuality of each version of a tale, his concern in this essay is with the process through which the stories assumed the form they came to have in the Grimms' *Kinder- und Hausmärchen.*

Among the types of changes made in their texts by the Grimms was the addition of folk sayings and curious figures of speech to which Wilhelm Grimm himself referred in the preface to the sixth edition (1850). This deliberate effort to incorporate proverbial expressions into the texts of the stories is investigated by Wolfgang Mieder. His aim is to demonstrate not only the frequency and type of such additions, but to show that they represented an attempt to conform certain tales to a style that reflects folk speech and, at the same time, to improve the telling of the stories artistically. Thus, while Mieder accepts the fact that the Grimms made changes for artistic reasons, he rejects Ellis's charge that they falsified their sources and attempted to deceive their readers.

Maria Tatar deals with another question about the Grimms' handling of their texts. Taking Charles Perrault's "Bluebeard" as her starting point, she argues that literary versions of the story consistently blame the victim for the murderer's criminality. Such versions, she claims, increasingly turned the story from a folktale about a maiden's rescue from a murderous ogre to a warning against female curiosity.

She supports this argument by referring to examples from the history of illustrations of the tale. With regard to the Grimms, she notes that, while they dropped the Bluebeard story from their collection beginning with the second edition (1819), the version of it they did include, "Mary's Child," stresses the theme of female curiosity even more. Tatar points out that, at the same time, two stories about beastly murderers in the Grimm collection do not emphasize that theme, but rather the heroines' successful defeat of their oppressors. She concludes that in oral tradition the Bluebeard story must have had this emphasis, too, before Perrault made it into a cautionary tale.

Among the Grimm texts that are considered to be closest to oral tradition are those they had from a retired soldier. Gonthier-Louis Fink examines the extent to which this soldier's tales reflect a particular social reality. Fink thus provides an example of the type of investigation that Röhrich and Dégh recommend in their essays, that is, a study that takes into account that in oral tradition stories are tailored to an audience in a given time and place. Accordingly, he comments not only upon the features that suggest that these stories especially reflect the lives and concerns of the common people; he also attempts to characterize this particular contributor's talents as a storyteller, that is, to comment on the artfulness of his narrative. In addition, he demonstrates the wisdom of Rölleke's admonition—that for proper understanding and appreciation of the Grimms' tales, the textual history of each individual story must be kept in mind—by examining the Grimms' changes that affected the soldier's tales over the course of subsequent editions.

With August Nitschke's essay, our attention is no longer focused on the art of storytelling in a given milieu, but squarely on the purpose such narratives served, especially in the context of family life. This is to ask, too, why folk narrative was so popular, and why it maintained that popularity throughout the early modern period and beyond. Nitschke attempts to provide answers to these questions by examining passages in autobiographical and epistolary writings, from the sixteenth century to the nineteenth, in which adults made reference to their experience of having popular stories told to them as children. He tries to discover how the function of this activity changed during the course of this period. From Luther's time to the early Enlightenment, he finds, children experienced great fright on hearing tales, whereas beginning with the late eighteenth century, adults typically began to tell the stories to transport the children to a better world, one that contrasts with depressing everyday reality. His essay thus raises the important question of how and in what directions the mode of storytelling had changed or was changing at the time the Grimms were collecting their tales.

The importance of telling or listening to folktales for the Grimms themselves, and for other young adults who engaged in this activity with them, is explored by Walter Scherf. As he points out, similar activity had given rise to the small collection of tales by Charles Perrault over a century before, at the court of Louis XIV. Scherf emphasizes that the enthusiasm for these stories owed virtually everything to the adults' memory of having heard such stories when they were children. Like Nitschke in his essay, Scherf is concerned to discover how the childhood experience of listening to folktales is described in letters and memoirs, or is indicated by the type of stories remembered and told. He finds that the tales that derived from the storytelling circle of friends around the Grimms' sister Lotte typically depict the passage from childhood to adulthood, and concludes that enthusiasm for folktales—especially the sort called fairy tales or *Märchen*—is closely bound up with a yearning to recapture the experience of being a child and the process of becoming an adult. He thus calls attention to age as a determining factor in the choice of the type of story told and cultivated, as well as to specific personal experiences, such as the Grimms' loss of their father and the breakup of the household when they were young.

The refined, or bourgeois, nature of the stories told among the Grimms' circle of friends in Kassel, which characterized the 1812 volume of tales, is the starting point for Ruth Bottigheimer's discussion of how, beginning with the 1815 volume, the trend was to coarser material, of a type to be associated rather with the folk than the middle or upper classes. She maintains that, as a result, the depiction and treatment of women in the collection became increasingly misogynistic and harsh. She attributes this shift to concern on the Grimms' part to make the collection a truer reflection of folk life and culture. While Nitschke and Scherf ask about folktale's function in the lives of children and young adults, Bottigheimer focuses on its role in the romantic yearning of middle-class, middle-aged adults in nineteenth-century Germany to return to the ways and culture of the folk. Her argument is that the Grimms' adjustment of their stories to the bourgeois tastes of their reading public was very much in this direction, with negative consequences for the image of women projected therein.

While Scherf makes a case for the importance of childhood experiences in the Grimms' passion for fairy tales, and Bottigheimer emphasizes their interest in promoting appreciation of traditional popular culture, Jack Zipes points to yet another aspect of the Grimms' enthusiasm for folktales: their very personal experience of material deprivation resulting from their father's sudden and premature death when they were about to enter adolescence. Zipes probes the question of how psychosocial elements influenced the Grimms' relationship to their activity of collecting and publishing folktales. As we become ever more aware of the extent to which the Grimms were not merely collectors and editors, but shapers and in some instances authors of tales (or parts of them), such questions pose themselves all the more urgently. Like their sources and informants, the Grimms, as transmitters, functioned also as storytellers. Their collection therefore bears the stamp of their psychological, social, and cultural makeup. Zipes's special concern is to argue for a connection between the personal suffering of a sudden loss of social status in childhood and their experience, as young adults, of Germany's political and cultural humiliation during the French occupation under Napoleon.

In the concluding essay, Betsy Hearne directs attention to the ways in which society's interests and concerns have further shaped the Grimms' tales over the course of their publication since the brothers' deaths. Her essay thus continues the chief theme of this volume, that a given folktale may be told in many ways, depending on time and place and the needs and purposes of the teller. In particular, Hearne discusses the effects of recent economic shifts in juvenile publishing on the way the Grimms' stories are presented. How, she asks, have the texts and accompanying artwork been modified in the competition for broader markets? She cites as an example the ending of the second story in the Grimms' collection, "Cat and Mouse Set up Housekeeping" (KHM 2). It was changed to avoid suggesting that "the aggressive gobble the gullible," as Hearne calls it, in order to appeal to an audience of three- to six-year-olds. She finds this same tendency to soften the stories in recent versions of Sleeping Beauty. Half of these, though, have altered the basic elements and tone of the tale, which she attributes to efforts to appeal to wider reading markets. Her focus is not the change in meaning that accompanies these adaptations and presentations; yet this question of course implicitly raises itself with each retelling and each job of illustration.

Taken together, the essays address the concern, expressed by Röhrich in the first piece, that careful attention be paid to who is telling the stories, at which time and place, and with which conscious or unconscious motives and purposes. Röhrich's point, however, is that what ultimately interests us is the question of meaning. The essays here, by and large, do not come to terms with that thorny problem itself—Dundes's essay being an obvious exception. Instead, this collection—the first volume of studies in English devoted solely to the Grimms and folktale—helps to lay a secure foundation for building sound interpretations and to suggest fruitful directions for searching after the meaning of the Grimms' stories and of their collection as a whole.

The Brothers Grimm and Folktale

LUTZ RÖHRICH

The Quest of Meaning
in Folk Narrative Research

What does meaning mean and what is the meaning of mean?

NOT ONLY the methods but also the aims of folk narrative research
have changed in many ways. The more difficult and unproductive
the answers to questions about age and origin of folk narrative proved,
the more one turned to the question of meaning, to the message of
legends and fairy tales. Time and again it was proposed that fairy tales
were not simply to be taken literally, but that they contained some
religious, philosophical, allegorical, metaphorical, or symbolic truth.
And the question was raised: What use is context if it cannot provide
the "clear text"—that is, to help us to a proper understanding of the
material. It is the nature of man to look for meaning. Aristotle said
that the purpose of art is to reveal the hidden meaning of things and
not their external appearance, for it is in this deeper truth that their
true form lies.

But folklore studies, it seems, still shy clear of the "quest of meaning,"
and we do not need to look far for the reason for this. In the last
hundred years rather too much emphasis was given to meaning, from
the mythological schools down to the psychological. Consequently,
interpretative approaches from fields such as psychoanalysis, anthroposophy, or Marxist theory have been treated by folklorists with critical
reserve.

The Historical Relativity of Meaning

Earlier generations would have had no hesitation in telling us what
the meaning of a story was. For centuries theologians were convinced,

1

for instance, that animals had a spiritual meaning, that the lion and the pelican represented Christ, for example, and the fox and the ape the devil. Alanus ab Insulis said: "Omnis creatura significans," or "Omnis natura Deum loquitur." If we turn for a moment to the quest of meaning in the Middle Ages, we can clearly see the historical relativity of meaning. For centuries the interpreters of Scripture agreed that the Old Testament was a typological prefiguration of the New: Christ was the new Adam and the Virgin Mary the new Eve. The Tree of Paradise corresponded to the cross of Calvary and Jonas's delivery from the whale foreshadowed the resurrection of Christ. In a similar fashion the Bible was seen to contain a threefold meaning: the literal level, the moral level, and the allegorical level.

In the nineteenth century, lunar and solar mythologists did not doubt for a moment that the tale of the hare and the hedgehog represented the evening skies—the moon and the shining stars. In the twentieth century it is quite clear to some psychoanalysts (following Sigmund Freud) that Rumpelstiltskin has a phallic meaning, or that the motif of the forbidden chamber and the bloody key refer to defloration. The Jungian school sees the straw doll made by alpine cowherds as a realization of their anima, that is, the confrontation with their unconscious in concrete form.

Today we might wonder about the audacity of some of the claims such schools made, in that we are more aware of the questions of relativity and subjectivity, and the role played by time in such interpretations. Consequently we may well question the validity of such fixed constructs of interpretation and of the "evidence" they produce. The history of ideologies can be read from that of interpretations. The meaning of a text is not a fixed constant but is a variable, determined by the development of culture and ideas, fashions and trends, and dependent on rulers and ruling ideologies, not to forget the education and cultural awareness, the sex, age, religion, and ethnic group of the consumer. Cultures are systems of meaning.

A single story or a single figure in a fairy tale or a legend will be reinterpreted through the centuries—and the meaning is indeed different for each time. A classic example is the different "meaning" given to the dragon in East Asia and in the western world, or the differences from age to age in our conception of the dragon within Europe. Is Hercules' or St. George's fight with the dragon able to tell us something about modern dragon tales? The message of dragon stories differs from culture to culture, but in each case dragons always represent the typical dangers for a period. In the oldest stories, in Babylonian myths, for example, the dragon threatens the populace. It guards the wells and rivers and threatens the population with drought, with infertility. In the medieval Christian version, the dragon is the devil, the enemy of faith. In historical legends it is the enemy of the state, while in legends of chivalry it is the knight's rival and holds the maiden captive. In modern versions, the dragon appears in cartoons, advertisements, or headlines as the dragon of inflation, of unemployment, of war, pollution, or whatever people are afraid of. As we have said, throughout the centuries one function remains constant: the concretization of fears and anxieties. While the figure of the dragon remains the same, the meaning changes to express the individual fears of each age. Obvious as this might seem, earlier research seems to have missed these connections: in his monograph FFC 114, Kurt Ranke investigates more than one thousand dragon-killer tales without displaying any curiosity as to the meaning the dragon might have for the different narrators and their audience.

What, we must ask, do folklore texts mean in their second or third "life" (*zweites oder drittes Dasein*), that is to say once they are no longer oral texts belonging to preindustrial lower classes, but have instead become intellectual entertainment, the subject of films and television programs, once they have been translated into other languages and are known far beyond the area or country they sprang from? New meanings are continually being given to traditional folk material. The question is whether these new forms can have the same meaning for urban societies as the traditional oral genres did for another time.

The Subjective Relativity of Meaning (Meaning for Whom?)

To historical relativity must be added subjective relativity. Fairy tales and legends are like a mirror: everyone sees his or her own face in them, that is, something of his or her own personality. From narrator to narrator and from listener to listener a single story can have vastly different meanings. The meaning of a story can even change for an individual in the course of his or her life, in that, while the objective meaning of a text may remain the same, the personal meaning changes. In fact, meaning means having a very personal relationship to the story. Everybody has only a limited sphere of experience, determined by knowledge, education, cultural context, sex, and so on. Consequently it is only natural that statements about the meaning of stories are highly contradictory. They can nevertheless be enlightening, provided we remember the limitations of our knowledge and the relativity of our perceptions.

We must distinguish clearly between individual meaning and general meaning. All folklore genres have a personal background; some more, some less. Even the fact that we remember and retell a certain story has personal reasons. Freud has demonstrated this for jokes, but it applies to every performance of a folk text.

One must ask, however, whether there are perhaps interpretations which have necessarily to be accepted. But then we must ask how the validity of an interpretation can be tested. How reliable is our subjective feeling about what counts as evidence? Is it not necessary to move from a "feeling" about evidence to knowledge if we want to consider ourselves as scholars and researchers rather than simply enthusiastic dabblers?

The Relativity of Meaning throughout the Genres

The genre is also very important in determining which meaning we can expect. There are metaphorical and what we will call nonmetaphorical folklore genres. Let us first consider the metaphorical genres. Some genres almost always have a double meaning, which is the very essence of the genre. Riddles, just like proverbs and jokes, clearly belong to such genres. They have a literal and a hidden meaning. A riddle which cannot be solved in some fashion would die and has no meaning in any case. Proverbs are different again: one thing is said, but something else is intended. A German proverb says: "Der Krug geht solange zum Brunnen bis er bricht" (a jug will go to the well until it breaks). The jug, on a literal level, is a container which is useless once broken. But in the proverbs and proverbial sayings of many cultures, in emblems and iconography, just as in art and literature (cf. Kleist's drama *The Broken Jug*) it is a symbol for lost virginity—representing the opposite of the Virgin Mary, who is often compared to a pure and unblemished vessel. Another example: "Wenn alte Scheuern brennen, hilft kein Löschen" (when old barns burn, you can forget the fire-brigade) has, of course, nothing to do with the fire-brigade; what is meant is that older people who fall in love do so particularly intensively and cannot be brought to reason. It has been said that proverbs are the clothes of ideas. In other words, we have to "undress" the proverb in order to get at a meaning.

In folk songs, too, there are keywords which mean something different from what they say. The subject of the majority of our songs is love—and this can be represented in many ways. Love can be an inflicted wound, an illness, it can be seen as death, obedience or service, a struggle or a war, as captivity, or as a fire, a burden, a light, a game, an animal, metal, or food, theft or trade. But the procedure involved here is not reversible: it would be misguided to equate every hunting motif or every physical injury with love. Nevertheless, we all understand what is meant by talk of plucking roses or blueberries, roaming in the gloaming, losing a slipper, spilling wine, or breaking a jug, namely, secret and forbidden love.

A short time ago an advertisement (*Heiratsanzeige*) appeared in the personals column of a well-known German weekly newspaper, which began with the first line of a folk song:

> "Es ist ein Schnee gefallen . . . "
> (Snow has fallen . . .)

This was followed by: "Where is the man who can complete the song for me? I'm academic, 37 years old, 165 centimeters tall and live in Switzerland; Box number. . . . " Now, the rest of the song goes as follows:

> "Es ist ein Schnee gefallen,
> wann es ist noch nit Zeit;
> ich wollt zu meinem Buhlen gan,
> der Weg ist mir verschneit.
>
> Es gingen drei Gesellen,
> spazieren um das Haus;
> das Maidlein was behende,
> es lugt zum Laden aus.
>
> Der ein der was ein Reiter,
> der ander ein Edelmann,
> der dritt ein stolzer Schreiber,
> denselben wollt es han.

Er tät dem Maidlein kromen
von Seiden ein Haarschnur;
er gab's demselben Maidlein:
Bind du dein Haar mit zu!

Ich will mein Haar nit binden,
ich will es hangen lan.
Ich will wohl diesen Sommer lang
fröhlich zum Tanze gan."[1]

What does the complete text tell us about the intention of the advertiser? First, the woman advertising here identifies herself with the person in the first verse. The snow hints at an unhappy past, and the snow-blocked road to the lover seems to indicate that the advertiser has had an unhappy love affair in which she lost the love of a man. Second, the three suitors in the folk song, a rider, a nobleman, and a scribe, indicate that the advertiser would prefer an intellectual, more specifically, a man who can complete her text.

Whether she wants to marry this person is left open. The maiden in the folk song, after all, doesn't want to bind her hair, that is, she does not want to attain married status. The advertiser, then, seems to be looking for a relationship without a ring.

Of course, it may be that the advertiser had another version in mind, because sometimes the song goes as follows:

"Ach Lieb, laß dich's erbarmen,
daß ich so elend bin,
und schleuß mich in dein Arme!
so fährt der Winter hin."

(O Love, have pity on me
because I feel miserable.
Keep me in your arms
and drive the winter away).

We can see the relativity of different meanings from version to version.

Even more than folk songs the didactic genres provide prime examples of texts with metaphorical meaning. The real significance of a parable or an exemplum is not the narrative itself. The narrative is not autonomous but contains some wisdom or moral. In fables, too, we find metaphorical meaning. On one level we have a story of the animal kingdom which serves as a vehicle for didactic instruction. The animals behave like human beings and reflect social norms. In contrast to the Christian lion of Physiologus, the lion in the fable stands for the king. As Roger Abraham puts it: "Man as an animal." This is what La Fontaine means by calling the fable the "disguise of truth."

The jests are also clearly metaphorical in character. The figure of the fool, for example, stands not only for foolishness, but, in effect, embodies truth and wisdom, as in the case with Eulenspiegel or Don Quixote, for instance. In the jest about Schlaraffenland, the folk land of milk and honey, the topsy-turvy world stands for the real world.

The problem of meaning in jokes is considerably more complex. The so-called linguistic jokes (like riddles) usually turn on ambiguity. But recognizing the ambiguity in a joke is not the same as understanding the significance of the joke. Freud has made us familiar with the mechanisms of repression and the reasons for our laughter. We know, too, how revealing someone's favorite joke can be about them. Recent studies have indicated the compensatory functions of jokes for both the teller and the culture in which the joke arises.

Legends

Legends and fairy tales are, in the first place, nonmetaphorical genres. Nevertheless they do have a message. The better known and the more widely spread a legend is, the more certain it is that it contains a message. The message of the Piper of Hameln is dangerous temptation and seduction, the meaning of the Tell legend is liberation from tyranny. The meaning of belief stories, the so-called demonological legends, is fear and overcoming fear. Creatures of lower mythology are usually embodiments of human fears, projections of anxiety, and the repression of these. Water sprites and water nymphs embody the enticement but also the danger and fathomlessness of water. Werewolf legends point to the wolflike traits in human beings. The werewolves are far worse than real wolves: they are homo homini lupus. The suffocating fear, experienced concretely, is transformed into the belief in succubi and nightmare demons. Belief in witches is the vehicle for a great many different fears and the attempt to find a scapegoat for these fears, often motivated by envy, hate, greed, and jealousy. Fear of bad weather led to the notion of weather-witches, who are responsible for hail, fog, frost, or heavy rain out of season. Other fears are connected with economic failure; it is witches who have put a spell on cattle or stolen the milk. The witch causes illness to befall man and animal. Repressed fear of these and similar dangers is transformed into aggression against suspect women. Envy of those who are more successful often plays a role here, and the responsibility for one's own failure is projected onto others. Projection, as Dundes points out, "refers to the tendency to attribute to another person or to the environment what is actually within oneself."[2]

Belief in witches also reflects the male fear of women who know more, of the superior woman, and fear of female sexuality. The so-called lace-knotting (*Nestelknüpfen*), thought to cause male impotence, was one of the chief charges against a witch in witch trials; and jealous husbands believed their wives had sexual relations with the devil or with other women. The devil's image was that of a sexual superman, complete with the appropriate attributes of horns, hair, and tail. It is only too evident that male fears of impotence and feelings of inferiority were often the motivation for belief in witches.

The supernatural beings of legends sanction the norms of human society. Legends recount fears about the consequences of breaking social and religious taboos. In each case we must ask what suppressed potential lies behind the taboos the legends call upon us to uphold. In this context one can speak of the "cultural language of fear." Legends and belief stories are oral communications in which people try to verbalize anxieties and fears and, by explaining these away, to free themselves from the oppressive power of their fears. One could call this the "shock effect of supra-normal experience." The telling of a legend can be compared to a therapeutic process and supranatural experiences constitute a kind of self-therapy.

Fairy Tales

If the genre of legends shows us the "cultural language of fear," that of fairy tales deals with the repression of fear and a world of wish fulfillment. Long ago the German philosopher Wilhelm Wundt called the genre "Glücksmärchen"—tales of happiness. This happiness can take many different forms, such as fulfillment in love, material wealth, and status, the choice of a partner, but also the happiness gained from being content with one's modest lot.

Certain themes and topics which could adversely affect the hero's happiness are simply absent in fairy tales. So fairy-tale heroes do not die or, at least, death is not final; death only applies to others, the hero remains exempt. These are the demands of the genre. With egocentric rigor the fairy tale pushes the fate of relatives, parents and brothers and sisters aside and concentrates solely on the hero, his self-realization and his attainment of happiness. In psychological terms this must almost be seen as a complete repression of death. On the other hand, although death is repressed in fairy tales, some motifs, such as the changing of shapes, petrification, getting lost in the woods, or not speaking for seven years, could in fact be understood as references to death. Other topics, too, are absent in fairy tales. There is, for example, no eroticism, although there is constant talk of winning a bride, choosing a partner, and of weddings. On the other hand, much in fairy tales can be understood sexually—and many a researcher has embarked upon the quest for hidden erotic meanings in fairy tales! For the psychoanalysts fairy tales are made of such stuff as dreams. Orthodox Freudians see in them a language of erotic metaphors.

The slippery, slimy frog-prince in the fairy tale, whom the princess does not want to take to bed with her, embodies her still-unconscious rejection of sexuality. Breaking the spell symbolizes the change from rejection to acceptance of love. And for some psychoanalysts—from Freud to Graf Wittgenstein—Rumpelstiltskin, the little mannikin, whose name no one knows and whose name changes from version to version, represents nothing less than the penis. Thus, according to the Grimm version, Rumpelstiltskin is a stiff being, rummaging a lumber room, hopping about on one foot, a being that bakes and brews and demands the queen's child.

Marxist ideologists approach fairy tales exclusively in terms of feudalistic power and exploitation. For the Rudolf Steiner school, fairy tales represent a higher and spiritual form of the individual's development. If, as none would deny, external objects in fairy tales stand for inner values, then the road to becoming king represents a psychological and emotional development; the crown is a symbol for a higher aim. The various adventures the hero meets with are confrontations with the metaphysical depths of one's own identity. Psychologists and educators see in almost every fairy tale a process of maturation.

In my opinion not only the monocausalists but also the dogmatists, the people who see an astral symbol or an anima or phallus in everything, the dogmatists propounding their Oedipus theories and jargon of mechanisms of suppression and basic drives, are dangerous. But above all we must beware of those who claim that their interpretation is the only right one. Many truths are sometimes better than one.

Fairy tales are so linear and simple in form that it is difficult to imagine that this simple structure and language could have any meaning beyond the literal. It is precisely the simplicity, the linearity, the one-dimensionality of the fairy tale which have led people to believe that fairy tales are allegories.

The concrete statement in a fairy tale often has an abstract meaning. Fairy tales avoid abstract representations; they speak, for example, of a maiden with golden hair, not of beauty, or of a maiden whose mouth drops toads with every word, which means she is ugly. Fairy tales do not speak of a bad conscience or worries, but rather of a king whose crown begins to wobble. In this way even the most simple elements in the fairy story mean more than the words themselves say.

Narrative folklore texts have something to do with human imagination and phantasy, just as dreams do. And they require to be interpreted like other products of our imagination. But dealing with phantasy stories does not permit us to make phantastical interpretations.[3] Why is it that psychoanalysis concerns itself so consistently with the phantastic genres such as legends and fairy tales? There is, to be sure, a parallel: the dreams and phantasies of the mentally sick seem to be just as illogical as the world of fairy tales. If somebody believes he is being followed by little green men in flying saucers and is therefore sent to a psychotherapist, this is because his environment (including the therapist) does not believe in the reality of his perceptions. Were his perceptions to be proved real, he would not require therapy. And the same is true of legends and fairy tales. We automatically ask: to what extent do they agree with objective data? If there is no correspondence, we resort to a psychological interpretation. Both psychology and folklore studies are trying to decode a message. Psychology attempts this for the individual, ethnology for groups. Hidden messages can only be understood if they are seen in context. In the case of the psychologist, context is to be sought in the case history of his patient. Folklorists find their context in the society involved.[4]

I want to mention only one example: in the Bluebeard fairy tale the motif of the forbidden chamber appears, entry to which is linked with a bloody egg or a bloody key. Both of these are symbols which point to an act of defloration. In other contexts, too, these motifs have a phallic or vaginal significance. Nevertheless, we cannot simply generalize about the interpretation of these symbols, since they appear as structural components in very different types of fairy tales: in Bluebeard, for example, in Faithful John, in Our Lady's Child, and also in stories of fairy love and the legend of Melusine. In the context of each story the motif of the forbidden door has a different function, and one interpretation is not valid for all types. More exact differentiation is required of the reasons for disobedience and the contents of the chamber, as well as the effect on the protagonist. Further questions to consider are: Who may impose a ban and what is the basis of their power? In most cases the ban is imposed by a supernatural being, such as Bluebeard, a dragon, the Virgin Mary, or Melusine.

What are the reasons for this taboo? Often the evil demon wants to hide his earlier crimes from his new victim. But in Faithful John the dutifully concerned father wants to protect his son from harm. In Our Lady's Child the forbidden chamber is almost a sacred place. Depending on the taboo involved, disobedience is seen as good or as bad. In Bluebeard for example, curiosity and disobedience are not necessarily faults. In contrast to her sisters and her predecessors, the heroine is both clever and wily. Cleverness is a positive quality when outwitting a demon. Any means of outwitting evil is morally good. In contrast, in "Our Lady's Child," disobedience is seen as a sin and absolution can only be gained through confession.

The motivations for opening the forbidden chamber, as well as its contents, differ from type to type. The commonest reason for breaking the taboo is curiosity. The desire to see the forbidden is basic to man. The structure involved here—the many things permitted and the one forbidden—is essentially that of the story of Adam and Eve in Genesis 2. Both men and women can be driven by curiosity. Bluebeard and Our Lady's Child concentrate on the curiosity often attributed to women. In Faithful John, Iron John, and The Swan Maiden, we find the same curiosity in men. In this narrative context gender-specific motivations are quite absent and this puts the interpretation of defloration in another light.

It is nevertheless striking that the test of the forbidden door often takes place in the context of puberty, on the threshold between childhood and adulthood. The motif of the forbidden chamber looks very much like a survival of an old initiation rite, to be understood not as a remnant of the rite itself but as a psychological equivalent.

The Validity of Interpretations

We are under no obligation to interpret motifs and figures in fairy tales in a certain way. We ought actually to be glad and grateful that in modern folklore studies there are no infallible dogmas and that there is no infallible pope and no orthodox creed: "Cuius est judicare de vero sensu de interpretatione scriptuarum sanctarum."

On the contrary, folklore texts allow for many diverse interpretations. What may seem valid for one version may not for another. What one scholar considers correct, another may not. There are, it seems, no objective standards. The problem lies, of course, in trying to approach in rational and objective terms the product of an irrational and imaginative process. It is quite possible that a storyteller does not perceive the significance of his story. On the other hand, no storyteller wants to relate nonsense and so even the most contaminated version has an individual meaning for its narrator. The scholar analyzing a tale necessarily finds a different meaning from that of the storyteller, quite simply because two different people will have two different interpretations.

Moreover, the storyteller can convey a meaning he himself does not understand. We might ask whether the meaning a text has for the narrator is perhaps not also the same meaning we should accept. It becomes clear that folk narratives have multiple levels of meaning: on a literal level accessible to everyone, on a higher level understood only by the initiated, and finally on a third level accessible only with the help of structuralist and psychological tools of interpretation. While the so-called metaphorical genres (like proverbs, riddles, and jokes) have an unambiguous ambiguity, fairy tales only seem to be unambiguous, and in reality involve multiple ambiguities which cannot be demonstrated. Most interpretations are only assessments of probability. Nevertheless the aim of the humanities is to arrive at valid interpretations. Yet certainty is not the same as validity, and recognition of ambiguity is not necessarily the same as uncertain knowledge.

Legends and fairy tales are, first and foremost, the narratives themselves and not their interpretations. The fact that folk narratives appear among so many peoples in such similar forms and ways shows that they have a common meaning which transcends language barriers. If narratives did not provide models for solving problems, they would never have survived for centuries, let alone the thousands of years some have. Only what is important and affects people directly enters folk narrative and tradition. Only what is meaningful is passed on. And finally, if folk narrative did not have a deep personal meaning for each of us, we would not have become folk narrative researchers. We surely have more meaningful things to do than classifying types and motifs. If that is all we were to do we would be like the man who tried to study the life of the fish by examining a tin of sardines.

The quest for meaning tries to explain why folk narratives are passed on: "Folklorists of the future must try to answer the difficult question of why an item of folklore exists now or why it existed in the past."[5] At the end of the drama *Der Tor und der Tod* by Hugo von Hofmannsthal, Death shakes his head over humanity, saying:

> "Wie wundervoll sind diese Wesen,
> Die, was nicht deutbar, dennoch deuten,
> Was nie geschrieben wurde, lesen,
> Verworrenes beherrschend binden
> Und Wege noch im Ewig-Dunkeln finden."

> (How wonderful these beings are,
> who interpret the uninterpretable
> who read the unwritten
> who regally order the unorderable
> and find their way in the eternal dark."

To know the knowable is the aim of all science, folklore research included. We have now seen how difficult the business of interpretation is. And we cannot be too careful when looking for meanings. Every new answer will lead to a hundred new questions. But we should remember that sometimes no answer is an answer too. To admit to knowing nothing is undoubtedly more honest than to pretend to know everything. Goethe's words to the all-too-eager interpreters are only intended ironically:

> Im Auslegen seid frisch und munter,
> Legt Ihr's nicht aus, so legt was unter!
> (Be bright and cheery in your interpreting and
> what you can't interpret—you can just invent!)

Notes

This essay appeared originally in the *Scandinavian Yearbook of Folklore*, 40 (1984), 127–38.
1. Erk and Böhme (eds.), No. 424a.
2. Dundes, p. 37.
3. Hirsch, p. 11.
4. Lévi-Strauss, p. 212.
5. Dundes, p. ix.

Bibliography

Bollnow, Otto F. *Das Verstehen: Drei Aufsätze zur Theorie der Geisteswissenschaften*. Mainz: Kirchheim, 1949.
Calame-Griaule, Geneviève, Veronika Görög-Karady, et al. "The Variability of Meaning and the Meaning of Variability." *Journal of Folklore Research*, 20 (1983), 153–70.
Douglas, Mary. *Implicit Meanings: Essays in Anthropology*. London: Routledge & Paul, 1975.
Dundes, Alan. *Interpreting Folklore*. Bloomington: Indiana University Press, 1973.
Erk, Ludwig, and Franz Magnus Böhme. *Deutscher Liederhort*. 3 vols. Leipzig, 1893–94. Rpt. Hildesheim: Olms, 1963.
Firth, Raymond William. *Symbols Public and Private*. London: Allen & Unwin, 1973.
Friedrich, Hugo. "Dichtung und die Methoden ihrer Deutung." In Dieter Steland (ed.), *Interpretationen 5*. Frankfurt am Main, 1968, pp. 14–27.
Guiart, Jean. "Multiple Levels of Meaning in Myth." In Pierre Maranda (ed.), *Mythology: Selected Readings*. Baltimore: Penguin Books, 1972, pp. 111–26.
Heidegger, Martin. *Unterwegs zur Sprache*. Pfullingen: Neske, 1969.
Hirsch, Erich Donald. *Validity in Interpretation*. New Haven: Yale University Press, 1967.
Holbek, Bengt. *Interpretation of Fairy Tales*. FFC 239. Helsinki: Academia scientiarum fennica, 1987.
Lévi-Strauss, Claude. *Mythos und Bedeutung*. Frankfurt am Main: Suhrkamp, 1980.
Lorenzer, Alfred. *Die Wahrheit der psychoanalytischen Erkenntnisse*. Frankfurt am Main: Suhrkamp, 1974.
Metzger, Michael M., and Katharina Mommsen (eds.). *Fairy Tales as Ways of Knowing*. Berne: Peter Lang, 1981.
Ogden, Charles Kay, and I. A. Richards. *The Meaning of Meaning*. New York: Harcourt, Brace & Co., 1923.
Ohly, Friedrich. *Schriften zur mittelalterlichen Bedeutungsforschung*. Darmstadt: Wissenschaftliche Buchgesellschaft, 1977.
Panofsky, Erwin. *Meaning in the Visual Arts: Papers in and on Art History*. Woodstock, N.Y.: Overlook, 1974.

Ranke, Kurt. *Die zwei Brüder: Eine Studie zur vergleichenden Märchenforschung.* FFC 114. Helsinki: Academia scientiarum fennica, 1934.

Röhrich, Lutz. *Sage und Märchen: Erzählforschung heute.* Freiburg im Breisgau: Herder, 1976.

Sperber, Dan. *Rethinking Symbolism.* Translated by Alice L. Morton. Cambridge: Cambridge University Press, 1975.

Staiger, Emil. *Die Kunst der Interpretation.* Zurich: Atlantis, 1955.

Wach, Joachim. *Das Verstehen: Grundzüge einer Geschichte der hermeneutischen Theorie im neunzehnten Jahrhundert.* 3 vols. Tübingen: Mohr, 1926–33.

ALAN DUNDES

Interpreting Little Red Riding Hood Psychoanalytically

VARIATION is a key concept in folkloristics. It is variation that in part distinguishes folklore from so-called high culture and mass culture. High culture and mass culture are fixed in print or on videotape or film. A novel, short story, or poem does not change over time although readers' perceptions and understandings of such literary products may well do so.

Folklore with its characteristics of multiple existence and variation is, in marked contrast, ever in a state of flux. There is no one single text in folklore; there are only texts. Folklore once recorded from oral tradition does not cease to be, but rather continues on its often-merry way from raconteur to raconteur, from generation to generation. It is precisely this continuous process of oral transmission (or learning by example in the case of gestural or material folklore) which makes it possible for flexible folklore to adapt to each individual or group among which it circulates.

Literature and mass or popular culture seem hopelessly rigid and inflexible in comparison with folklore. In studying them, one must either seek to reconstruct the intellectual *Zeitgeist* or governing worldview paradigm present when the literary effort or popular/mass cultural product was created, or else abandon such a historical approach in favor of "new criticism" or its successors in an attempt to investigate how an old literary favorite is understood by yet one more set of readers.

The lack of flexibility of the texts of literary and popular culture is compensated for by the flexibility in interpretive approaches. Egyptologist Van Baaren has sagely observed that because biblical myths (e.g., in Genesis) are fixed and are part of a written tradition of organized religions, they cannot vary with each generation as an oral myth might. Instead the variation can occur only in the critical interpretation of biblical myths.[1] New generations are not really free to tamper with the sacred text, but they can occasionally offer new critical perspectives on the fixed texts, as the history of biblical criticism over many centuries attests.

In folkloristics, the scientific study of folklore, the overwhelming amount of variation in texts—we have more than one thousand versions of many of the standard Indo-European *Märchen,* first indexed or catalogued by Finnish folklorist Antti Aarne in 1910—may have discouraged those interested in interpretation. The comparative method, or Finnish method as it is sometimes termed, rarely leads to interpretation, that is, to the interpretation of a folktale's content. It is a tedious task merely to assemble all one thousand versions of the Kind and Unkind Girls (AT 480) or Cinderella (AT 510A) and further to arrange to have all these texts translated into the native language of the researcher carrying out the comparative study.[2] At best or at most, the exhausted comparative folklorist may reluctantly guess at the possible (historical) relationships existing between subtypes of a given tale type or at the possible direction of diffusion—did a particular European tale type move from the Near East to continental Europe or from continental Europe to the Near East?

The failure of folklorists to interpret the data they so assiduously gather from informants in the field and which they afterwards so painstakingly classify has left the field of interpretation by default to nonfolklorists. These nonfolklorists, including students of literature, anthropologists, historians, and psychoanalysts, among others, have been more than willing to venture interpretations of folklore. As a result, we usually find in terms of the two methodological steps essential for the study of folklore in literature and culture, *identification* and *interpretation,* one of two extremes.[3] The folklorists who delight in flaunting their expertise in identification are quick to point out that a specific text is a version of a particular tale type, but they utterly fail to interpret that text. In contrast, literary critics, anthropologists, historians, and psychoanalysts are unable or unwilling to identify a text in terms of tale type, but they feel perfectly free to interpret a given text. Identification without interpretation, as practiced by too many folklorists, is sterile—publishing collections of tales with the notes limited to enumerating the relevant tale type numbers; but interpretation without proper identification may be equally unfortunate.

One might, for example, wrongly assume that a tale had been invented by a particular author or was peculiar to one culture or historical period whereas in fact the existence of earlier versions of the same tale type in other cultures could easily disprove such an unwarranted initial assumption.

Germanicists and psychoanalysts, for example, have had a long tradition of interpreting the Grimm tales. Since the founder and early practitioners of psychoanalysis were native speakers of German, it made sense for them to choose samples from the celebrated Grimm canon on those occasions when they sought to consider folklore as grist for the psychoanalytic mill. From the folkloristic perspective, the problem of limiting one's data base to a Grimm tale is twofold. For one thing, it is never appropriate to analyze a folktale (or any other exemplar of a folklore genre) on the basis of a single text. Literary scholars, accustomed as they are to working with "the" text rather than with "a" text, have simply taken the Grimm (or if of the French persuasion, the Perrault) text as "the" text for analysis. Psychoanalysts have done much the same.

The second problem from the folklorist's perspective is that the Grimms' versions of tales are at least one full step from pure oral tradition. Although the Grimms claimed that they were recording authentic unadulterated tales as they fell from their informants' un-tutored lips, source criticism over the years, thanks in part to the Grimms' own notes on their tales, has conclusively disproved this claim. When the Grimms, especially Wilhelm, who was more concerned than Jacob with the later editions of the *Kinder- und Hausmärchen,* began to combine different versions of the same tale type, to "present many versions as one" as they put it, they committed a cardinal sin in folklore, though to be sure it was one often committed by nineteenth-century collectors. Such a composite text—made up of different portions of different versions of the same tale type—constitutes what folklorists call fakelore.[4] What this means is that many of the tales in the Grimm canon were never actually told in precisely that form before the publication of the Grimms' doctored texts.

It is well to keep in mind that fairy tales are first and foremost an *oral* form. So from that point of view, any written version is suspect. I am speaking here of *Volksmärchen,* not *Kunstmärchen. Kunstmärchen* constitute yet another area of inquiry, that is, artistic or literary tales composed by known authors, perhaps inspired by a folk model. But there are varying degrees of accuracy in the written texts of oral tales collected in the nineteenth century. Some nineteenth-century collectors, e.g., E. T. Kristensen (1843–1929) of Jutland, one of the greatest folklore collectors who ever lived, made a serious attempt to record oral fairy tales verbatim.[5] The Grimm brothers, regrettably, did not report their tales verbatim from their informants. Comparisons of the "same" tale in different editions of the *Kinder- und Hausmärchen* show just how much rewriting was done.[6]

What this means is that the error of studying an international oral fairy tale on the basis of one single text is compounded by the fact that the Grimm version is not even an authentic oral version of that tale type. The folklorist would accordingly ask Germanicists and psychoanalysts who have written on fairy tales the following questions: why, if there are one thousand versions of a tale type in print or readily available in folklore archives, would one want to limit one's analysis to a single version of the tale under investigation? And if one did want to limit one's analysis to a single version, why would one choose the Grimm text as that single version when we have indisputable evidence establishing that the Grimm version is *not* an authentic oral version of that tale?

Now it can certainly be argued that the Grimm fairy-tale canon has its own existence as a kind of literary creation based in part on oral sources, and that as a separate and unquestionably important and influential literary creation it deserves study by literary critics. The essential point is that while one may, of course, legitimately analyze a Grimm tale, one should not delude oneself that one is analyzing the most common or most authentic form of that particular tale. The difficulty has been that some ambitious scholars have sought to extrapolate general German values and worldview from the tales in the Grimm corpus. If someone wanted to seek reliable sources of German values and worldview, he or she would be far better off examining the substantial body of bona fide German oral fairy tales in print. This is the fundamental distinction between analyzing literature and analyzing folklore.

But all this is wishful thinking. By far the majority of the interpretations of fairy tales published depend almost exclusively upon the Grimm canon. Certainly this is true in the case of psychoanalytic studies of folktales. There are dozens and dozens of psychoanalytic readings of fairy tales, most of which are totally ignored by literal-minded folklorists frightened and evidently greatly threatened by any thought that fairy tales might have a symbolic import. Nearly every one of these psychoanalytic readings of fairy tales uses the Grimm version as the sole point of interpretive departure. A few folklorists have bothered to read Bruno Bettelheim's *The Uses of Enchantment* (1976), but not many have read earlier psychoanalytic treatments of fairy tales by Géza Róheim and others. Róheim was actually trained as a folklorist and was much more conversant with comparative folkloristics than Bettelheim, but his brilliant if somewhat erratic readings of fairy tales remain largely ignored by professional folklorists.

I should like to illustrate the pitfalls of relying too heavily upon literary, derivative, and bowdlerized renderings of what are wrongly believed to be authentic folktales by considering the case of Little Red Riding Hood (AT 333). In this particular instance, we are victimized by not one but by at least two distinct reworkings of the original oral tale.

The first was that of Perrault. His literary versions of 1695 and 1697 omitted many of the details of the oral tale. French folklorist Paul Delarue, among others, has established that the oral tradition which preceded Perrault told of a girl (who wore no red hood) carrying a hot loaf of bread and a bottle of milk to her grandmother. On the way, she meets a wolf who asks her what path she is taking to her grandmother's house: the path of needles or the path of pins? The girl indicates that she will take the path of pins. Meanwhile the wolf enters the grandmother's house, kills the grandmother, and puts some of her flesh in the cupboard and a bottle of her blood on the shelf. The girl finally arrives and gives the bread and milk to the wolf disguised as grandmother, who invites her to eat some of the meat and wine. After she does so, a little cat remarks, "A slut is she who eats the flesh and drinks the blood of her granny." The wolf then instructs the little girl to undress herself. When she asks where to put her apron, bodice, dress, petticoat, and long stockings, the wolf replies each time with "Throw them into the fire, my child, you won't be needing them any more." Then comes the celebrated dialogue which begins, "Oh, Granny, how hairy you are!" "The better to keep myself warm, my child." Hereafter come nails to scratch oneself, shoulders to carry firewood, ears to hear you with, nostrils to sniff tobacco with, ending with a mouth to eat you with. At that point, the little girl, in danger, says, "Oh, Granny, I've got to go badly. Let me go outside." The wolf replies, "Do it in the bed, my child!" "Oh no, Granny, I want to go outside." "All right, but make it quick." The wolf attaches a woolen rope to her foot and lets her go outside. When the little girl is outside, she ties the end of the rope to a plum tree in the courtyard. The wolf becomes impatient and says, "Are you making a load out there? Are you making a load?" When he realizes that nobody is answering him, he jumps out of bed and sees that the little girl has escaped. He follows her, but arrives too late at her house, just at the very moment she enters.[7]

Perrault left out such "crude" elements as the cannibalistic eating of grandmother's flesh, the ritualistic striptease, and the ploy of going outside to defecate to escape the wolf's clutches.[8] Perrault also changed the ending of the story by having the little girl devoured by the wolf.

The overtly cannibalistic component of AT 333 is dramatically affirmed in a north Italian version of the tale collected in 1974. In this version a dialogue between Little Red Riding Hood (henceforth LRRH) and the wolf takes place which parallels and to some extent prefigures the traditional dialogue known to all devotees of the tale. Arriving at the grandmother's house, LRRH tells the wolf, whom she does not recognize under the grandmother's clothing, that the long trip has made her very hungry. "If you are hungry," says the wolf, "open the kneading trough and eat two or three tortellini which remain on a plate." While she eats, the wolf murmurs, "Eat the ears of your grandmother!" "Are you still hungry? In a pan are two or three lasagne," and he murmurs, "Eat the intestines of your grandmother!" "Are you still hungry? In a pan are remaining two or three manfettini," and he murmurs, "Eat the teeth of your grandmother." "Are you thirsty? In the corner is a bottle of red wine. . . . Drink the blood of your grandmother."[9]

Despite the existence of numerous oral versions of this tale type—Delarue examined more than thirty-five French texts—scholars continue to insist upon the priority of the Perrault telling of the tale, following in the steps of folklorist Alexander Haggerty Krappe, who maintained in *The Science of Folklore* (1930) that "The story of Little Red Riding-Hood seems to be an invention of Perrault: at least no earlier variants are known, and the other French and Central European variants, not very many, to be sure, in all, show the unmistakable influence of the classical French text."[10] This statement articulates a typical literary bias—contending that oral traditions derive from an original written source—but it is demonstrably false. Perrault's source was oral tradition.

The alleged literary origin of LRRH was even espoused by Stith Thompson, who said in *The Folktale* (1945): "This tale of Little Red Ridinghood has never had wide circulation where folktales are learned by word of mouth. Even in France and Germany, where the largest number is reported, practically all are based upon Perrault or Grimm. It does not extend east beyond the Russian border." This too is in error. Even a most cursory examination of Chinese, Japanese, and Korean versions of tale type 333 will establish that the oral tale *does* exist "beyond the Russian border" *and,* what is even more fascinating, this examination will document that some of the salient features of the pre-Perrault French oral tales are to be found in the Chinese, Japanese, and Korean traditions. Delarue, among European folklorists, appears to be one of the very few scholars to have been at all aware of the Asian versions of the tale type.[11]

The Chinese tale type 333C, The Tiger Grandma, as summarized in Nai-Tung Ting's *A Type Index of Chinese Folktales* (1978), presents a curious combination of The Wolf and the Kids (AT 123, Grimm #5) and The Glutton (Red Riding Hood) (AT 333, Grimm #26). Here is the plot synopsis: an ogress, often a tiger, claims to be a relative of the children, usually a grandmother. The mother, leaving home, warns her children to watch the house and not open the door to strangers. The ogress, usually a wolf or tiger, comes to the house and asks the children to open the door. In some versions, the children meet the ogress on the way to see their grandmother and are invited to the house of the ogress, who claims to be their grandmother. Inside the house, the ogress's strange physical features are noticed by one or two of the older children. The surviving child hears the sound of crunching, biting, and so on in the dark and asking to have some of the supposed grandmother's snack is given a part of her sibling's body, usually a finger. She obtains permission to leave, typically with a rope tied to her body which she later unties and puts around another object. When the ogress finds out she has been deceived, she searches and locates the fugitive, but the child talks her into letting a rope be tied to her body, after which the helpless ogress may be killed by having sharp or heavy objects thrown at her or having lime, salt water, or hot liquid poured on her body or into her mouth.[12]

Wolfram Eberhard has written a monographic account of this popular Chinese tale type based upon some 241 Taiwanese texts of "Grandaunt Tiger." Some of the details he reports cannot help but remind us of the oral French versions. For example, in several Taiwanese texts, after the heroine asks to be allowed to leave to go to defecate, "the tiger tells the girl to relieve herself in the bed or in the room, but the girl objects saying that it would smell." Eberhard is able to illuminate the tiger's technique of tying a rope to the girl when she leaves to defecate. According to Eberhard, "The idea of the rope is nothing unusual to a Chinese. Toddlers are often prevented from getting into mischief or danger by having a rope tied to their legs, so that they can walk or crawl around but cannot get too far away."[13]

It is worth remarking that the elements common to the French and Chinese oral traditions, namely, the cannibalistic eating of a relative's flesh, the wolf or tiger's suggestion that the girl defecate in bed, and the device of escaping by tying a rope around a substitute object, could not possibly have been transmitted by the Perrault literary version since these elements are *not* found in that version.

A summary of some seventy-three versions of AT 333A, The Gluttonous Ogress and Children, from Japan, as reported in Hiroko Ikeda's *A Type and Motif Index of Japanese Folk-Literature* (1971), reveals some of the same distinctive features. An ogress comes upon a woman, eats all the food she has, and then she eats the woman too. The ogress proceeds to the woman's house to eat the children; she is disguised as their mother. The ogress is asked by the suspicious children to put her hand through a hole and is told that the mother's hand is not so rough. The ogress leaves and returns after rubbing her hand with a taro leaf. This time the children claim that the ogress's voice is too hoarse to be that of their mother. She goes and returns after drinking oil (or sugar or honey) and is finally admitted. After they have all gone to bed, the ogress eats the baby. Hearing the munching sound, one of the children asks for the food and is given the baby's finger. The children insist that they need to go to the outhouse and are let out after ropes have been tied to them. They untie the ropes and climb up a tall tree. The ogress asks them how to climb the tree and following their false instructions falls from the tree to her death. In some versions, the children come down from the tree, cut the ogress open, and rescue their mother inside.[14]

The tale is equally popular in Korea. Eighteen versions are cited in In-Hak Choi, *A Type Index of Korean Folktales* (1979). They too include the detail that the children escape from the tiger by saying they have to go to the toilet.[15]

Even from these abbreviated summaries of the Chinese, Japanese, and Korean traditions, it should be obvious that the Perrault literary reworking of AT 333 is far from being the most typical version of the tale type. Once one admits that the Perrault version does not contain many of the most distinctive and essential traits of the oral tale, one may then turn to the Grimm version. A series of scholars have documented that the Grimm version came from Marie Hassenpflug, a woman with a French Huguenot background. Textual comparisons tend to substantiate the claim that the Grimms essentially reworked the Perrault version. Jack Zipes reminds us, "As is generally known, the major change made by the Grimms in their version of Little Red Cap was the happy ending. Here the Grimms borrowed a motif from the folk tale The Wolf and the Seven Kids. A hunter saves Little Red Cap and her granny and they proceed to fill the wolf's belly with stones. When the wolf tries to jump up and escape, the stones cause his death."[16] If the Grimms simply altered the Perrault version, then we would appear to have a case of a literary reworking of a literary reworking of an oral tale. The Grimm version of LRRH would thus be "twice removed" from genuine oral tradition.

The "twice removed" status of the Grimm version of AT 333 should serve to illustrate the distinction made earlier between analyzing pure oral tradition and literary reworkings of that tradition. On the other hand, it should also be pointed out that the Grimms' restoration of the happy ending is entirely in accord with fairy-tale morphology. Nearly all *oral* fairy tales end happily. Moreover, if we assume that AT 123 and AT 333 are probably cognates, possibly subtypes of the same general tale type (with the critical difference depending upon whether the wolf comes to the house of the children or the children come to the house of the wolf), then the fact that the Grimms may have borrowed the ending of AT 123 to affix to the Perrault version of AT 333 may not be such a heinous literary crime. We have seen that in the Japanese versions of AT 333 the children in some instances cut the ogress open and rescue their mother inside.

The possible cognate relationship between AT 123 and AT 333 is actually hinted at by Stith Thompson insofar as he cross-references the two types in his revision of the tale type index. One of the weaknesses of the Aarne-Thompson tale type index system stems from the decision (by Aarne) to classify folktales on the basis of dramatic personae rather than upon plot structure. Because of this arbitrary decision, AT

9B, In the Division of the Crop the Fox Takes the Corn, the Bear the More Bulky Chaff, is classified as an animal tale while the very same tale, if told of man and ogre rather than fox and bear, becomes AT 1030, The Crop Division. It is obvious that AT 9B and AT 1030 should be considered under the rubric of a single unifying tale type. In the same way, one can see that AT 43, The Bear Builds a House of Wood, the Fox of Ice, is equivalent to AT 1097, The Ice Mill. As a matter of fact, Thompson's synoptic summary of the latter tale type reads: "Like Type 43 with man and ogre in place of animals." In the same fashion, one may compare AT 34, The Wolf Dives into the Water for Reflected Cheese, with AT 1336, Diving for Cheese. Again, Thompson's summary of the latter includes "This is Type 34 with human actors."

The point in the present context is that it may not be at all unreasonable to consider AT 123 and AT 333 as part of one and the same tale type. Eberhard, an expert in Chinese folklore, comments "The use of the Aarne-Thompson types involves . . . some difficulties when non-European tales are studied. In our case, the Grandaunt Tiger story is classified as AT 123, but one form of our tale is very similar to AT 333. . . . Yet for the Chinese, both variants are the same story, not different stories."[17]

If tale type AT 123 and AT 333 should prove to be cognate, then one must reexamine Jack Zipes's claim that "research has proven rather conclusively that Little Red Riding Hood is of fairly modern vintage. By modern, I mean that the basic elements of the tale were developed in an oral tradition during the late Middle Ages, largely in France, Tyrol, and northern Italy."[18] AT 123 goes back to classical antiquity, as Haim Schwarzbaum reminds us in *The Mishle Shu-Alim (Fox Fables) of Rabbi Berechiah Ha-Nakdan* (1979).[19] For instance, the tale is an Aesopic fable. In Perry's *Aesopica*, we find a version of AT 123 with a curious phrase strangely reminiscent of the cannibalistic content of some of the oral versions of AT 333. When the wolf comes to the goat's door, he tries to imitate the mother goat's voice. The smart kid's response is "Vocem matris audio; sed tu fallax et inimicus es, et sub matris voce nostrum quaeris sanguinem bibere et carnes edere."[20] Specifically, the kid's taunt that the wolf's disguise is just so he can "drink blood and eat flesh" is strikingly similar to the inversion in AT 333 where it is the wolf who dupes LRRH into drinking the blood and eating the flesh of her grandmother. French folklorist Marie Louise

Tenèze, in an essay devoted to AT 123 based upon some sixty French versions, considers it one of the most popular animal tales in France.[21] I cannot forbear remarking that the first word in Perry's Latin text in *Aesopica* is Capella, which means she-goat, and I wonder if there could possibly be any phonetic connection between this word and set of names for the heroine of AT 333 in the Romance-language tradition, e.g., in Italian she is Cappuccetto. Stranger things have happened than to have original Latin words transformed into puzzling neologisms—for example, "hoc est corpus" becoming "hocus pocus," through parody of the Eucharist, although this may be only a folk etymology.

In any event, I trust that this discussion of versions of AT 333 (and AT 123) shows conclusively that all those interpreters of LRRH who have based their respective analyses on just the Grimm version or even just the two Grimm and Perrault versions have unnecessarily handicapped themselves. What are these various interpretations of LRRH?

Perhaps the earliest were solar in nature. In 1865, Edward B. Tylor, regarded by some as the founding father of modern cultural anthropology, mentioned LRRH in his *Researches into the Early History of Mankind,* comparing the story to other accounts of swallowed protagonists and suggesting that it might have solar significance. The protagonist representing the sun was swallowed by night; the release from the monster's stomach signified the sun being set free at dawn. Tylor took up the subject again in his discussion of sunset and sunrise myths in *Primitive Culture* (1871): "Stories belonging to the same group are not unknown in European folk-lore. One is the story of Little Red Ridinghood, mutilated in the English nursery version, but known more perfectly by old wives in Germany, who can tell that the lovely little maid in her shining red satin cloak was swallowed with her grandmother by the Wolf, but they both came out safe and sound when the hunter cut open the sleeping beast. Anyone who can fancy with prince Hal, 'the blessed sun himself a fair hot wench in flame-coloured taffeta,' and can then imagine her swallowed up by Skoll, the Sun-devouring Wolf of Scandinavian mythology, may be inclined to class the tale of Little Red Ridinghood as a myth of sunset and sunrise."[22] George W. Cox, in the *Mythology of the Aryan Nations* (1870), offered a slight variant of this interpretation: "In Teutonic folk-lore the night or darkness is commonly the ravening wolf, the Fenris of the *Edda.* This is the evil beast who swallows up Little Red Cap or Red Riding Hood, the evening with the scarlet robe of twilight."[23] Here LRRH is the evening rather than the sun. It is somewhat ironic that Max Müller, the indefatigable champion of solar mythology, urged caution in interpreting LRRH in this way. In a review of solar mythologist Hyacinthe Husson's *La chaîne traditionelle* (1874) in which Husson had suggested that LRRH was the dawn, Müller remarked that without proper supporting philological evidence, "It would be a bold assertion to say that the story of Red Riding Hood was really a metamorphosis of an ancient story of the rosy-fingered Eos."[24] Note well the diversity of solar mythological opinion as to whether LRRH is the sun, the evening, or the dawn. Then there was also the lunar school of interpretation, competing with its earlier solar counterpart, which insisted that LRRH, who disappeared and reappeared, was a moon figure.[25]

The pioneering Danish folklorist Axel Olrik published an essay in 1894, "Den lille Rødhaette," in which he took Tylor's comparative approach as a point of departure.[26] Assembling various examples of swallowing-monster narratives, Olrik sought to show that the monster represented death. Hence, he concluded that such stories constitute life-and-death struggles and that is why the protagonist might be associated with "light" and the "sun" as rebirth images in contrast to "darkness" and "night." Olrik's interpretation drew fire from fellow Dane V. Holst, who contended that the monster in such tales represented spiritual and material oppression as manifested in unfair political and social conditions. This 1895 rejoinder would appear to be an early Marxist reading of folklore materials. Olrik in his rebuttal of Holst strongly opposed such allegorical readings—at the same time refusing to admit that his own interpretation of LRRH was highly allegorical.[27]

Ritual or myth-ritual interpretations of LRRH are of two types. The first argues that the tale reflects a seasonal ritual in which typically spring conquers winter. This calendrical battle is the interpretation proposed by Saintyves.[28] Here LRRH is spring (or the month of May) escaping from the winter-wolf. It is not unlike Olrik's life-and-death reading of the tale. The second type of ritual interpretation insists that fairy tales are remnants or reflections of puberty initiation rites. Vladimir Propp, for example, in his 1946 *Historical Roots of the Fairy Tale,* contended that fairy tales stemmed from an early matriarchal cultural stage of evolutionary development. The gist of this form of ritual interpretation might be summarized as follows: a girl leaves her childhood home, experiences the onset of menses, fulfills set tasks (especially those involved in cleansing a donor figure or a donor figure's dwelling), and finally marries, signifying maturation. One can readily see how Propp's 1928 *Morphology of the Folktale* led to this interpretation even though Alfred Winterstein had already proposed just such an interpretation of female fairy tales in his 1928 essay "Die Pubertätsriten der Mädchen und ihre Spuren im Märchen."[29]

Ritual interpretations of LRRH have continued unabated. In his 1963 essay, "La fiaba al lume della psicoanalisis," Glauco Carloni combines ritual and psychoanalytic approaches to LRRH, relying upon Saintyves and Propp for the ritual theory.[30] In similar fashion, Anselmo Calvetti, in his 1980 essay, "Tracce di Riti di Iniziazione nelle Fiabe di Cappuccetto Rosso e delle Tre Ochine," relies not only on Propp and Lévi-Strauss, but also on Van Gennep's rites of passage insofar as he sees LRRH's departure from home as a rite of separation, her time in the woods as a marginal or liminal period, her initiation test in the grandmother's house when she is eaten by the wolf, and finally her rebirth or readmission into adult society when she is rescued from the wolf's stomach.[31] Yvonne Verdier's 1978 essay (which appeared in slightly abridged form in 1980), "Le Petit Chaperon Rouge dans la tradition orale," also adopts a ritual stance: "The sojourn in the little house of the grandmother presents all the characteristics of an initiation . . . her entrance is death, her leaving is birth . . . the little girl is instructed about her feminine future."[32]

There is simply no end to the interpretations offered of LRRH. Marianne Rumpf in her 1951 doctoral dissertation, "Rotkäppchen —Eine vergleichende Märchenuntersuchung," based, however, on only forty versions of the tale, dismisses the interpretive efforts of Olrik and Saintyves and suggests that the tale is simply a warning or cautionary tale.[33] According to such a functional approach, the tale is told to keep young girls from straying from home into dangerous forests. The contrast between home and forest has also been a point of departure for structural and semiotic readings of LRRH, with home representing "culture" and the outside world of the forest representing "nature."[34]

The nature-culture dichotomy reminds us of one of the most curious sets of folktale interpretations of all those proposed. These interpretations are inspired by anthroposophy, a school of spiritual science founded by Rudolf Steiner (1861–1925). Anthroposophical reasoning, similar to Jungian theory, argues that primeval man was in touch with nature and that this intuitive sense has been continually dulled by the inevitable encroachment of civilization. To get back in touch with archetypal reality—and Steiner does employ the term *archetype*[35]—one is advised to rediscover fairy tales and partake of the spiritual wisdom contained therein. Wisdom is one of the key words in anthroposophy and most of the numerous German books in this vein contain "Weisheit" somewhere in the title.[36]

In one typical reading of LRRH, first published by N. Glas in 1947, we are told: "The fairy stories collected by the brothers Grimm are an infinite source of . . . pictures of events taking place within the human soul. In modern times, as a result of childhood spent in towns and of the mechanisation of life, it becomes more and more difficult to apprehend the intimate stirrings of the soul and the spirit."[37] The essence of the interpretation is that grandmother is an old woman who is "weak and ill and in need of succour." Red Riding Hood comes to the rescue carrying "bread and wine." "In the Christian Church the Christ comes to the human being in the Bread and Wine; through the Bread and Wine sickness shall be healed."[38] The huntsman signifies *wisdom* (not to be confused with "mere intellectual cleverness"). In another anthroposophical reading of LRRH, the hunter is said to be reminiscent of the Holy Ghost.[39] In the end, the grandmother "eats the cake, the bread and drinks the wine; in other words, she receives the Holy Communion." Glas concludes, "The fairy tale 'Red Riding Hood' describes thus in a most wonderful way the victory of the human soul over the wild and tempting forces of the wolf which want to prevent it from treading the true path into the future."[40]

Steiner and his followers, it must be noted, have produced a large number of interpretative books on fairy tales in various languages going back at least to Steiner's own lecture "The Interpretation of Fairy Tales," given in Berlin in December, 1908. Anthroposophists are not much interested in criticisms of their approach. Indeed, some of their books, for example, Rudolf Steiner's own *The Mission of Folk-Souls (in Connection with Germanic Scandinavian Mythology)* (1929) bears a clear caveat on its title page: "Printed for Members of the School of Spiritual Science, Goetheanum, Class I. No person is held qualified to form a judgment on the contents of this work, who has not acquired—through the School itself or in an equivalent manner recognised by the School—the requisite preliminary knowledge. Other opinions will be disregarded; the authors decline to take them as a basis for discussion."[41]

The psychoanalytic study of LRRH began with Freud, not just because he was the founder of psychoanalysis but also because he specifically commented on the tale. In "On the Sexual Theories of Children," a paper published in 1908, Freud described the so-called cloacal theory of creation. Children ignorant of the birth process might logically assume that "babies" who grow in the body of the mother must exit the body in the same way that all objects located in the general area of the stomach leave the body, namely, via the anus: "The child must be expelled like excrement. . . . If in later childhood the same question is the subject of solitary reflection or of a discussion between two children, the explanations probably are that the baby comes out of the navel, which opens, or that the belly is slit and the child taken out, as happens to the wolf in the tale of Little Red Riding-Hood."[42] Freud continues, "If babies are born through the anus then a man can give birth just as well as a woman. A boy can therefore fancy that he too has children of his own without our needing to accuse him of feminine inclinations." Freud's remarkable insight about male pregnancy envy and how it might be manifested in anal terms has inspired analyses of creation myths, e.g., the creation of earth or man from mud or dust.[43] In the present context, we can only regret that Freud knew only the Grimm version of AT 333. What might have he thought in the light of versions of the same tale with explicit anality!

In his 1913 essay "The Occurrence in Dreams of Material from Fairy-Tales," Freud deals more extensively with LRRH. A young male patient had a dream in which white wolves appeared in a tree. The patient remembered being "tremendously afraid of the picture of a wolf in a book of fairy tales. . . . He thought this picture might have been an illustration to the story of 'Little Red Riding Hood.' " Freud's knowledge of the Grimm canon stood him in good stead for he suggested to the patient that the childhood image probably referred not to LRRH but to "The Wolf and the Seven Little Goats": "The white, too, comes into this story, for the wolf had his paw made white at the baker's after the little goats had recognized him on his first visit by his grey paw." Freud goes on to say, "Moreover, the two fairy-tales [that is, what folklorists now call AT 123 and AT 333] have much in common. In both there is the eating up, the cutting open of the belly, the taking out of the people who have been eaten and their replacement by heavy stones, and finally in both of them the wicked wolf perishes."[44]

Freud was not only interested in helping his patients but also in the analysis of folklore. For Freud, folklore was an aid to understanding patients just as psychoanalysis was an aid to understanding folklore. Folklore and psychoanalysis were understood to be mutually or reciprocally beneficial. Freud concluded his essay: "If in my patient's case the wolf was merely a first father-surrogate, the question arises whether the hidden content in the fairy-tales of the wolf that ate up the little goats and of 'Little Red Riding Hood' may not simply be infantile fear of the father." Freud remarked that his patient's father had the habit of indulging in "affectionate abuse" and that he may have threatened in fun to "gobble him up." Another of Freud's patients told him that her two children could never get to be fond of their grandfather "because in the course of his affectionate romping with them he used to frighten them by saying he would cut open their tummies."[45] Freud reiterated his remarks about LRRH in the longer write-up of the same case in his 1918 paper "From the History of an Infantile Neurosis."[46]

The psychoanalytic treatment of LRRH continued with brief contributions by Otto Rank and Carl Jung. In 1912, Rank, no doubt influenced by Freud's 1908 paper "On the Sexual Theories of Children," attempted to survey what he termed "folk psychological parallels to infantile sexual theories." In his extensive consideration of myths and folktales, Rank judged LRRH to be the best-known illustration of the infantile notion of either opening or cutting the stomach to induce birth. In 1913, the year that Jung began to reject psychoanalytic theory in favor of what was to become analytical psychology, he published "Versuch einer Darstellung der psychoanalytischen Theorie," in which he interpreted the wolf as the father with the fear of being swallowed as an expression of a fear of intercourse. Jung at this point was still very much under the influence of Freud.[47]

Perhaps the first significant psychoanalytic interpretation of LRRH was that written by Erich Fromm in 1951 in *The Forgotten Language*. He claimed, as so many psychoanalysts arrogantly do, that "Most of the symbolism in this fairy tale can be understood without difficulty." According to Fromm, "The 'little cap of red velvet' is a symbol of menstruation. The little girl of whose adventures we hear has become a mature woman and is now confronted with the problem of sex. The warning 'not to run off the path' so as not 'to fall and break the bottle' is clearly a warning against the danger of sex and of losing her virginity. The wolf's sexual appetite is aroused by the sight of the girl and he tries to seduce her."[48]

Fromm argues that the fairy tale is more than simply a moralistic tale warning of the danger of sex. He claims that the "male is portrayed as a ruthless and cunning animal, and the sexual act is described as a cannibalistic act in which the male devours the female." According to Fromm, this view is not held by women who like men and enjoy sex. It is an expression of a deep antagonism against men and sex. Fromm continues, "But the hate and prejudice against men are even more clearly exhibited at the end of the story . . . we must remember that the woman's superiority consists in her ability to bear children. How, then, is the wolf made ridiculous? By showing that he attempted to play the role of a pregnant woman, having living things in his belly. Little Red-Cap puts stones, a symbol of sterility, into his belly, and the wolf collapses and dies. His deed, according to the primitive law of retaliation, is punished according to his crime: he is killed by the stones, the symbol of sterility, which mock his usurpation of the pregnant woman's role."[49]

Fromm concludes, "This fairy tale, in which the main figures are three generations of women (the huntsman at the end is the conventional father figure without real weight), speaks of the male-female conflict; it is a story of triumph by man-hating women, ending with their victory."[50]

Robert Darnton, in his 1984 book *The Great Cat Massacre,* writes a devastating critique of Fromm's interpretation, a critique based in part upon source criticism. Darnton notes that the symbols Fromm "saw in his version of the text were based on details that did not exist in the versions known to peasants in the seventeenth and eighteenth centuries." Darnton explains, "Thus he makes a great deal of the (nonexistent) red riding hood as a symbol of menstruation and of the (nonexistent) admonition not to stray from the path into wild terrain where she might break it. The wolf is the ravishing male. And the two (nonexistent) stones that are placed in the wolf's belly after the (nonexistent) hunter extricates the girl and her grandmother, stand for sterility, the punishment for breaking a sexual taboo. So, with an uncanny sensitivity to detail that did not occur in the original folktale, the psychoanalyst takes us into a mental universe that never existed, at least not before the advent of psychoanalysis."[51]

Darnton argues like a folklorist when he points out the fallacy of

Fromm's analyzing a single version, namely, the Grimm version of a tale type, but he himself errs when he seeks to extrapolate social history from such tales. Fairy tales are by generic definition "fiction," *not* fact. Although occasional ethnographic or social facts may certainly be extracted from fairy tales, it is a methodological mistake to assume a one-to-one relationship between fairy tales and reality. A purely literal or historical approach to fairy tales yields precious little hard data. For one thing, it is not possible to "date" fairy tales in one particular century. Assuming, for example, that the Chinese, Japanese, and Korean versions of AT 333 cited earlier in this essay are indeed cognate with the French and other European versions of the tale type, one must assume a far greater time depth for the tale than the seventeenth century. Eberhard refers to a seventeenth-century Chinese version of AT 333, for example.[52] It would therefore be the height of folly to assume that most of the incidental details of the tale represent seventeenth-century peasant France.

Quite a different psychoanalytic interpretation of LRRH is offered by Géza Róheim. In a 1940 essay, "The Dragon and the Hero," he offers brief exegeses of both AT 123 and AT 333. His basic view is that the tales reflect oral aggression on the part of infants. He cites a Romanian version of AT 123 in which the she-goat reveals to her children before leaving them what she will later say as a password so that they will let her in. "It is all about the good things she is going to give them to eat. She has milk in the breast and cheese on her lips." Evidently, Róheim contends, "the narrative has something to do with the oral trauma. An absent nipple is a wicked child eating mother and whenever the she-goat is not at home 'the wolf is at the door.' The youngest kid is probably the oldest and instead of wishing to rescue all the other kids swallowed by the wicked wolf-mother it really wishes to cut them out of its mother's body. As the wolf has become a wolf by not nursing its children, it dies in the attempt to assuage its thirst."[53] Róheim's preliminary analysis of LRRH is a bit more cryptic, although it is along similar lines. "The point is that Little Red Riding Hood (as Wolf) eats the grandmother first and is then eaten by the grandmother-wolf in the phase of talio-anxiety."[54] What is significant about Róheim's first attempt at analyzing AT 333 is that it draws attention to the cannibalistic component of the oral tales.

In the oral tales, the female protagonist does eat the body of her grandmother. One might object that LRRH does so unwittingly, but that is a necessary device in folktale projections of psychological traumas. In folklore fantasy, characters typically do what they would like to do but which everyday society forbids or interdicts. The sad part about most analyses of folklore is that the emphasis is wrongly put on the moralistic interdictions. Yes, the interdictions are surely present, but what is critical in folklore is that they are always violated. It is a mistake to see only that the norms of a society are reflected in that society's folklore. Folklore articulates social sanctions at the very same time that it permits, through wishful thinking, escape from those very same social sanctions.[55]

Infants who breast-feed eventually learn that when their teeth are in place, they possess their first real weapon. Any mother or wet nurse can testify to the pain that such little teeth can inflict when a nursing baby becomes satiated or unhappy during nursing. Through the principle of *lex talionis,* a guilty act is punished by the same means as those employed in the commission of the original crime. Hence biting or eating the mother's breast would be punishable by the mother's (or father's) biting or eating the naughty infant. (It is my contention, incidentally, that the psychological origin of the wide-spread vagina dentata motif comes from a projection of the first weapon of the infant, that is, the teeth that bite the breast. As a male infant bites a female body protuberance so later his fear of females finds expression in an imagined toothed vagina which threatens to bite his phallus.)

In 1953, the year of his death, Róheim published short separate essays on both AT 123 and AT 333. In his study of AT 123, "The Wolf and the Seven Kids," Róheim, unlike most psychoanalysts, makes good use of comparative data. Accordingly, he cites an interesting version from Lorraine in which the wolf jumps down the chimney into a cauldron of boiling milk. Róheim's analysis concludes, "The objectively good mother does not, moreover, satisfy the insatiable cravings of the child and to that extent becomes *ipso facto* an ogress. The infant's fantasy of being devoured by the mother is a fear through retaliation of its wish to devour the mother."[56] This remark would certainly apply to the story of LRRH. LRRH's attempt to devour her grandmother is followed immediately by the wolf-grandmother's attempt to devour her. This is precisely the plot of the oral French versions of the tale. Róheim, in his essay "Fairy Tale and Dream," offers an interpretation of LRRH. After commenting upon the forced *moralité* added to Perrault's story which makes the wolf into the typical symbol of male aggression and sexuality, Róheim acutely remarks that such tales end in disaster for the young girl because they "are written from a pedagogical angle." When he returns to the oral versions, Róheim reiterates the same theory he proposed for AT 123: "Aggression is combined with regression and it follows that the idea of being swallowed, being eaten, is the talio aspect of this aggression. The cannibal child creates a cannibal mother."[57]

In the above discussion of Róheim's psychoanalytic interpretation of LRRH, I have intentionally omitted some of the more controversial aspects of his analysis. For example, Róheim believes that fairy tales come from dreams. Such parts of his interpretation are extremely hard to substantiate. He remarks, "To go on sleeping after its stomach has been cut open several times is quite an achievement, even for a folk-tale wolf. We can only understand this if we assume that the wolf, the grandmother, and the little girl, are essentially the same person."[58] Róheim continues, "Red Riding Hood is swallowed into her own 'sleep-womb' which is at the same time the inside of her mother. The hunter would then be correctly interpreted as the father figure, as a rival for the inside (or breast) of the mother."[59]

A number of other psychoanalytic treatments of LRRH can be mentioned briefly. In 1955, Elizabeth Crawford, inspired by Róheim's analysis of AT 123, wrote "The Wolf as Condensation." She argued that the wolf in that tale "is father and mother simultaneously." In her analysis of LRRH, she continues her efforts to see the wolf as a complex figure, representing "good and bad, giver and taker, sexual object desired and feared." The complexity is summarized by her statement that "The wolf seduces, but the children invite seduction and danger."[60] Much the same argument could be sustained about the parental-seduction-of-children fantasy. Parents may act seductively toward their own children, but children also engage in seductive behavior toward their own parents of the opposite sex.

Carloni's insightful psychoanalytic treatment of LRRH (1963) draws heavily from Róheim, combining this approach with a ritual-initiation analysis deriving from Saintyves and Propp.[61] Also in 1963 appeared Julius E. Heuscher's *A Psychiatric Study of Fairy Tales*. Heuscher, with his mixture of Jungian theory, anthroposophy, and psychoanalysis, is not always clear. With respect to LRRH, his interpretation is in part Oedipal. He disagrees with Fromm's opinion that the huntsman is a weak figure. Rather he sees the huntsman as a "*strong* Father-image." According to Heuscher, "The huntsman who carries off the wolf's skin combines now the human and sexual aspects of the male without being threatening. He shows that he has control over his animal drives."[62]

In 1966, Lilla Veszy-Wagner published her "Little Red Riding Hoods on the Couch" in the *Psychoanalytic Forum,* accompanied by comments by four discussants and a final response by the author. Here we find the usual parochial lack of knowledge of tale types. The author begins by saying, "There seems to be no particularly relevant folkloristic materials available to this story outside Europe so we may infer that problems pertaining to this tale seem to be more connected with the unconscious of the European mind."[63] One of her discussants, Mark Kanzer, offers the following psychoanalytic "translation" of LRRH: "The pubescent girl, at the time of menstruation, defies her mother's warnings and enters into conversation with a strange man who accosts her. Taken to his room (which fuses in her unconscious with the bedroom of her parents), she inspects his body and is consumed sexually (just as mother has been by father). There follows (foreshortened in time) a pregnancy and delivery. However, a denial element is registered at this point: not the girl but the 'wolf' becomes pregnant while she is delivered from his body by a good man, the hunter. The wolf, justly enough, succumbs to the perils of the pregnancy he has engendered."[64] Kanzer adds that he finds some support for Fromm's suggestion that there is an allusion to the inability of the male wolf to bear children: "With the aid of the well-known equation, stones = feces, we find that he cannot, after all, convert his feces into children."

Another discussant, Thomas Mintz, proposes that the tale be looked at as a dream, in which case "one might see all the characters in the story as representing the dreamer: the wolf would represent sexual temptation and cannibalistic desires (the id) which must be killed off by the punishing huntsman (the superego) in order that the small child (the ego) will not be consumed and overwhelmed."[65]

No doubt the best known psychoanalytic interpretation of LRRH is that written by Bruno Bettelheim in his 1976 book *The Uses of Enchantment.* To his credit, Bettelheim is aware that there are versions (e.g., French) other than those of Perrault and the Grimms, but he makes absolutely no reference to any of the previous psychoanalytic treatments of the tale, e.g., those cited in this essay. Bettelheim's interpretation differs radically from Róheim's. For example, he claims that, in contrast to Hansel and Gretel, who suffer from an oral fixation, "Little Red Cap, who has outgrown her oral fixation, no longer has any destructive oral desires."[66] I suggest that the overt cannibalistic details of the oral versions of AT 333 would not support Bettelheim's contention. When the protagonist devours her grandmother's body, that would seem to be prima facie "destructive oral desires."

Bettelheim, aware of the versions of the tale in which LRRH has to choose between taking the road of needles and the road of pins, remarks in a footnote that pins represent the pleasure principle while needles represent the reality principle. His reasoning is that it is easier to fasten things together with pins; it is much more work to fasten things by needles, that is, by sewing. From this viewpoint, LRRH's decision to take the path of pins signals her intention to indulge in the pleasure principle.[67]

For Bettelheim, the wolf is "not just the male seducer, he also represents all the asocial, animalistic tendencies within ourselves. . . . Little Red Cap's danger is her budding sexuality, for which she is not yet emotionally mature enough."[68] Bettelheim maintains that LRRH's giving explicit directions to the wolf as to how to find grandmother's house is an admission that she is not ready for sexuality, but that grandmother, a mature woman, is. Bettelheim feels that the tale of LRRH is basically an Oedipal one: "With the reactivation in puberty of early oedipal longings, the girl's wish for her father, her inclination to seduce him, and her desire to be seduced by him, also become reactivated. Then the girl feels she deserves to be punished terribly by the mother, if not the father also, for her desire to take him away from Mother."[69] Thus as long as mother or grandmother is around, the girl is not free to seduce/be seduced by the wolf. According to Bettelheim, the story "on this level deals with the daughter's unconscious wish to be seduced by her father (the wolf)."[70] This is why so many of the illustrations of the tale concentrate on the scene with Little Red Riding Hood in bed with the wolf. For Bettelheim, the father is present in the story in two forms: the wolf "which is an externalization of the dangers of overwhelming oedipal feelings, and as the hunter in his protective and rescuing function."[71]

There have been psychoanalytic interpretations of LRRH since Bettelheim, for example, that included by Carl-Heinz Mallet in his

Kennen Sie Kinder? (1981).[72] However, few new insights have emerged. Not mentioned in this survey are various Jungian-inspired readings of LRRH which, true to analytical psychology (as opposed to psychoanalysis), disavow the sexual content of fairy tales, preferring instead to emphasize individuation and maturation.[73]

What has been the reaction to these various psychoanalytic readings of LRRH? We may consider that of Jack Zipes to be representative. Zipes's response to Bettelheim's treatment of LRRH is colored somewhat by his primary concern with the Grimms (and also Perrault's) manipulation of an oral tale. Zipes insists that these males twisted what was originally a girl-centered fairy tale (in which she triumphs unaided over the villainous wolf figure) into a story in which female sexuality is squelched and in which either a naughty female is killed by a male punishing wolf (Perrault) or a victimized female must await rescue at the hands of a male huntsman. Zipes traces these "civilizing" and moralizing trends through a host of literary editions of LRRH and moreover adduces convincing evidence for his thesis from the illustrations in these children's books, illustrations drawn mainly by males, of course. From Perrault's conversion of LRRH into a cautionary tale to the Grimms' revision of the Perrault tale at the beginning of the nineteenth century, Zipes sees a reflection of a shift of emphasis reflecting the growing impact of bourgeois morality. As Zipes remarks near the end of his important introductory essay in *The Trials & Tribulations of Little Red Riding Hood,* "Little Red Riding Hood is a *male* creation and projection. Not women but men—Perrault and the Brothers Grimm—gave birth to our common image of Little Red Riding Hood."[74] Zipes says further, "Viewed in this light, *Little Red Riding Hood* reflects men's fear of women's sexuality—and of their own as well. The curbing and regulation of sexual drives is fully portrayed in this bourgeois literary fairy tale on the basis of deprived male needs. Red Riding Hood is to blame for her own rape. The wolf is not really a male but symbolizes natural urges and social nonconformity. The real hero of the tale, the hunter-gamekeeper, is male governance."[75]

In a reprise essay of 1983–84 entitled "A Second Gaze at 'Little Red Riding Hood's Tribulations,' " Zipes reiterates his view that the Perrault and Grimm versions of LRRH "have served as models for numerous writers of both sexes throughout the world who have either amplified, distorted, or disputed the facts about the little girl's rape." In Zipes's words, "Instead of being raped to death, both grandma and grand-daughter are saved by a male hunter or gamekeeper, who polices the woods. Only a strong male figure can rescue a girl from herself and her lustful desires."[76]

From this perspective, we can more easily appreciate Zipes's reaction to Fromm's and Bettelheim's psychoanalytic readings of LRRH. First of all, Fromm and Bettelheim do not realize that the tale they analyze is "*not* an ancient and anonymous folk tale reflecting 'universal' psychic operations of men and women, but rather it is the product of gifted male European writers, who projected their needs and values onto the actions of fictitious characters within a socially conventionalized genre."[77] Secondly, Zipes contends that Fromm, Bettelheim, and others have exacerbated the problem because they—as males—have interpreted the Perrault and Grimm versions "to reaffirm conventional male attitudes towards women; the girl is guilty because of her natural inclinations and disobedience."[78] Fromm, it may be recalled, claimed the tale displayed hate and prejudice against men and that it constituted a story of triumph by man-hating women while Bettelheim felt that Little Red Cap's danger is her budding sexuality for which she is not yet emotionally mature enough.[79] In other words, both the male-altered tale *and* the male interpretations of this tale constitute a kind of male conspiracy to stereotype and dominate women.

Support for Zipes's position may be found in Eric Berne's pop(ular) psychology manual, *What Do You Say after You Say Hello?* (1972). Berne gives what he pretends might be a Martian's reaction to the tale:

> What kind of a mother sends a little girl into a forest where there are wolves? Why didn't her mother do it herself, or go along with LRRH? If grandmother was so helpless, why did mother leave her all by herself in a hut far away? But if LRRH had to go, how come her mother had never warned her not to stop and talk to wolves? The story makes it clear that LRRH had never been told that this was dangerous. No mother could really be that stupid, so it sounds as if her mother didn't care much what happened to LRRH, or maybe even wanted to get rid of her. No little girl is that stupid either. How could LRRH look at the wolf's eyes, ears, hands, and teeth, and still think it was her grandmother? Why didn't she get out of there as fast as she could? And a mean little thing she was, too, gathering up stones to put into the wolf's belly. At any rate, any straight-thinking

girl, after talking to the wolf, would certainly not have stopped to pick flowers, but would have said to herself: "That son of a bitch is going to eat up my grandmother if I don't get some help fast."[80]

In similar fashion, Berne makes the Martian ponder the motivations of all the dramatis personae in the tale. The mother is evidently trying to lose her daughter "accidentally"; the wolf, instead of eating rabbits and such, is obviously overreaching himself; grandmother lives alone and leaves her door unlatched, so she may be hoping for something interesting to happen; the hunter is obviously a rescuer who enjoys working over his vanquished opponents with sweet little maidens to help; and LRRH tells the wolf quite explicitly where he can meet her again, and even climbs into bed with him. She is obviously playing "Rapo"—Berne is famous for coining the "Games People Play" metaphor—and ends up quite happy about the whole affair.[81]

Berne concludes his Martian musing as follows: "The truth of the matter is that everybody in the story is looking for action at almost any price. If the payoff at the end is taken at face value, then the whole thing was a plot to do in the poor wolf by making him think he was outsmarting everybody, using LRRH as bait. In that case, the moral of the story is not that innocent maidens should keep out of forests where there are wolves, but that wolves should keep away from innocent-looking maidens and their grandmothers; in short a wolf should not walk through the forest alone. This also raises the interesting question of what the mother did after she got rid of LRRH for the day."[82]

This would certainly seem to be a fine example of Zipes's point that males insist upon projecting their sexual fantasies upon women. Men do not rape women; instead women ask to be raped. In Berne's terms, LRRH is playing "Rapo."

The problem for the folklorist with all this is that Zipes is really interested only in the particular impact of the Perrault and Grimm versions of AT 333 upon European society from the seventeenth century to the present. There is nothing wrong with such a scholarly concern, but it is *not* the same thing as being interested in the underlying, original oral folktale as such. We return to a theme mentioned at the outset of this essay. The study of one or two literary versions of an oral tale, no matter how important those literary versions may be, is no substitute for a full-fledged folkloristic study of the oral *and* literary versions of a given tale.

What then is one to make of all the various interpretations of LRRH? While they are not all mutually exclusive, one might wish to argue that some are more persuasive than others. Certainly the solar interpretations and others which depend upon one particular trait, e.g., the red cap or hood, which in fact does *not* occur in the vast majority of available versions, are suspect. Within the more limited category of psychoanalytic interpretations, we clearly find discrepancies. Fromm suggests the tale is about the battle of the sexes; Róheim sees the tale as basically pre-Oedipal with an emphasis upon infantile oral aggression; Bettelheim specifically denies such a theme. Recall his claim that Little Red Cap had outgrown her oral fixation and that she "no longer has any destructive oral desires." Bettelheim opts for a more Oedipal or Electral interpretation of LRRH. One could, of course, argue that fairy tales, like dreams, are overdetermined, that is, they stem from more than one cause. In that event, a particular tale could contain both pre-Oedipal (in this case oral) *and* Oedipal elements.

From the vantage point afforded by folkloristics, we can see that most of the interpretations cited failed to make use of the full panoply of oral texts of LRRH available. No psychoanalytic (or any other) interpretation of the tale has utilized the numerous versions of the basic tale type found in China, Japan, and Korea. (There are also many African versions of the tale type.)[83] The indisputable evidence of the existence of the tale in Asia would seem to militate against the notion that the tale was somehow a reflection of personality features restricted to Europe. Such a narrow Europocentric approach to folklore in general and to fairy tales in particular would benefit greatly from taking account of cognate tales found in other parts of the world.

My own view, admittedly influenced by the various psychoanalytic essays devoted to the tale, is that there is good reason to believe that wishful thinking and regression abound. Any fairy tale with a female protagonist will have a female antagonist. Hence I tend to agree with Verdier's interpretation of the tale as essentially an intergenerational conflict between daughter and mother. (The grandmother is an extended form of the mother imago.) But whereas Verdier sees this conflict only in terms of LRRH, I would use the Proppian model to suggest that same-sex rivalry is a standard feature of all oral fairy tales. Thus young girls have to contend with wicked stepmothers and witches while young boys have to struggle with male dragons or giants. The sexual identity of the donor (when he or she is distinct from the villain) may

vary, but even here there is commonly a split parent with the donor
figure in "female" fairy tales being a kind female (e.g., a cow) and the
donor figure in "male" fairy tales being a helpful, wise old man.

In LRRH, we find tremendous antagonism between heroine and
female foe. We begin with a mother sending a hapless girl away from
the safety of the home. This enforced abandonment (cf. weaning)
leads the girl to take her revenge by eating her grandmother's flesh. If
one stops to think about it, one can see that breast-feeding constitutes
a kind of eating of maternal flesh in order to obtain the necessary
nourishing mother's milk. In oral versions of LRRH, the heroine eats
the flesh and blood of her grandmother, an unquestionably oral
aggressive act on the part of the girl. The infantile regression is also
signaled by the desire to defecate *immediately* after eating. Here we
have the first of a whole series of projective inversions or reversals. It is
not the infant who seeks to "do it" in bed, but the wolf-grandmother
who urges the child to do it in bed. In other words, it is the parent
who is not toilet trained while the child is. This explicit anal component of LRRH has received virtually no attention from commentators,
probably because it was one of the "ruder" elements presumably intentionally omitted by Perrault in his version.

Eberhard observes that in the Chinese context, "it is also common
that a grandmother or a mother shares her bed with one or two
children."[84] In some of the Taiwanese versions of the tale type, we find
a curious competition motif. "The tiger wants to eat the children, but
cannot possibly eat both children at once and thus must try to eat one
without arousing the suspicion of the other. Therefore the tiger
declares that only one child may sleep with 'her,' the one who wins in
a competition. The competition is usually that the girls must wash
themselves, or more specifically, wash their feet. The one who is
cleaner may sleep with the visitor."[85] The older girl, suspicious, remains
"dirty on purpose" so as to discourage the tiger from sleeping with
her. From a psychoanalytic perspective, we can see here an instance of
projective inversion. In the infantile experience, the infant associates
defecating in bed with the withdrawal and absence of the parent who
normally sleeps with it. In the fairy-tale projection, it is not the parent
but the infant who withdraws from the bed through the threat of
defecation. Indeed, in the fairy-tale projection, the parent-surrogate
actually urges the infant to "do it in bed." This explains why the
feigned wish to defecate in the tale is a reasonable and appropriate
means of escaping from the parental bed.

The reversal of the parent-child toilet-training schema—in which it is the parent who recommends doing it in bed while the child goes outside to the outhouse—is paralleled by other reversals in which the parent and child exchange places. Once outside, the child-heroine frees herself from the toddler's safety-line (rope) and later induces the tigress to have a similar line tied around her. In this way, it is the parent-figure who assumes the role of toddler-infant. Finally, in many of the Chinese versions of AT 333, the tiger grandma is killed by having hot liquid poured on her body "or into her mouth." Remember the French (Lorraine) version cited by Róheim in which the wolf jumps into a cauldron of boiling milk. The original oral aggressive tendencies of the infant are displaced or projected onto the parent-figure. It is then not the child who is hungry, but the parent. LRRH begins her adventure carrying food to her grandmother. As Róheim correctly observed, it is not the child who wants to eat up the parent; it is, through projective inversion, the parent who wants to eat up the child. Through *lex talionis,* the hungry parent is killed by having boiling fluid poured into his or her mouth, or the wolf dies by drowning in hot milk! Even in the peculiar Grimm addendum to their version of the tale which tells of a second encounter with a wolf, that second wolf is duped by oral temptation. Following her grandmother's instructions, LRRH pours the water in which yesterday's sausages were boiled into a trough. The wolf smells the scent of the sausages and falls down from the roof where he was ensconced to drown in the sausage-water.

The sequence of oral, anal, and finally genital themes in oral versions of LRRH would indicate that the application of psychoanalytic theory is not inappropriate. In Chinese, Japanese, and Korean versions of the tale, there is the added sibling rivalry component in which the hero or heroine's siblings are swallowed by the ogress.

All this leads me to conclude that the tale of LRRH is full of infantile fantasy. I believe that the evidence of the infantile nature of LRRH has been available for centuries, but folklorists and literary scholars have chosen not to consider such evidence. The oral cannibalistic eating of the mother's body, the reference to defecating in bed, the toddler's rope (which is a direct allusion to LRRH being a *very* young child), and for that matter the very insistence upon Red Riding Hood's being called *little*. Illustrators may very well depict her as a young girl approaching adolescence, but the name of the central character calls attention to her littleness, as in Le *petit* chaperon rouge and Rotkäpp*chen*.

But such clues have gone unnoticed by commentators, perhaps in part because of their resistance to psychoanalytic interpretations of fairy tales.

Some may feel that the present psychoanalytic reading of the tale somehow spoils the story by reducing it to a series of infantile wishes. Such individuals should keep in mind that all of us begin life as infants and that there is nothing wrong or unusual in retaining or even celebrating infantile desires and fears in fairy-tale form. Fairy tales are *always* told from the child's point of view, never the parents' (except in some literary versions). Furthermore, adults (no matter how old they are) never cease to be the children of their own parents. Giants and giantesses are nothing more than the infant's-eye view of adults. The fairy-tale form is sufficiently symbolically disguised so that adults seeking to fathom the depths of meaning in fairy tales can pretend to ignore or forget their earliest infantile thoughts. Perrault simply chose to edit out what he considered to be overly rude or earthy elements from the oral tale, but the basic tale, like all genuine folklore, survived.

The unconscious content of LRRH was not entirely removed by the efforts of either Perrault or the Grimm brothers. The extensive number of updatings, parodies, short stories, poems, and even cartoons based upon LRRH as documented by Hans Ritz, *Die Geschichte vom Rotkäppchen: Ursprünge, Analysen, Parodien eines Märchens* (1981); Jack Zipes, *The Trials and Tribulations of Little Red Riding Hood* (1983); and Wolfgang Mieder's essay, "Survival Forms of 'Little Red Riding Hood' in Modern Society" (1982), all reveal how much a part of contemporary culture LRRH is.[86] Even the scholarship dedicated to LRRH can provide a source of amusement, as we see in Heinrich E. Kühleborn, *Rotkäppchen und die Wölfe: Von Märchenfälschern und Landschaftszerstörern* (1982), in which the research efforts of a certain Professor Wainbrasch [= brainwash] are reported in detail.

To the extent that some of the poetic and cartoon derivatives of the tale are sexually explicit, I would argue that the moralizing effects of Perrault's cautionary tale version and the Grimm brothers' recension have not been successful in stifling the underlying content of the oral tale. The projective nature of LRRH with respect to key familial conflicts has survived the literary reworkings of the tale. While the oral versions are ever so much more explicit than most of the tame children's book adaptations, the basic infantile content remains intact. Perrault and the Grimms may have truncated the tale, but they could not destroy it. Folklorists know well that folklore once recorded does not cease to be. Little Red Riding Hood is a delightful and psychologically meaningful piece of folklore fantasy. It will remain a factor for children and adults in decades to come—even if the more explicit and direct oral versions should continue to remain in the shadow of the better-known Perrault and Grimm texts.

Notes

1. Th. P. Van Baaren, "The Flexibility of Myth," *Studies in the History of Religions*, 22 (1972), 199-206, reprinted in Alan Dundes (ed.), *Sacred Narrative: Readings in the Theory of Myth* (Berkeley: University of California Press, 1984), pp. 217-24.

2. For representative comparative studies of folktales made by folklorists, see Warren E. Roberts, *The Tale of the Kind and Unkind Girls* (Berlin: Walter de Gruyter, 1958) and Anna Birgitta Rooth, *The Cinderella Cycle* (Lund: C. W. K. Gleerup, 1951).

3. For a discussion of this methodology, see Alan Dundes, "The Study of Folklore in Literature and Culture: Identification and Interpretation," *Journal of American Folklore*, 78 (1965), 136-42.

4. The term "fakelore" was coined by Richard M. Dorson. See his "Folklore and Fakelore," *American Mercury*, 70 (1950), 335-43. See also his article "Fakelore," *Zeitschrift für Volkskunde*, 65 (1969), 56-64. For a consideration of the Grimms' tales as fakelore, see Alan Dundes, "Nationalistic Inferiority Complexes and the Fabrication of Fakelore: A Reconsideration of Ossian, the *Kinder- und Hausmärchen*, the *Kalevala*, and Paul Bunyan," *Journal of Folklore Research*, 22 (1985), 5-18.

5. For an introduction to this extraordinary collector, see Joan Rockwell, *Evald Tang Kristensen: A Lifelong Adventure in Folklore* (Aalborg: Aalborg University Press, 1982).

6. For considerations of the differences from edition to edition of the Grimms' tales, see Heinz Rölleke (ed.), *Die älteste Märchensammlung der Brüder Grimm* (Cologny-Genève: Fondation Martin Bodmer, 1975) and John M. Ellis, *One Fairy Story Too Many: The Brothers Grimm and Their Tales* (Chicago: University of Chicago Press, 1983). For a small sample of the changes in Little Red Riding Hood in the different editions, see Marianne Rumpf, "*Rotkäppchen: Eine vergleichende Märchenuntersuchung*" (Diss., Göttingen, 1951), pp. 97-98.

7. See Paul Delarue, "Le Petit Chaperon Rouge," *Bulletin folklorique d'Île-de-France*, n.s. 12 (1951), 221-28, 251-60, 283-91, where he considers some thirty-five French versions. See also his essay, "Les contes merveilleux de Perrault et la tradition populaire," *Bulletin folklorique d'Île-de-France*, 14 (1953), 511-17. For a summary in English of some of Delarue's conclusions, see his note to The Story of Grandmother (T 333) in his *Borzoi Book of French Folk Tales* (New York: Knopf, 1956), pp. 380-83. It is this version of the tale, which dates from circa 1885, which I have summarized in this essay. Literary scholars unfamiliar with

folkloristics are genuinely puzzled by Delarue's claim that this "1885" text is the "source" of Perrault's seventeenth-century tale. How can a tale collected in the nineteenth century be "older" than one recorded in the seventeenth century? The answer is that comparative studies of many, many versions of a given tale type can establish with reasonable certainty what some, if not all, of the most ancient traits or details of a tale are or were. Delarue explains this when he notes that an examination of French and Italian-Tyrolean versions shows that they share common traits which are absent from Perrault's version. He concludes that it is plausible to assume that Perrault eliminated some of those salient traits which would have shocked the society of his period. For the skeptical view, see Carole Hanks and D. T. Hanks, Jr., "Perrault's 'Little Red Riding Hood': Victim of the Revisers," *Children's Literature,* 7 (1978), 76–77, n. 2. For Delarue's remarks, see *Borzoi Book of French Folk Tales,* p. 383.

8. The idea of "striptease" I have borrowed from Marc Soriano, "Le petit chaperon rouge," *Nouvelle Revue Française,* 16 (1968), 429–43.

9. The version was first reported in Anselmo Calvetti, "Una versione romagnola di Cappuccetto Rosso," *In Rumâgna,* 2 (1975), 85–94. The dialogue cited in the present essay is also found in Calvetti, "Tracce di Riti di Iniziazione nelle Fiabe di Cappuccetto Rosso e delle Tre Ochine," *Lares,* 46 (1980), 487–96. (The dialogue is on p. 488.) For similar Italian versions of the tale, see Delarue, "Petit Chaperon Rouge," pp. 257–59. For statistics demonstrating the frequency of the cannibalistic eating of the grandmother's flesh and blood, see ibid., p. 260, and Rumpf, "Rotkäppchen," pp. 51–54.

10. Alexander Haggerty Krappe, *The Science of Folklore* (New York: Dial, 1930), p. 38.

11. For Thompson's comments, see *The Folktale* (New York: Holt, Rinehart and Winston, 1946), p. 39. For Delarue's discussion of the Asian analogues, see "Petit Chaperon Rouge," pp. 286–89. See also Rumpf, "Rotkäppchen," p. 68. Although both Delarue and Rumpf tend to see the Asian tales as related to AT 123 rather than AT 333, Delarue does state that the Chinese tales have analogous traits with LRRH which are so particularized that they cannot possibly be attributed to coincidence. In other words, they are cognate. See Delarue, "Petit Chaperon Rouge," p. 289. To be fair, it should be noted that Thompson does comment on AT 123's distribution in China, Japan, and Africa. See Thompson, *Folktale,* p. 40.

12. Nai-Tung Ting, *A Type Index of Chinese Folktales,* FFC 223 (Helsinki: Suomalainen Tiedeakatemia, 1978), pp. 61–64.

13. Wolfram Eberhard, *Studies in Taiwanese Folktales,* Asian Folklore and Social Life Monographs (Taipei: Orient Cultural Service, 1970), pp. 152, 54.

14. Hiroko Ikeda, *A Type and Motif Index of Japanese Folk-Literature,* FFC 209 (Helsinki: Suomalainen Tiedeakatemia, 1971), pp. 91–92.

15. See tale type 100 in In-Hak Choi, *A Type Index of Korean Folktales* (Seoul: Myong Ji University Publishing, 1979), pp. 27–28.

16. Jack Zipes, *The Trials and Tribulations of Little Red Riding Hood* (South Hadley, Mass.: Bergin and Garvey, 1983), p. 15. See also Rolf Hagen, "Perraults

Märchen und die Brüder Grimm," *Zeitschrift für Deutsche Philologie,* 74 (1955), 392–410. For LRRH, see pp. 402–6.

17. Eberhard, p. 166.

18. Zipes, *Trials and Tribulations,* p. 2.

19. Haim Schwarzbaum, *The Mishle Shu-Alim (Fox Fables) of Rabbi Berechiah Ha-Nakdan: A Study in Comparative Folklore and Fable Lore* (Kiron: Institute for Jewish and Arab Folklore Research, 1979), pp. 119–22.

20. Ben Edwin Perry, *Aesopica,* vol. 1 (Urbana: University of Illinois Press, 1952), p. 614, # 572.

21. Marie Louise Tenèze, "Aperçu sur les contes d'animaux les plus fréquemment attestés dans le repertoire français," in Georgios A. Megas, ed., *IV International Congress for Folk-Narrative Research in Athens, Lectures and Reports, Laographia,* 22 (1965), 569–75.

22. Edward B. Tylor, *Researches into the Early History of Mankind,* ed. Paul Bohannon (Chicago: University of Chicago Press, 1964), p. 206; *The Origins of Culture,* Part I of *Primitive Culture* (New York: Harper, 1958), pp. 340–41.

23. George W. Cox, *The Mythology of the Aryan Nations,* vol. 2 (London: Longmans, Green & Co., 1870), p. 351, n. 1.

24. F. Max Müller, "Note B. L'Aurore et le Jour," in *Selected Essays on Language, Mythology and Religion,* vol. 1 (London: Longmans, Green & Co., 1881), p. 564. For the interpretation criticized by Müller, see Hyacinthe Husson, *La chaine traditionelle* (Paris: A. Franck, 1874), p. 7. For references to other solar interpretations of LRRH, see Zipes, *Trials and Tribulations,* p. 59, n. 1.

25. Ernst Siecke, *Indogermanische Mythologie* (Berlin: P. Reclam, 1921), p. 66. According to Siecke, the wolf as swallower is the dark of the moon while the LRRH is the bright moon which comes back to life after being released from the wolf's stomach.

26. Axel Olrik, " 'Den lille Rødhaette' og andre Aeventyr om Mennesker, der bliver slugt levende," *Naturen og Mennesket,* 11 (1894), 24–39.

27. V. Holst, "Aeventyr om menneskeslugende Uhyrer," *Naturen og Mennesket,* 11 (1895), 187–89. For Olrik's rebuttal, see "Om Betydningen af Aeventyr," *Naturen og Mennesket,* 11 (1895), 189–204. For these Danish references, I am greatly indebted to Bengt Holbek's important 1984 doctoral dissertation, published as *Interpretation of Fairy Tales: Danish Folklore in a European Perspective,* FFC 239 (Helsinki: Academia Scientiarum Fennica, 1987), p. 233. Inasmuch as Holbek uses LRRH as a sample tale to illustrate diverse approaches to content analysis, his dissertation provided many of the sources utilized in the present essay. The point about Olrik's inconsistency, however, is mine.

28. Pierre Saintyves, *Les contes de Perrault et les récits parallèles* (Paris: Émile Nourry, 1923), pp. 215–29.

29. Propp's 1946 book as yet has not been translated into English. Two chapters, however, appear in Vladimir Propp, *Theory and History of Folklore* (Minneapolis: University of Minnesota Press, 1984), pp. 100–123, where his myth-ritual bias may be observed. For a more extreme argument that LRRH is the product of matriarchy, see M. Pancritius, "Aus mütterrechtlicher Zeit: Rotkäppchen,"

Anthropos, 27 (1932), 743–78. The validity of Propp's brilliant morphological analysis of fairy tales fortunately is independent of his myth-ritual theorizing. See *Morphology of the Folktale* (Austin: University of Texas Press, 1968). For Winterstein's essay, see *Imago,* 14 (1928), 199–274.

30. For Carloni's essay, see *Rivista di psicoanalisi,* 9 (1963), 169–86. The analysis of LRRH is pp. 177–86.

31. For the application of Van Gennep's classic scheme to LRRH, see Calvetti, "Trace di Riti di Iniziazione," p. 489.

32. Yvonne Verdier, "Le Petit Chaperon Rouge dans la tradition orale," *le débat,* no. 3 (juillet-août 1980), 31–61. The initiation interpretation appears on p. 54. The original article appeared as "Grands-mères, si vous saviez: le Petit Chaperon dans la tradition orale," *Cahiers de Littérature Orale,* 4 (1978), 17–55.

33. Rumpf, "Rotkäppchen," pp. 113–18, 121. See also her *Ursprung und Entstehung von Warn- und Schreckmärchen,* FFC 160 (Helsinki: Suomalainen Tiedeakatemia, 1955). Although this approach has its advocates, e.g., Gottfried Henssen, "Deutsche Schreckmärchen und ihre europäischen Anverwandten," *Zeitschrift für Volkskunde,* 50 (1953), 84–97, it says little or nothing about the possible symbolic meaning(s) of the tale. According to Propp's *Morphology,* a great many fairy tales involve interdictions. The point is, however, *not* that fairy tales have interdictions (to teach morality), but that the interdictions are invariably *violated.* It is the violation of the interdiction which makes the plot of fairy tales possible. This suggests that it is a truism but a gross oversimplification of LRRH to say it is a warning to little girls to stay out of the forest!

34. For a structural study of LRRH, see Carsten Høgh, "Dansk på seminariet— 'Rødhaette' som metodeeksempel," *Kursiv,* 20 (1982), 9–18. For a semiotic study, see Victor Laruccia, "Little Red Riding Hood's Metacommentary: Paradoxical Injunction, Semiotics and Behavior," *Modern Language Notes,* 90 (1975), 517–34. For an essentially linguistic exercise in analyzing LRRH into sentences, see Gerald Prince, *A Grammar of Stories: An Introduction* (The Hague: Mouton, 1973), pp. 84–100.

35. See Rudolf Steiner, *The Interpretation of Fairy Tales* (New York: Anthroposophic Press, 1929), p. 20. According to this 1908 lecture, "in a proper explanation of fairy tales it should always be recognised that we must go back to the archetype and identify it."

36. Representative titles include: Rudolf Meyer, *Die Weisheit der Schweizer Märchen* (Schaffhausen: Columban, 1944); Marie Brie, *Das Märchen im Lichte der Geisteswissenschaft* (Breslau, 1922); Fritz Eymann, *Die Weisheit der Märchen im Spiegel der Geisteswissenschaft Rudolf Steiners* (Berne: Troxler, 1952); Ursula Grahl, *The Wisdom in Fairy Tales* (East Grinstead: New Knowledge Books, 1955); and Rudolf Meyer, *Die Weisheit der deutschen Volksmärchen* (Frankfurt: Fischer Taschenbuch, 1981) first published in 1935. The Christian bias in anthroposophy is explicit. Grahl, p. 39, remarks, "Moreover, these stories contain a deeply Christian element, as indeed there lives in all genuine fairy tales. This is true even of the stories that date back to pre-Christian times; for Christ was always known to men on earth." For those interested, a major collection of Steiner-inspired books and monographs is to be found in the Steinerbiblioteket which is a part of the Donnerska Institutet för Religionshistorisk och Kulturhistorisk Forskning located in Turku, Finland.

37. See Norbert Glas, *Red Riding Hood (Little Red Cap)* (East Gannicox: Education and Science Publications, 1947), p. 3.

38. Ibid., pp. 10-11.

39. See Mellie Uyldert, "Roodkapje," in *Verborgen Wijsheid van het Sprookje,* 2d ed. (Amsterdam: De Driehoek, 1969), pp. 19-27. The interpretation of the hunter is on p. 26. For the same author's interpretations of children's rhymes, see *Verborgen wijsheid van oude rijmen* (Amsterdam: De Driehoek, [1972]).

40. Glas, p. 24. For additional anthroposophical readings of LRRH, see the discussion in Holbek, pp. 226-28. For another such reading, see Roy Wilkinson, *The Interpretation of Fairy Tales* (East Grinstead: Henry Goulden, 1984), pp. 18-19.

41. Rudolf Steiner, *The Mission of Folk-Souls (in Connection with Germanic Scandinavian Mythology* (London: R. Steiner Pub. Co., 1929). The preface was written in 1918 for the series of lectures which were given in Christiania (Oslo) in 1910.

42. Sigmund Freud, *Collected Papers,* vol. 2 (New York: Basic Books, 1959), pp. 68-69.

43. See, for example, Alan Dundes, "Earth-Diver: Creation of the Mythopoeic Male," *American Anthropologist,* 64 (1962), 1032-50, reprinted in Dundes, *Sacred Narrative,* pp. 270-94.

44. Freud, *Collected Papers,* vol. 4 (New York: Basic Books, 1959), p. 242.

45. Ibid., p. 243.

46. Freud, *Collected Papers,* vol. 3 (New York: Basic Books, 1959), pp. 473-605. The clinical discussion of LRRH is on pp. 498-515.

47. See Otto Rank, "Völkerpsychologische Parallelen zu den infantilen Sexualtheorien: Zugleich ein Beitrag zur Sexualsymbolik," *Zentralblatt für Psychoanalyse,* 2 (1912), 372-83, 425-37. The discussion of LRRH occurs on pp. 426-27. See also C. G. Jung, "The Theory of Psychoanalysis," in *The Collected Works of C.G. Jung,* vol. 4, Bollingen Series, 20 (New York: Pantheon, 1961), pp. 83-226. The consideration of LRRH is found on pp. 210-11.

48. Erich Fromm, *The Forgotten Language: An Introduction to the Understanding of Dreams, Fairy Tales and Myths* (New York: Rinehart, 1951), p. 240.

49. Ibid., p. 241.

50. Ibid.

51. Robert Darnton, *The Great Cat Massacre and Other Episodes in French Cultural History* (New York: Basic Books, 1984), p. 11.

52. Eberhard, p. 4.

53. Géza Róheim, "The Dragon and the Hero," *American Imago,* 1 (2) (1940), 40-69. The discussion of AT 123 occurs on pp. 61-62 and of AT 333 on p. 63.

54. Ibid., p. 63.

55. This is what William R. Bascom referred to as "the basic paradox of folklore." He concluded his classic statement on the functions of folklore by observing that while folklore "plays a vital role in transmitting and maintaining the institutions of a culture and in forcing the individual to conform to them, at the same time it provides socially approved outlets for the repressions which these same institutions impose upon him." See "Four Functions of Folklore," *Journal of American Folklore,* 67 (1954), 333-49, reprinted in Alan Dundes (ed.), *The Study of Folklore* (Englewood Cliffs, N.J.: Prentice-Hall, 1965), pp. 279-98.

56. Róheim, "The Wolf and the Seven Kids," *Psychoanalytic Quarterly,* 22 (1953), 253–56. The quotation is from p. 255.

57. Róheim, "Fairy Tale and Dream," *The Psychoanalytic Study of the Child,* 8 (1953), 394–403. LRRH is treated on pp. 394–98. The quotation comes from p. 397.

58. Ibid., p. 395.

59. Ibid., p. 396.

60. Elizabeth Crawford, "The Wolf as Condensation," *American Imago,* 12 (1955), 307–14.

61. Carloni, "La fiaba al lume della psicoanalisis." Carloni is one of the very few interpreters of LRRH to acknowledge Róheim's brilliant analysis of the tale, although he unaccountably omits a formal reference in his footnotes.

62. Julius E. Heuscher, *A Psychiatric Study of Fairy Tales: Their Origin, Meaning and Usefulness* (Springfield, Ill.: Charles C. Thomas, 1963), pp. 73–79.

63. Lilla Veszy-Wagner, "Little Red Riding Hood on the Couch," *Psychoanalytic Forum,* 1 (1966), 400–415. The quotation is from p. 400.

64. Ibid., p. 410. Kanzer also refers to Róheim's essay although his own summary of the content of LRRH owes little to Róheim's emphasis upon orality.

65. Ibid., p. 411.

66. Bruno Bettelheim, *The Uses of Enchantment: The Meaning and Importance of Fairy Tales* (New York: Alfred A. Knopf, 1976); the discussion of LRRH runs from p. 166 to p. 183. The comment that LRRH has outgrown her oral fixation is found on p. 170.

67. Ibid., p. 171n. For further discussion of the needles and pins alternatives, see Bernadette Bricout, "Les deux chemins du petit chaperon rouge," in James C. Austin et al. (eds.), *Frontières du Conte* (Paris: Éditions du Centre national de la recherche scientifique, 1982), pp. 47–54.

68. Bettelheim, pp. 172, 173.

69. Ibid., pp. 174, 175.

70. Ibid., p. 175.

71. Ibid., p. 178.

72. See Carl-Heinz Mallet, *Kennen Sie Kinder?* (Hamburg: Hoffmann und Campe, 1981). The discussion of LRRH is on pp. 81–112. The English translation is *Fairy Tales and Children* (New York: Schocken, 1984). Not all psychoanalytic studies are truly psychoanalytic. See J. Geninasca, "Conte populaire et identité du cannibalisme," *Nouvelle Revue de Psychanalyse,* 6 (1972), 215–30.

73. Jungian treatments of LRRH would include David L. Miller, "Red Riding Hood and Grand Mother Rhea: Images in a Psychology of Inflation," in James Hillman, ed., *Facing the Gods* (Irving, Texas: Spring, 1980), pp. 87–99; Marzella Schäfer, *Märchen lösen Lebenskrisen: Tiefenpsychologische Zugänge zur Märchenwelt für Eltern und Erzieher* (Freiburg: Herder, 1983) (LRRH is the subject of the second chapter, pp. 43–55); and Verena Kast, *Märchen als Therapie* (Olten and Freiburg: Walter, 1986) (LRRH is the first tale analyzed, pp. 14–45).

74. Zipes, *Trials and Tribulations,* p. 56.

75. Ibid., p. 57.

76. Jack Zipes, "A Second Gaze at 'Little Red Riding Hood's Tribulations,'"

The Lion and the Unicorn, 7–8 (1983–84), 78–109. The quotation is from p. 81.

77. Ibid., pp. 81–82.

78. Ibid., p. 83.

79. Fromm, p. 241; Bettelheim, p. 173.

80. Eric Berne, *What Do You Say after You Say Hello?: The Psychology of Human Destiny* (New York: Bantam, 1972), p. 43.

81. Ibid., p. 44.

82. Ibid., pp. 44–45.

83. For references to African versions (especially of AT 123), see May Augusta Klipple, "African Folk Tales with Foreign Analogues" (Diss., Indiana University, 1938), for more than a dozen versions of AT 123, pp. 86–92, 202–4. See also Erastus Ojo Arewa, *A Classification of the Folktales of the Northern East African Cattle Area by Types* (New York: Arno, 1980), pp. 223–24, type 4024.

84. Eberhard, p. 44.

85. Ibid., pp. 46, 82.

86. Hans Ritz includes discussions of both scholarship and parodies in his *Die Geschichte vom Rotkäppchen* (Emstal: Muriverlag, 1981). The same is true of Zipes, *Trials and Tribulations.* Zipes, however, has a special interest in political interpretations of LRRH. Accordingly, he summarizes the argument of Hans-Wolf Jäger who hypothesizes that the Grimms, having collected their tales during a period of French occupation, infused LRRH with anti-French sentiments. See "Trägt Rotkäppchen eine Jakobiner-Mütze? Über mutmaßliche Konnotate bei Tieck und Grimm," in Joachim Bark (ed.), *Literatursoziologie,* vol. 2 (Stuttgart: W. Kohlhammer, 1974), pp. 159–80, or Zipes, *Trials and Tribulations,* pp. 17–18. Wolfgang Mieder's extensive compilation of poems, parodies, and cartoons deriving from LRRH documents the tale's continuity in the twentieth century. See "Survival Forms of 'Little Red Riding Hood' in Modern Society," *International Folklore Review,* 2 (1982), 23–40. Also of interest are the eight poems referring to LRRH contained in Mieder, *Disenchantments: An Anthology of Modern Fairy Tale Poetry* (Hanover, N.H.: University Press of New England, 1985), pp. 95–114. Lutz Röhrich includes twelve parodies of LRRH in his *Gebärde–Metapher–Parodie: Studien zur Sprache und Volksdichtung* (Düsseldorf: Schwann, 1967), pp. 130–52. For a serious review of LRRH scholarship, see Hans T. Siepe, "Rotkäppchen einmal anders: Ein Märchen für den Französischunterricht," *Der Fremdsprachliche Unterricht,* 65 (1983), 40–48; for a lighthearted review, see Heinrich E. Kühleborn, *Rotkäppchen und die Wölfe* (Frankfurt: Fischer Taschenbuch Verlag, 1982).

KAY STONE

Three Transformations of Snow White

THE STORY of Snow White became popular with readers at the first publication of tales by the Grimm brothers, and retained its favored position as the German tales were translated into other languages. Thus it was already an obvious choice for the Disney brothers (Walter and Roy) when they created their first feature-length cartoon in the early 1930s. The story is now so widely known in North America that we tend to forget that it did not originate with either the Grimms or the Disneys, but in oral tradition.

The intention here is to examine the necessary transformations of a story—in this case Snow White—in the differing media of oral composition, print, and film. My emphasis is on process rather than on content, as I wish to show as objectively as possible how alterations are a natural result of transformation from one medium to another. While it may seem obvious that contextual change results in content modification, both the Grimms and the Disneys have been castigated for altering this tale in order to meet the needs of new expressive forms intended for new audiences. The Grimms, for example, reworked traditional stories for an urbane audience of readers unfamiliar with oral material. Scholars have criticized their modifications as inappropriate and also as dishonest, since they claimed to be offering genuine traditional tales "straight from the lips of the peasants."[1]

The Disney brothers also intended to reach a new audience with the now-familiar Grimm material by reinterpreting the story from print into film. While they made no false claims as to their source, the final film carried Walt Disney's name in place of the Grimms' (Walt Disney Presents *Snow White and the Seven Dwarfs*).

The apparent dishonesty of both Grimm and Disney brothers has fascinated scholars and popular writers for decades. It is popularly known and accepted that the Disneys fundamentally altered the sense of the Grimm tale,[2] but only recently have the Grimms' modifications and misrepresentations become known beyond the narrow walls of academe.[3] Alan Dundes frankly identifies the Grimm tale collection as "fakelore," a concept originated by Richard M. Dorson to distinguish material falsely claiming origins in genuine folk tradition. According to Dundes: "It does seem sacrilegious to label the Grimms' celebrated Kinder und Hausmärchen as fakelore, but to the extent that oral materials are rewritten, embellished and elaborated, and then presented as if they were pure, authentic oral tradition, we do indeed have a prima facie case of fakelore."[4]

Dundes goes on to urge folklorists not to reject fakelore as unworthy of serious attention but instead to "study it as folklorists, using the tools of folkloristics."[5] I accept this challenge. Including the Disneys in such an approach allows me to compare the final Grimm and Disney versions of Snow White as well as examples of oral variants.

In recent years folklorists have attempted to clarify the vibrant relations between text, texture, and context, thus providing a useful framework in which to survey variations of Snow White.[6] The text is the basic story of Snow White; its texture is the specific language (visualization in the case of film) of a particular story; context is any relevant personal, social, historical, and other influences. There might be countless oral texts of Snow White, each with its own texture and context. The storytelling event, or actual verbal composition of a story, is extremely sensitive to immediate contexts that might motivate changes in texture. Thus Snow White in oral tradition is multi-textural and multicontextual. There is no single "original" or "authentic" oral text. The story would never be told in precisely the same words even by the same person. A unique context for each telling produces different textures, and thus a variety of oral texts.

Print and film, on the contrary, take on a final form combining text and texture in an unchanging unity. Also, the contexts of creating and of receiving are separated so that the readers of the story and the viewers of the film did not share directly and simultaneously in the creation of these versions of Snow White. Thus this particular story in print and film is rigid in text and texture and has no inherent context except when actually created and then received. Unlike oral variants, the printed and filmed tale of Snow White can exist indefinitely in storage, quite free of direct human context.

In considering content I find the literary concept of open and closed texts valuable in exploring Snow White variations.[7] A closed text is one that carefully develops details and connections, leaving readers or viewers little chance for active participation and interpretation. An open text, on the other hand, presents itself in such a way that a full story is told without elaborating every detail of plot, character, or motivation. Thus receivers can take a more active role by making their own connections, by "filling in the gaps." The open or closed nature of the text is influenced by the medium in which it exists. In general, told stories have more possibility for openness than do those in printed and filmed media.

It seems to be current folk wisdom that "the medium is the message." This oft-quoted observation by Marshall McCluhan emphasizes the critical role any medium plays in determining the message of its content.[8] While his own message is not always clearly expressed, he does articulate his basic concept in terms that folklorists can easily comprehend. He explains that his observation that the medium is the message "can, perhaps, be clarified by pointing out that any new technology gradually creates a totally new human environment. Environments are not passive wrappings but active processes."[9] In other words he is not looking at a medium as a product but rather as a process. McCluhan meant to challenge interpreters who rely on content alone to discover the "message" of a story. Like folklorists who see context as a critical creative force, McCluhan insists that the message or meaning can be found in the actual process of creation and dissemination rather than in its textural content.

The story of Snow White would naturally be altered as it passed from one medium to another. The Grimms could not have furnished an esthetically powerful printed version of the oral tale any more than the Disneys could have produced an exact filmed version of the printed Grimm story. The difficulties of accurate translation can be felt in films which have laboriously attempted to reproduce a complex novel, or in careful transcripts of oral texts recorded by professional folklorists. This problem of shifting artistic products from one medium to another has bedeviled folklorists for generations. In maintaining accuracy of transcription from oral to printed forms, textural and contextual impact must often be sacrificed.[10]

The basic story of a girl's blossoming, apparent death, and miraculous rebirth may persist no matter how it is expressed, but its particular concrete manifestations must vary according to the medium of its expression.

Snow White in Oral, Printed, and Filmed Media

If we consider any medium of narrative creativity as a bridge of communication between creators and receivers, and understand that the structure of any bridge determines the traffic it can bear, then the dynamic concept of "message" or meaning can be seen to extend well beyond content. Each medium has its own requirements and potential for communication, and each—as McCluhan observes—creates a new environment in which the communication takes place.

The fullest and most direct bridge of communication would be the orally composed story of Snow White. In this context both creators and receivers participate simultaneously in the storytelling event,[11] while print and film split the experience of artists and audiences. The oral bridge allows a constant flow of two-way traffic while the bridges of print and film permit only separated flows of traffic, first one way and then the other. In other words, the audience has a far greater opportunity to take part in the telling of a story than is possible while reading a book or viewing a film. This alone could not help but influence the formation of a story in any particular medium.

Since both Grimm and Disney versions could not have come into being without orally composed interpretations of Snow White, let us begin with a consideration of verbal creativity.

Snow White in Oral Tradition. Stories created verbally are continually fluid and adaptable according to time and place, tellers and listeners, and other contextual factors. Some folklorists describe this vibrancy as "emergent quality," meaning that the precise text of any story emerges at the actual event of its telling.[12] At the same time these stories maintain a firm stability that has allowed them to exist for uncountable years of ongoing narration and recreation. Narrated tales balance between traditional stability and individual innovation so long as they remain in oral currency. No one story can be considered original in the sense of either primacy or individual innovation. Every traditional teller of Snow White is as original as any other. The concept of original and authoritative texts is applicable only to print or film.

The oral story of Snow White has been examined by Steven Swann

Jones, who searched through more than one hundred traditional texts
from printed collections of European, African, Asian, and New World
tales.[13] He chose to focus on twenty-four representative texts in order
to demonstrate precisely how Snow White manages to exhibit both
stability and variability. As he observes: "It is remarkable that a story
should travel such great distances, be told by many different peoples,
and undergo apparent changes and yet remain recognizably the same
tale. I suggest that folktales such as "Snow White" are not simply
muddied or muddled up the more they are retold by subsequent
tellers."[14] He identifies distinctive formalistic elements that provide
the unique pattern of Snow White. To simplify his detailed enumeration:
these begin with the heroine's expulsion from home, the various
threats on her life culminating with apparent death, and her rescue
and reawakening.

Jones finds this elemental narrative pattern in all the texts he surveys,
though of course the exact expression or texture varies from story to
story. For example, a Norwegian variant has a giant's daughter prick
her finger and, inspired by red blood on white snow, wish for a
daughter with pure white skin and red lips; a Celtic tale features a
jealously beautiful queen named Silver-Tree, who threatens the young
heroine, Gold-Tree; an Icelandic heroine named Vildridr Fairer-than-
Vala escapes to a small house carved of stone and inhabited by only
two dwarfs. Each of these texts is equally authentic in terms of its
contribution to the larger generalized story type of Snow White (AT
709).[15] It matters not a bit if the French-Canadian "Le Miroir Qui
Parle" (The Speaking Mirror) is different in detail from the Louisiana
story of "King Peacock." They are both authentic and easily recogniz-
able variants of Snow White.

Unfortunately we do not know, since the Grimms do not tell us,
how many oral texts might have been available in Germanic oral
tradition at the time of their collecting activities. We can only assume
that the potential variety of details would have provided them with
a wealth of material for their single printed text, "Snow White."

The oral medium, then, provides a potentially direct bridge between
tellers and listeners that encourages the ongoing re-creation of the
story in an infinite variety of emergent texts, each with unique texture
and context.

Snow White in the Printed Medium. Stories composed in writing tend
to become fixed and unchanging, and authors and readers no longer

share simultaneously in the creative event. When texts become attached to specific creators, the notion of originality in the dual senses of primacy and uniqueness come into play. Because a single text entitled "Snow White" was included in the Grimm collections, and because the collection itself was original in both meanings of the word, we arrive at the concept of "the Grimm version" as the "authentic" variant of Snow White (excluding oral sources).

If the Grimms had either drawn directly from oral tradition (as they claimed) or completely fabricated their tales, then we might indeed expect to find only one authoritative text for this story. However, the brothers combined both oral and written traditions to produce a new literary form. Apparently they were sincerely committed to re-creating what they conceived as a pre-Christian Teutonic literature. Alan Dundes's article on "fakelore," cited earlier, suggests that countries with a weak sense of nationhood, like Germany in the early nineteenth century, sometimes produced a consciously composed literature deliberately passed on as genuine "folklore."[16]

The Grimms responded to the forces of romantic nationalism by fashioning a unique genre. Interestingly, they offer several variant texts of their "Snow White," altering the story somewhat in each of their seventeen editions from 1812 to 1856. The earliest known text is in a manuscript of 1810, sent to Clemens Brentano but never published.[17] Here the handsome queen is the girl's natural mother, who first wishes for her and is then dismayed by her ever-increasing beauty. It is the mother herself who takes Snow White to the forest on the pretext of picking flowers, and abandons her there. Except for some changes of wording the basic story is the one already familiar to us, until we reach the death-rebirth motif at the conclusion. Here it is Snow White's father who finds and removes the coffin, and then orders his royal physicians to revive her by tying her body to ropes connected to the four corners of a room. After this surprising climax we find the more familiar marriage to a prince and the queen's dance of death in heated iron shoes.

In the first published edition of 1812 the natural mother is still the villain, but this time she orders her huntsman to destroy Snow White in the forest, and to return with her lungs and liver as proof. The escape to the dwarfs' house and the three attempts on her life are unchanged, but this time the prince himself carries away the coffin. Two of his disgruntled servants accidentally revive Snow

White when they strike her in anger, thus dislodging the apple.

With each edition other minor changes were made, until the final text, which became the "authoritative" version, separated the good and bad aspects of the queen into independent characters. Since the wording of the various texts is much the same, we cannot assume that different oral sources are represented, since these would employ variant wording. Instead it is clear that literary editing is at work. Thus the Grimms have not actually provided the variety of texts that might exist in actual oral tradition, but offer only revisions of one basic text. It is possible that some of the revisions were inspired by additional oral sources encountered over their decades of work, but we cannot know this because none of their original manuscripts before 1809 remain in existence.

The Grimms unknowingly demonstrate the communication problems that can arise when we have only a printed document removed from the context of its creation. As the story was increasingly edited by a single writer it became more his story and less the people's story. And we, long trained to accept only one text as "original," consider the Grimm version of Snow White as authoritative. We have no prior printed text that challenges it. But in its transformation from oral to printed media it has lost its emergent quality, despite the appearance of variety in the Grimm editions. Separated from the actual context of composition—here in time as well as in space—we no longer experience the multitextural advantages of narration. Snow White in print becomes frozen into the wording of the 1857 edition.

The medium of print offers a narrower bridge of communication than does narration. Artistic traffic moves in two separate streams, from the authors to the book and then from the book to the readers. There can be no direct interchange, but only subordinate reactions.

Snow White in the Filmed Medium. Films create an even greater separation of makers and viewers, giving the latter even less possibility for interaction. Both story-listening and story-reading give us the opportunity to provide our own visual, oral, emotional, and other elaborations, but film provides these all ready-made for our consumption.

The Disney film in particular is exquisitely explicit in its visualization, as well as in its aurally and emotionally manipulative aspects. My own childhood memories are still clear, all the more so since this was my first "moving picture." My aunt Val took me and my younger sister

Janet to a downtown theater in Detroit in 1944; in my memory Snow White is still scrubbing the palace steps and singing sweetly about her dream-prince; then she is dashing in terror through the dark forest to escape from her stepmother; and at last she finds the dwarfs' house with its wonderful child-sized furniture and exquisite background details. Even sharper in my mind is the dramatic transformation of the handsome queen into a hideous hag, one of the Disneys' stunning elaborations on the Grimm tale. At this point Janet's four-year-old voice still echoes in my ears as she yells "I want to go home!" But we remained to the melodramatic end.

Many years later I found myself in the small archives of Walt Disney Productions in Burbank, California, exploring file folders full of planning transcripts and preliminary sketches from the three years of production (from 1934 to 1937).[18] It is now commonly known and proudly acknowledged by the Disney studio that the film was initially dubbed "Disney's Folly" even by some of those close to the Disney Brothers. People simply could not believe that adults, who formed the large majority of film audiences, would pay to see a long cartoon based on a children's fairy tale. But because of the careful and explicitly detailed work that went into all aspects of the film, it became an overnight success that is rereleased every few years.

The very first transcript I explored was a list of suggestions for characterizations.[19] Snow White was to resemble actress Janet Gaynor, while Douglas Fairbanks was suggested as the model for the prince. Interestingly the Queen had no living models, but was to be a "mixture of Lady Macbeth and the Big Bad Wolf." She is finally developed as "a very majestic, cold, tiger-lady type."[20] The individualized dwarfs were also a challenge to the filmmakers, who swung between extremes of buffoonery and sentimentality, eventually arriving at a compromise. By the end of the first year of planning all the major characterizations were well established, and the seven dwarfs had become central characters.

The only significant changes between 1934 and 1937 were with important secondary characters like the queen's mirror, her huntsman, and the prince. The mirror and the huntsman were shifted between unwilling complicity in the queen's evil plots to acquiescent conspiracy with her, until the former attitude was finally chosen. The prince was even more intriguing in his various manifestations. Initially Walt Disney suggested a key role for him and his horse, who were to be imprisoned in the queen's dungeon and rescued by birds and animals.

These sequences eventually disappeared from organizational sessions, only to resurface two decades later in the Disney *Sleeping Beauty*.

The final film *Snow White and the Seven Dwarfs* closely follows the general pattern of the Grimm tale, despite the various changes motivated by visualization. For example, two significant scenes featuring the queen were modified for increased visual impact: the transformation from a beauty to a hag (in the Grimm tale she merely disguises herself as a peasant) and her fatal plunge over the cliff (instead of dancing to her death in heated iron shoes). These modifications would not exclude the filmed tale from Jones's list of Snow White texts described earlier.

The years of preparatory conferences contributed a number of alternate texts for the filmed rendition of Snow White, each a very faint echo of the variability found in oral tradition. And while an actual audience did not contribute to these preparations, the film was undoubtedly successful because the Disneys had come to know their potential audience from past animated successes. Herbert Gans reminds us that such a projected, ideal audience plays an important though indirect role in such variability: "Every creator is engaged to some extent in a process of communication between himself and his audience, that is, he is creating *something* for *somebody*. This somebody may be the creator himself, other people, or even a nonexistent stereotype, but it becomes an *image* of an audience which the creator develops as part of every creative process."[21]

But of course film viewers see only the final "text" agreed upon by the Disneys and their co-workers; they do not experience textural variability. Like the Grimms' tale, the Disneys' film has no serious challengers to its status as the authoritative film version of the story. (An intriguing but dated parody entitled *Coal Black and the Seben Dwarfs* is known only to film historians.)[22]

In summary, the Disney film isolates creators and receivers, and offers them even less possibility of interaction since it furnishes sights, sounds, and motivations. The filmed text thus provides the narrowest bridge of all, with the most closed text and context. There is only one *Snow White and the Seven Dwarfs*.

As we have seen, the conceptual bridge of creative communication narrows progressively from oral to printed to filmed versions of Snow White. As well, the openness of text and texture also becomes more confined. Yet even the film, the most rigid and manipulative interpretation of Snow White, does not prevent viewers from interacting in one way or another. The traffic is always two-way, even when the creative and receptive streams are separate. Because readers and viewers do indeed respond, the neatly drawn lines between the three media considered above lose the sharp definition delineated here.

My son was five years of age when he saw *Snow White and the Seven Dwarfs* while we were visiting Madrid.[23] He understood not a word of the Spanish dialogue, nor was he familiar with the story in any form, yet he followed the action with complete accuracy due to Disney's explicit visualization. He was disturbed by the wicked queen's death, however, and insisted that we sit through the film again, hoping (though as an experienced moviegoer he knew it was futile) that the story would end differently. It did not, of course, so we had to find a printed text of "that story." The best we could do in Madrid was a simplified picture book with no clear treatment of the queen.

When we returned home I found and read him the Grimm tale, but this was no more satisfactory. I was then asked to tell him the story in my own words, which I did for the next several nights. Finally he informed me that when I told "that story" I was to have the queen fall asleep for one hundred years and then "wake up a nice lady."

By working through all three media and their possibilities he created his own version of the story. He was responding not only to the explicit and implicit content of the story, but also to the differing means in which this content was expressed through film, books, and narration. He created his own multitextual and multitextural tale by experiencing it through a variety of contexts. His text is worthy of the same consideration as those we have surveyed here.

If the medium is the message, the reaction to that message is still in the minds of individual receivers.[24] As we have seen, each of the means of textual formulation has inherent possibilities and limitations for inviting creative participation. The oral tale, and particularly a *Märchen* like Snow White, has the greatest potential for attracting such a response, not only because of its emergent quality and the immediacy of its continual re-creation, but also because of its abstract nature. As with abstract, nonrepresentational art, the *Märchen* implies its message rather than explicity revealing itself. Max Lüthi speaks eloquently about this "open text" aspect of traditional oral tales: "Any attempt at a detailed description gives rise to the feeling that only a fraction of all that could be said has in fact been told. A detailed description lures us into the infinite and shows us the elusive depth of things. Mere naming, on the other hand, automatically transforms things into simple, motionless images. The world is captured in a word; there is no tentative amplification that would make us feel that something has been left out."[25]

For the *Märchen*, more is less. Lüthi reproaches the Grimms for the literary embellishments that pushed them away from the genuine, unselfconscious folk tradition: "they speak of the red eyes and wagging head of the witch and of her long bespectacled nose (KHM Nos. 15, 69, 193). Genuine folktales speak only of an 'ugly old hag,' an 'old witch,' an 'evil witch,' or simply an 'old woman.' "[26] The more detail put in by a creator, the less abstract and open the story. The Disney film, of course, is even more elaborately representational than was the Grimm tale. Yet, as my son has illustrated, the power of the *Märchen* can still be felt, even in an explicit movie like *Snow White and the Seven Dwarfs*.

When I began formulating this paper, the content of the story of Snow White as interpreted by the Grimms and Disneys was central to my thinking. As I tried to understand more fully how their respective interpretations came into being, the critical impact of the particular medium of presentation became increasingly obvious. Exploring the process of translating Snow White from oral telling to print to film allows us to see the dynamics of human creativity from a wider perspective than that inspired by content analysis alone.

It is not useful to think of the Grimm and Disney versions in terms of faithfulness to any particular sources. More valuable, and considerably more interesting, is a broad conception of human expressive creativity. Both filmed and printed versions of Snow White take on their specific characters as influenced by the interplay of text, texture, and context, and by the dynamics of medium and message.

Linda Dégh reminds us of Lüthi's observation that *Märchen* have survived exploitations and intrusions of all kinds (including those of the Grimms and Disneys) without losing the powerful essence of the ancient oral tales that inspired them: "The common knowledge of the tales is so profound, so deeply ingrained, that, even without the story being told in full, a reference or casual hint is enough to communicate the meaning of the essential message of the tale."[27] She suggests that even an amusing television commercial in which the jealous queen consults her mirror to see the effects of her new beauty soap can call back the powerful death/rebirth principle of the whole of Snow White.[28] Thus any "text" of Snow White, whether full or partial, serious or humorous, contributes to the continued life of this seemingly simple story.

Certainly the context in which Snow White is created affects the texture of its content in oral, printed, and filmed "texts." Still, neither the medium nor the content can fully define the message of Snow White for any active receiver. Each new context simply adds another text for consideration. And this of course includes the medium of the academic essay.[29]

Notes

The comments of L. Danielson, J. Harrell, N. Dancis, and D. Stone have aided greatly in enriching this brief essay.

1. Linda Dégh, for example, specifies their "embellishments and elaboration of details . . . , polishing of rough edges . . . ," and the composition "of one perfect tale out of several less complete variants." See Linda Dégh, "Grimm's *Household Tales* and Its Place in the Household: The Social Relevance of a Controversial Classic," *Western Folklore,* 38 (April, 1979), 83–103; also, John M. Ellis, *One Fairy Story Too Many: The Brothers Grimm and Their Tales* (Chicago: University of Chicago Press, 1985); Heinz Rölleke, "Die 'stockhessischen' Märchen der 'alten Marie': Das Ende eines Mythos um die frühesten KHM–Aufzeichnungen der Brüder Grimm," *Germanisch-Romanische Monatschrift,* n.s. 25 (1975), 74–86.

2. See, for example, Richard Schickel, *The Disney Version: The Life, Times, Art and Commerce of Walt Disney* (New York: Avon, 1968).

3. See in particular Ellis, *One Fairy Story Too Many* for an enthusiastic attack on the Grimms for their alterations and false claims.

4. Alan Dundes, "Nationalistic Inferiority Complexes and the Fabrication of Fakelore: A Reconsideration of Ossian, the *Kinder- und Hausmärchen,* the *Kalevala,* and Paul Bunyan," *Journal of Folklore Research,* 22 (1985), 9.

5. Ibid., pp. 15–16.

6. For a clear explanation of these terms see Alan Dundes, "Text, Texture, and Context," *Southern Folklore Quarterly,* 28 (1964), 251–65.

7. In particular see Umberto Eco, *The Role of the Reader: Explorations in the Semiotics of Texts* (Bloomington: Indiana University Press, 1979).

8. See in particular Marshall McCluhan, *Understanding Media: The Extensions of Man* (New York: McGraw-Hill, 1964). Here he states: "In a culture like ours, long accustomed to splitting and dividing all things as a means of control, it is sometimes a bit of a shock to be reminded that, in operational and practical fact, the medium is the message. This is merely to say that the personal and social consequences of any medium—that is, of any extension of ourselves—results from

the new scale that is introduced into our affairs by each extension of ourselves, or by any new technology" (p. 7).

9. Ibid., p. vi.

10. For an eloquent exploration of the problem of intermedia translation, see (among others): Dennis Tedlock, *The Spoken Word and the Work of Interpretation* (Philadelphia: University of Pennsylvania Press, 1983), and Dell Hymes, "*In Vain I Tried to Tell You*": *Essays in Native American Ethnopoetics* (Philadelphia: University of Pennsylvania Press, 1981).

11. Much recent folklore scholarship focuses on the importance of examining stories in their full oral context. See in particular Richard Bauman, *Verbal Art as Performance* (Prospect Heights, Ill.: Waveland, 1984). Originally published in 1977.

12. For example see ibid., pp. 37–46.

13. Steven Swann Jones, "The Construction of the Folktale: "Snow White" (Diss., University of California at Davis, 1979).

14. Ibid., p. 218.

15. Antti Aarne and Stith Thompson, *The Types of the Folktale: A Classification and Bibliography* (Helsinki: Suomalainen Tiedeakatemia, 1961), p. 245.

16. Dundes, "Nationalistic Inferiority Complexes and the Fabrication of Fakelore." For a more general examination see also Eric J. Hobsbawm and Terence O. Ranger (eds.), *The Invention of Tradition* (Cambridge: Cambridge University Press, 1984).

17. For complete English texts of both the 1810 and the 1812 variants of "Snow White" see Alfred David and Mary Elizabeth David, *The Frog King and Other Tales of the Brothers Grimm* (New York: Signet Classics, New American Library of World Literature, 1964), pp. 303–15.

18. A small grant from the University of Winnipeg allowed me to spend several days in 1978 in the archives of Walt Disney Productions in Burbank, California. I am grateful to archivists Paula Sigman and David R. Smith.

19. From a one-page outline dated Oct. 22, 1934.

20. Document entitled: SNOW WHITE AND THE SEVEN DWARFS, Transcribed from verbatum [sic] notes on General Continuity as talked by Walt, 12/22/36, p. 1.

21. Herbert J. Gans, "The Creator-Audience Relationship in the Mass Media: An Analysis of Movie Making," in Bernard Rosenberg and David Manning White (eds.), *Mass Culture: The Popular Arts in America* (New York: Free Press of Glencoe, 1957), pp. 315–24.

22. I am grateful to Richard J. Leskosky, assistant professor of Cinema Studies at the University of Illinois, for allowing me to view this 1942 Warner Brothers parody in April, 1986.

23. Viewed in Madrid in April of 1976.

24. McCluhan seems to be far less interested in active responses of viewers, regarding them in the main as placid consumers of any media expressions.

25. Max Lüthi, *The European Folktale: Form and Nature*, translated by John D. Niles (Philadelphia: Institute for the Study of Human Issues, 1982), p. 25.

26. Ibid., pp. 25–26.

27. Dégh, "Grimm's *Household Tales,*" p. 102.

28. Ibid., p. 102. She further develops the relation of *Märchen* and advertising in "The Magic Tale and Its Magic," in Michael M. Metzger and Katharina Mommsen (eds.), *Fairy Tales as Ways of Knowing* (Berne: Peter Lang, 1981), pp. 54–68 (esp. pp. 66–68).

29. Claude Lévi-Strauss develops this challenging concept in all of his writing. See in particular *Structural Anthropology,* trans. C. Jacobson and B. G. Schoepf (London: Allen Lane, 1968), esp. chaps. 2 and 11.

LINDA DÉGH

What Did the Grimm Brothers Give to and Take from the Folk?

A RE ORAL and literary tradition two separate entities which can be studied independently from each other or must their interdependence be taken into consideration when looking at a folklore genre, the *Märchen* in particular, as it evolved and developed through the ages?

This question touches upon essentials about the nature of folklore and its study. In view of a chronological process of interaction between folk and elite, oral and written sources, we may look at the folk-product and its managers: scholars, artists, educators, politicians, and marketers who shape the product in service to their diverse goals. I will try to evaluate the influence of the Grimm tale corpus on oral tale production from the viewpoint of the folklorist.

At the beginning of folklore study, the subject of interest consisted of materials edited and formulated in the service of nationalistic ambitions from both literary and oral sources. Later, at a more emancipated stage of ethnic consciousness, folklore theory developed the notion of authenticity and the criterion of genuineness, striving after the elicitation of exclusively oral texts, from the illiterate tradition of the "folk," that is, the peasant untouched by literary intrusion. It was assumed that the "folk," as a primitive human contingent, unwittingly preserved elements of a forgotten, superior, national poetic heritage. Thus, for a long time individual contributors of folklore were only marginally recognized as reservoirs and retellers, not inspired artists. Schools were established to trace unilinear avenues of the anonymous oral tradition and determine the role of collective and personal memory in its survival or erosion. Field collectors looked for archaisms, "pure" items, free of what they judged to be folk-alien urban pollutants.

Following World War II, however, folklorists had to realize that the designated "folk" in the isolation of the rural countryside could not be the exclusive target of a discipline. Technological advancement invaded most remote areas of the world. Diverse strings of traditions obtained through print contained orally learned and performed folklore. The celebrated and promoted folklore genres, whose identification, classification, and analysis was the main routine of scholarly practitioners, dwindled under the pressures of industrialization. Changed life-style and worldview of peasants did not allow time for the singing of archaic ballads or the telling of magic tales for recreation as before. There was no other choice but either to declare that folkloristics had reached the limits of its inquiry and had to resort to the study of the past, preserved in manuscripts, or to realize that the meaning of the "folk" and its "lore" must be extended beyond the narrow confines of pre-industrial, preliterate peasantries. Folklorists chose to lift the old boundaries of their trade. Instead of the continued search for relics of the past "anachronistically still living in vestigial forms," scholars switched to living folklore in the here and now.[1] The new folklore was discovered as an integral, inseparable constituent of culture striving in contemporaneous social groups to serve as meaningful and creative expressions of relevant ideas. This new conception of folklore not only revealed the naiveté of purist fixation on a hypothetical, untainted, self-perpetuating oral tradition, it also opened new perspectives for tracing folklore as a product of social reality in continual processes of change.

If, at the outset, folklore was defined as a fading, perilous oral tradition of national significance which must be saved, restored, and preserved by the literati in order to maintain cultural distinctiveness, it is now defined as the product of people taking advantage of a variety of available auditive and visual media in order to bring oral and literary tradition into synthesis in communicating relevant messages.

All this seems clear and obvious. Nevertheless, it might seem outrageous to some folklorists who are divided according to their interests in diverse developmental stages and do not recognize the logic of the inevitable process of change. Marxist theorists still maintain that folklore is an art of the exploited classes and succumbs only when social oppression ceases to exist,[2] whereas modern European theorists do not trust their own judgment. They tend to see mass society as producing only normalized and secondhand, instead of "real," folklore,[3] and some mention the term "folklorism" disparagingly as something inferior to folklore.[4] Those who are not ready to deal with the problem of adjustment in folklore theory resort to the study of marginal groups where no disturbing questions concerning the nature of folklore must be raised.

Any folklorist who wishes to define the *Märchen* in its historic development and current existence will somehow relate it to the *Kinder- und Hausmärchen* of the Grimm brothers. This collection is a landmark, deeply rooted in sociocultural conditions of nineteenth-century Germany. But, at the same time, it is also a source for the scrutiny of previous history of the European folktale, and a point of departure for the study of its worldwide dissemination. The *KHM* was the most complete, representative collection of miscellaneous narratives, chosen from literary and oral tradition in and outside of diverse social contexts.[5] It is an irony that the documents from which folklorists infer the primacy of an oral tradition come from fixed literary and artistic versions. The themes can be traced back to literary documents of early simple narration, and there is little unanimity concerning when the oral genre *Märchen* emerged. Wesselski cautiously marks the beginning of the *Märchen* as a distinct genre with Straparola's *Nights,* or even later with Basile and Perrault,[6] whereas Schenda points out that the *Märchen,* earlier far less popular than jokes, horror, or personal experience accounts, became the literary fashion of high society only as late as the eighteenth century.[7]

It was within the nineteenth-century romantic milieu that a new "folk" tone was attributed to the *Märchen,* that its rustic simplicity was highlighted and viewed as a survival of ancient poetry preserved by the lower classes. The Grimm brothers earned recognition for their "rescue mission" to save "these innocent household tales" (*diese unschuldigen Hausmärchen*)[8] from oblivion.[9] Their activities were taken as models by the early schools of folklore and harshly criticized by later schools, which did not take into account that they worked before the discipline was established. In celebrating the two-hundredth birthday of the Grimm brothers in 1985 and 1986, new research efforts contributed to our better understanding of their work technique and philosophy of tale collection and edition and their influence on folk narrative scholarship. Special studies also threw new light on the most popular pieces of the *KHM,* their meaning, continued social relevance, modification, and travesties in modern urban society. My discussion will focus on a rather neglected area which concerns the fieldwork-based folk narrative: the complex relationships of oral and written folk tradition in the light of our recognition that orality is just one of the means of tale transmission. The question I will raise concerns the influence of the Grimm tales on oral folk tradition.

As is well known, the Grimms created the artistic form of the *Märchen* by gradual improvement of their text, until it reached perfection in the 1857 version. During the process of variation, a distinctive short narrative genre emerged which contained a characteristic episodic structure, style, and tone. Once set in print, the whole collection and its individual pieces became models for both scholarly and literary authors—a source for both told and written *Märchen,* influential in reinvigorating fading oral tradition, in creating regional variables, and in the general adaptation and spread of the genre in the modern world.

The Grimms never made a secret of their data-compiling method, which exploited both literary and oral sources. The collectors—the Grimms and their friends and acquaintances—retold and rewrote what they had remembered from childhood or obtained through questioning. The new variants, taken as raw data, were shared with the members of the circle the Grimms called their "Märchengesellschaft," by definition a folklore communicating group in itself, and those variants were subjected to continuous polishing. In his recent book, Heinz Rölleke lists the members of this cooperative team and also appends Jacob Grimm's appeal to others he hoped to include from the whole German-speaking territory.[10] However, as Ranke observed, time was not yet ripe for such an undertaking: no one joined the Grimms. The Austrians and the Swiss wanted to work on their own.[11]

Grimm philologists and folklorists have criticized the brothers for merging oral and literary traditions indiscriminately. From Berendsohn's cautionary note that the collection is far removed from living oral telling and may be used only for the study of content,[12] to Ellis's recent attack on the honesty of the brothers,[13] many comments were made. Critics who stated their belief in an oral tradition free from book influence, however, were not so far from the Grimmian principle in their own work. They did not record total storytelling events as social acts, as modern ethnographers do.[14] We cannot speak of authenticity in our sense before the 1940s. The general public did not distinguish between oral narrator and tale writer and regarded published stories as common property free for anyone to change.[15] Scholarly recording of oral tales from the folk, at the same time, meant notation of a skeleton content of stories judged to be genuine. Style editing along the lines of existing models then embellished the tales to reflect more the style of the collector than that of the raconteur. Texts the scholars regarded as folk-alien, nonauthentic, corrupt, or retold from a book were omitted. Small wonder that most published collections reflect the wishful thinking of folklorists, not the real folk repertoire: an oral tradition of miscellaneous provenience.

The influence of the Grimms' work on subsequent generations of folk narrative scholars, in spite of repeated criticisms, was decisive and determinant. National and regional collections assembled, revised, and published in the Grimmian manner appeared one after the other in Europe. Since the Grimm model was disseminated early through diverse print media in many countries,[16] partial or full adaptation of texts was common. Early collectors subscribed to the editorial principle summarized in the 1840s by the Hungarian classical poet, János Arany (1817–82): "The good collector must have the genius of a perfect storyteller. Being there, at the fireside, the spinnery, he must know the language, expressions, and the style of narrating. He must have the imagination and the knowledge of how the folk-mind works. He must be as gifted and as inspired as the native folk and become as good as the best narrator of the region."[17]

While the Grimm corpus was always regarded as literary, it soon became a standard for comparative tale philology. Since Köhler and Bolte-Polívka's type listings and annotations,[18] the titles of the tales appear as type names to which oral variants are compared. Several Grimm titles and type descriptions were adapted by the Aarne-Thompson index, such as Hansel and Gretel (327/A), Godfather Death (332), Jorinde and Joringel (405), Snow White (709), Ferdinand the True and Ferdinand the False (531), and so on.

Furthermore, German folklorists in their tale studies often still depend on the Grimm texts and cite the *KHM* instead of the Aarne-Thompson index numbers in referring to international tales. Scholars to this day often analyze the Grimm version as representative of its kind, in complete disregard of the limitless number of oral variants. In his analysis of Snow White, N. J. Girardot uses the Grimm version with reference to Max Lüthi. Admitting that cultural and individual variations may be important, he felt that, since "every single fairy tale has a particular message,"[19] in the case of Snow White the Grimm text particularly controlled oral variables: "its basic frame of formulaic form, main events, and episodic sequence remains generally constant."[20] In the same vein, Steven Jones follows the Grimm outline in his Snow White study. Over one hundred versions he examined "eschew most of the 'traditional' motifs taken from the Grimms."[21]

Robert Darnton convincingly criticized Bettelheim's reading of the Grimm variant of Little Red Riding Hood as "flattened out, like patients on a couch, in a timeless contemporaneity,"[22] irrespective of other versions of the type. He calls for "rigorous documentation—the occasion of the telling, the background of the teller, and the degree of contamination from written sources."[23] One can agree with such a demand, but Darnton, a cultural historian, commits similar mistakes, using the Grimm tale to illustrate German mentality in contrast to the prerevolutionary French mentality he deduces by analyzing two late nineteenth-century notations from oral informants.[24]

Separation of oral and written forms in considering the life history or the just-performed variant of oral art, particularly the *Märchen,* is and always was problematic. "Folkloristics lives in literature," observed Schenda, "oral literature is a paradox, it freezes when fixed in writing."[25] Obviously, the two can live only in interdependence, influencing content, composition technique, style, situational details, and the rules of performance. "Whoever sees folklore communication intact only where it involves clearly illiterate tradition bearers," writes Bausinger, "is as mistaken as those who believe forms and contents of oral folklore communication are in all cases offshoots of literary production."[26]

Nothing is really new about this. In 1931 Wesselski had already taken issue with adherents of the Finnish school for claiming the existence of an independent oral channel which would account for the extraordinary stability of tales. The scholar of medieval *Märchen* argued that Walter Anderson's hypothetical "magic tale village" (*Märchendorf*), in which tales are common pastime, cannot exist because "*Märchen* in folk-telling can survive only if bearers and preservers of tales (*Märchenträger* and *Märchenpfleger*) appear at brief intervals."[27] According to Wesselski, these can be gifted raconteurs as well as literary authors like the Grimms. Wesselski claims, "without the crutches of a book," the *Märchen* would not have blossomed in modern Europe.

It seems that the complex and untraceable relationship between oral and literary traditions accounts for the stabilization of tales into story units and types. The agents within the transmission process together perform conventional creative acts, producing myriads of variants by repeatedly telling, retelling, reading, editing, printing, illustrating, translating, and thereby adapting and disseminating seeds of the folktale around the world. In their utilization of sources that were partly "literary art form" and partly "popular oral tradition,"[28] the Grimms met the criteria according to which folklore creation is being defined today.[29]

In the course of 130 years since the final form of the *KHM* left the press, the processes of selection, variation, and spread, corrosion and restoration, innovative formulations, translation, and reinterpretations according to innumerable conduits and microconduits[30] took their course not only through telling and print, but also through the more effective electronic media of mass communication. While tales travel from medium to medium and meet the expectations of diverse population groups in the world, one feature remains constant. It is in the nature of the tale that at a certain stage of its life it is told orally, or read aloud, in face-to-face proximity. Modern society established its institutional storytelling services through professional and amateur performers, in addition to the traditional and natural narrators, whose primary repertoires have been sanctioned by the Grimm collection.[31] This also presents the *KHM* as a stabilized version of a genuine folktale repertoire, a sourcebook for adaptation and a link in the continuing chain of tradition. In essence the *KHM* does not differ from the repertoire of any illiterate master storyteller whose performance in front of his village listeners is also the product of previous literary and folk manipulations and whose artistry reasserts fading traditions and determines future ramifications. The "genuine" tale is the one told and listened to irrespective of its literary antecedents.

My long-term fieldwork in a village community in Hungary where traditional storytelling maintained its popularity after World War II as a socially important act with regular performances by prominent illiterate and semiliterate narrators gave me a representative example of the nature of standard literary influence. The folktale corpus I collected from major, minor, and occasional tellers consisted of some 450 items. Most were complete stories in active use; others were fragments, faintly remembered or in the process of formation. On the basis of information from the narrators, as well as my own examination of the texts, I found 40 percent of the total body directly or indirectly related to book tales.[32] Narrators were actively seeking to expand their repertoires by listening to the reading of stories, which they then kept retelling and gradually shaping. In addition to classic literary themes mediated through chapbooks and pious exemplum collections, storybooks constituted the major sources. In 1894, Elek Benedek compiled a five-volume book whose influence on oral tales was comparable to that of the Grimms. Benedek, himself a member of the first team of fieldworkers, stylized the stories, intended for juvenile and uneducated popular audiences, written down by himself and others. Many of the folktales were originally adapted from the Grimms, but Benedek did not hesitate to add direct translations of his own.[33] His books became the most influential source for Hungarian village narration in the twentieth century. His style-editing and acceptance of the Grimmian principles helped homogenize rules of narration through innumerable editions of selected tales. There are eighteen tales in Mrs. Palkó's repertoire[34] from the Benedek collection and eleven Grimm tales among the current favorites of Mrs. Fábián.[35]

The impossibility and futility of separating oral and literary phases in folktale transmission is obvious. Considering the crucial impact of the *KHM* on live narration in the twentieth century, folktale research needs to take another direction. It needs to recognize that the comparative study of direct or indirect literary influences and processual stages of retroaction between written and oral variants can offer new insights into the nature of creative processes in storytelling. As a matter of fact, examples at our disposal indicate that most folklorists minimized the influence of the booktale and only very few experimented with comparing oral tales to their literary models.

As early as 1912, Elizabeth Róna-Sklarek discussed the striking similarity of five tales in the Berze-Nagy collection from North Hungary with five from the Grimms' collection (the Grimms' nos. 4, 21, 47, 80, and 129).[36] She found that the verses in the tales are identical with those of a specific translation from 1889. In an article on acclimatization of foreign tales, S. Solymossy identifies other Grimm tales mediated indirectly through chapbooks to literate peasants, despite structural and compositional modifications. Referring to these, Ortutay observed: "It would be fruitful even today to follow the avenues of Hungarian peasant adaptation of the Grimm tales."[37]

Wesselski reported how the "retelling" of "Little Red-Cap" (Red Riding Hood) in his experiment with thirty-eight schoolgirls resulted in a variety of versions.[38] Twenty years later Max Lüthi convincingly demonstrated that "the substance of a literary form changes according to specific tendencies." In the case of Rapunzel, writes Lüthi, the basic folk stratum provides the driving power to sustain the story. It is no accident that the additions of the ladies of the French court and German upper class could not survive. Once returned to the folk, tales gradually lost the traces of literary revisions. Lüthi regards the work of Jacob Grimm as a link in this transaction: "he created what he assumed would have been created 'by itself' among the folk, consciously developing the story in a new direction for the retellers. His version, even if scholarly and scanty, selects essential images and trends, erases arbitrary embroidery inherent in literary narration."[39] In his comparison, Lüthi shows how two oral narrators—one from Danzig, another from Hajós, a German-Hungarian village—dropped banalities in folklorizing the Grimm tale.

Working with narrator Egbert Gerrits, Gottfried Henssen examined the retelling of four Grimm tales which Gerrits had learned in his early youth from his grandmother in the Netherlands. "Contrary to the literary archetype," writes Henssen, "the tales were brought closer to the real world, made more reasonable and logical, while maintaining the outlook of the *Märchen*. Formulas are also more genuinely folkloric than those of the Grimms."[40]

Vladimir Propp reports two kinds of adaptation by master storytellers. They either internalize whole tales from the Grimms, or adapt single motifs and ingredients learned from storybooks. He illustrates both, citing young narrators.[41]

Felix Karlinger found two versions of the Grimms' no. 161 ("Schneeweisschen und Rosenrot") directly adapted by Sardinian storytellers who drastically removed most of the artificiality of the original.[42]

In a monograph description of the Danish redaction of AT 1640 (The Brave Tailor), Bødker asserts that Grimm no. 20 has been read since 1821, and has exerted its influence on the oral form of every subsequent generation.[43]

These examples of willingness to consider possible literary origin or influence are not free of bias and depart from the convictions that (1) the folk has an independent oral tale tradition free of literary intervention, and (2) the folk rejects and corrects artificial elements of booktales and restores the canon of hereditary types. This rigidity of scholars led also to the narrow view that real folktales are transmitted by illiterate peasants in isolated communities, and texts suspect of literary reminiscences need to be omitted from scholarly collections. The book influence, however, was not determined by rigorous comparative analysis of materials but on the basis of the folklorist's sensitivity as to what is and what is not a real folktale.

An interesting case in point is that of American tale collectors. They ignored Dorson's verdict that no American group corresponds to what is denoted by the term "folk" in Europe: "a deeply rooted, traditionally minded community, with a direct ancient past with its accumulated heritage."[44] They also ignored the fact that for the American folk "masses of popular narrative became accessible in print, in almanacs and magazines, especially, for example, after the Civil War."[45] Following the example of Cecil Sharp, who journeyed to the southern Appalachian mountains in search of British ballads preserved by emigrants in their primitive retreat,[46] folklorists visited the mountaineers to find the residues of the European oral *Märchen*. What they found was, to a considerable extent, retelling of the most popular, often reprinted pieces of the *KHM*. Two prominent Kentucky fieldworkers, Marie Campbell (1958) and Leonard Roberts (1969, 1974), depicted in compassionate colors the traditional life and wisdom of the settlers, giving the impression that the tales in "oral tradition" "are all from 'across the ocean waters' brought to Kentucky 'by our foreparents way back in time.' "[47] In the introduction to their collection, neither Campbell nor Roberts gave accounts of the personality and educational level of their informants or the sources of their folklore. Many of the tales were privately, so to speak discreetly, told by very old people upon the insistence of the inquisitive outsider[48] or written down by the informant and sent to the folklorist by mail.[49] It is quite remarkable that while the collectors provided type and motif numbers for each item and made reference to international variants including the Grimm collection, they never raised a question concerning the conspicuous closeness of the texts to the Grimm tales. One cannot tell whether the brevity, lack of coherence, yet almost slavish retention of Grimmian features was due to fading memory or inability of the narrators to integrate storybook materials into local oral tradition. The retold Grimm texts from Kentucky are nevertheless valuable documents worthy of source-critical analysis.

Prejudice weakens considerably Kurt Ranke's surprising statement that the Grimm tales influencing narrative tradition throughout Europe had little or no effect at all on the living German tale tradition.[50] In his rebuttal of von der Leyen's observation that "Das Volk hat den Brüdern für ihre Märchen in seiner Weise gedankt. Es hat sie aufgenommen und weiter erzählt und neu verschlungen und durch die ganze Welt geschickt,"[51] Ranke examined one hundred post-Grimmian collections from marginal peasant villages and concluded that the Grimms' modifications were alien to tradition and therefore unacceptable to the folk, which continued its mouth-to-mouth transmission undisturbedly. His findings were based on variant comparison, not on the microanalytical measurement of cultural revision by individuals and their supporting communities. The examples—that out of thirty-one variants of AT 451 only two have seven ravens like the Grimms' no. 25, all others retained the original number three; that out of sixteen versions of The Girl without Hands only one accepted Wilhelm Grimm's contamination of this type with the introductory episode of another; that out of thirty-six variants of Godfather Death only four follow the Grimms' conclusion (extinction of the candle of life of the doctor)—do not even prove that the few identical elements came from the Grimms. The subjectivity of the argument is obvious and justifies the question: Is there a more dependable way to observe processes of narrative development than in a book-to-teller and teller-to-book relationship?

It sounds almost a commonplace to repeat that the *KHM* is "still the most often reprinted and translated German book, next to the Bible."[52] Yet, perhaps this fact is the strongest evidence of its efficacy in keeping the world of the *Märchen* alive. Although it has been stated that the tales were translated into 140 languages and reached thirty million editions, we have no accurate figures to show how many modern language translations were made; how many are in current circulation; what tale selections were made for abridged editions or for miscellaneous storybooks; and which individual tales have appeared separately for educational or other purposes. The limited number of available bibliographies, mostly from Europe, reveals little.[53] We may gather impressions from the multitude of reprints and paraphernalia that appear annually on the European Christmas market. Evidently, the popularity and applicability of the tales to diverse needs in diverse types of societies keeps the *KHM* viable and exportable.

We sometimes tend to consider oral tales moribund on the basis of our own experience: modern urban society cannot accommodate traditional village-style narration and has replaced it with other kinds. It must be remembered, though, that the rest of the world continues oral narration the way nonurbanized cultural styles require. According to a UNESCO estimate, there are 900 million adult illiterates and the number is increasing. To give folklorists the opportunity to study live, emergent, variable oral tradition,[54] UNESCO's Sector on Culture delegated a subcommission to protect and safeguard the natural flow of folklore.[55] Here again, folk, folklorist, and cultural managers join forces to redefine and mark out the boundaries of folklore for future generations.

With this prospect of manipulation for the future in mind, I would like to illustrate the adaptation of Grimm tales by master storytellers in their radically diverse cultural settings. This will show the continued viability of the *KHM* beyond our world. It seems the messages these stories convey are of general validity and cross the narrow confines of ideological systems. Because we lack systematic research materials, the examples are drawn from accidental and impressionistic observation that serves only to indicate the possibilities of research in folk narrative adaptation, choice, and rejection. Much must be done before we can attempt anything more.

1. Storyteller Minya Kurcsi spent his life in the Transylvanian mountains working as a lumberman. For half a century he traveled on foot to work sites and entertained fellow workers with his tales at night around the campfire. He had a sixth-grade education and loved to read storybooks. Although as a youth he listened to many narrators, he never retold any of their tales. József Faragó, who recorded thirty-seven of Kurcsi's tales, discovered that these were Elek Benedek's versions of Grimm tales. "Old Minya is living witness to the folklorizing process of which not only the tales but also the Grimm translation of 'Grandpa Elek' ultimately became a part."[56] Kurcsi chose thirty of the forty items from the book he had read. Faragó's exploration revealed that Kurcsi, at the age of sixty-four, now retired from the lumberyards but performing in schools for children and clubs for adults, does not remember the source of the tales after so many years. His adaptation of the best-known pieces—Snow White, Hansel and Gretel, Little Goose Girl, Frau Holle, Godfather Death, Learn What Fear Is,

The Twelve Brothers, Seven Ravens, Cinderella, The Clever Peasant Girl, among them—consists of stylistic embroidery, the addition of dramatic dialogues between the main characters, change of episodic construction, and the introduction of elements from everyday life.

For a well-liked migrant narrator of his type, Kurcsi's dependence on the *KHM* as the source of his total repertoire is quite unique. It is unusual that he did not care to learn from the storytelling of other lumbermen at the alpine log shelter—one of the classic places for story exchange among adult men.[57] Perhaps Benedek's book decisively influenced him to become a storyteller, and he wanted to be different from the others? But was he different? Were others also learning from books without telling the collector? Were folklorists naive enough to believe in exclusive orality even if the classic "liars" often referred to book sources in their playful introductory formulas? Or were folklorists disposed to accept the run that stated: "Once upon a time in the world there was a large tree. On the top of this tree there was a smaller tree. On the top of the little tree there were three hundred and sixty-six ravens and tied around its trunk, three hundred and sixty-six stallions. Whoever doesn't listen to my tale, may the three hundred and sixty-six ravens pick out their eyes and may the three hundred and sixty-six stallions scatter their bodies . . . in the hut underneath there was a big book whose three hundred and sixty-six pages I read through. I read this tale from it"?[58] Is this common formula not a bantering reference to a book source? Be that as it may, over the years Kurcsi's choice of tales, variation, and stabilization through retelling, and his influence on others, is what counts. Unfortunately, the collector did not ask the pertinent questions.

2. In his doctoral dissertation, Robert Adams gave an account of a Japanese woman's change in social identity from a story listener to a storyteller. At age forty-seven, Mrs. Tzune Watanabe, owner of a tea shop and grandmother to her son's eight children, began to lose her hearing. Isolated by deafness, this former farm girl who had once enjoyed listening to and telling folktales decided to teach herself how to read because, in Adams's words, "her deafness had deprived her of the mental stimulation she demanded from social contact in an intensely oral community. As soon as she began reading she was able to use the stories in the books, not only for her own enjoyment but as additions to her repertoire of tales. With this new material she renewed her activity as village raconteur insofar as societal conditions allowed, and

was able to completely integrate the tales into her storytelling style and into the Japanese milieu."[59] All this took place while she was operating the tea shop.

The first storybook she was able to read contained seven European *Märchen,* among them Snow White, Snow-White and Rose-Red, Rapunzel, and Hansel and Gretel. Mrs. Watanabe continued to tell stories, despite illness, and acclimatized Grimm tales to her repertoire. Her mastery of traditional narration enabled her to carry on and develop her style within a speedily changing urbanized milieu. Not essential episodic substitution but rather intricate elaboration of small details characterizes her skill. Seven years after reading Rapunzel, she had expanded the Grimm sentence describing what the prince over-hears the girl singing into a lengthy account and a song. Mrs. Watanabe "appropriated the tale as an expression of her own personal experience when she detailed the subject of the song which Rapunzel sang, and related it to the objects which she supposed constituted the totality of Rapunzel's world."[60] Furthermore, the raconteur did not omit ele-ments of the Grimm tale, except those which did not fit her cultural and personal biases. For example, she dropped the cruel torture of the stepmother in the Snow White story. Her restructuring of tales "to conform to a pattern established by her versions of tales heard from her mother and grandfather reflect the influence of the internalized pattern which governs all her tales."[61] The modifications give insight into techniques of cultural, communal, local, and personal acclimatiza-tion. Adams's penetrating comparative analysis of tale passages—repetitive exchanges of dialogue in the Grimm version compared to Watanabe's version of several tales—is revealing and suggestive.

3. In the Philippine Islands, the Ilianen Monobo represent an ethnic minority culture without a written language. Although their Moslem neighbors, the Magindanao, enslaved them for a while, in the 1970s the Monobo fled from Islamic unrest to safer valleys where they made contact with more recent immigrant groups who have had a history of four hundred years of Western influence. The team of linguists who wrote down the Monobo language recorded forms of oral art and discovered a blooming storytelling tradition maintained by a number of master storytellers and supported by community acclaim. Hazel Wrigglesworth, a member of the team, wrote her dissertation on the tale repertoire of two prominent Monobo story-tellers as an expression of native rhetoric within a system of an exclusively oral culture.[62]

How is it possible that the repertoire of these Monobo narrators (Mr. Ampalid told sixteen, Mrs. Mengsenggild twenty-three stories) consists of a majority of European-type *Märchen?* Although the tales are set in a mythological context with culture heroes as actors and contain genealogical episodes and references, the European influence in story content and structure cannot be mistaken. The presence of AT 300 (Dragonslayer), AT 400 (Swan Maidens), and AT 425 (Cupid and Psyche) may be attributed to an oral tradition, but can this also be the case with AT 566 (Fortunatus, widespread through chapbook reprints), AT 314 (Goldener), AT 130 (Bremen City Musicians), and above all AT 480 (Frau Holle)? There are chances of monogenetic transmission of course, and such triviality as the recent telling by a visiting missionary is always possible. Mr. Ampalid's grade-school education in a regional compound cannot be overlooked either. But hearing an unusual foreign story does not account for its reception and integration, as happened in this case. We have seen many examples of how long it takes for an imported popular literary story to lose its exotic features.

The Grimm version of Frau Holle was recorded twice from Mrs. Mengsenggild. She learned it from an aunt, and it seems to be one of the community's favorites. It is also known under the title of "Good Character Girl—Bad Character Girl." Since Monobo culture and language have been influenced mainly by Malaysian and Indonesian sources via contact with Islamized tribes, Wrigglesworth compares the basic elements of Mrs. Mengsenggild's tale with a Javanese and an Indonesian version and Grimm's "Frau Holle." Examination of the amount of elaboration shows that the Grimm and the Javan texts consist of 1,100 words each, the Indonesian has 3,000, and the Monobo contains over 7,000. The embroidery and modification of the Grimm story is considerable in all Asian versions, resulting mainly from cultural dissimilarities, but the Monobo text displays quite a bit of personal creativity. The chief means by which the Monobo variant is amplified is a fourfold repeated encounter for each of the two girls in which a new set of dramatis personae and events appears. Unlike the three other versions, the two girls are not identified in the Monobo version as the real daughter and the stepsister; the journey is not taken for the acquisition of wealth but for a more basic commodity, food. In both the Indonesian and Monobo texts the girls encounter an alligator or crocodile who asks them to care for her child in return for granting their request. Also, the lullabies sung first by the kind and then by the unkind girl to the alligator's baby bear strong resemblance in the Indonesian and the Monobo texts. The old woman's tasks are relevant only to the German and Javanese versions, while the cock's song assumes the form of a lullaby in both the Indonesian and the Monobo versions and is sung by the girls themselves, thus retaining the contrast between the golden and the filthy appearance. Finally, the reward of wealth in the other three versions becomes a "reward of both food and beauty" in the Monobo. Additionally, in the Monobo story the Bad Character Girl does not limit herself to one journey, but repeats her attempt to succeed four times.[63] Considering lasting historical contacts, Wrigglesworth believes there is a likelihood that European folktales were introduced to the Philippines via Malaysian immigrants.[64]

4. Peter Pandur was a transient between worlds; a man of many trades, a dreamer, and an accomplished storyteller. Born in Transylvania in 1881, the son of estate servants, he began his career as a hired hand at twelve. After domestic service at the home of local nobility, he entered military service. Following his discharge, he traveled to Budapest and worked at construction sites. He married a girl he met at work, settled in her home village thirty miles from the city, and continued to accept odd jobs at diverse locations. He spent four years on the Eastern front during World War I. In 1938 an injury took his eyesight.

I met Pandur and his wife in their village on my first field trip and recorded his total repertoire of 108 tales.[65] I recorded his life history twice in fifteen years, the second time shortly before he died at seventy-nine. The couple lived in the "poor quarter" of a well-to-do peasant village. As a in-migrant poor man, Pandur remained a misfit, never accepted by the villagers. His days of glory, of storytelling in migrant workers' camps, were over; occasional drunks in the pub, Gypsies, and children were his listeners.

Pandur's education, following his four years in school, was unlike that of the classic type of narrator. Most tradition-minded folklorists would have judged him uprooted and urbanized; and indeed his exposure to a great variety of social groups through employment had influenced to a great extent the stylistic shaping of his tale repertoire.

Yet in content this repertoire reveals stronger roots in oral tradition than the convoluted style indicates. Seventy percent of his narratives are classic *Märchen,* 20 percent show haphazard, forced accumulation of episodes lacking a consistent frame, and 10 percent originate in the Grimm collection.

In Pandur's case, certainty about the origins of his stories would be hard to establish. Unlike most narrators who name their sources, he emphatically denied that he learned his stories from someone else and claimed he made them up himself. He demonstrated this to me by changing episodes or conclusions whenever I commented on an unusual turn. He saw himself as an author and planned to dictate a book to me. We would be joint authors and make much money.

The stories borrowed from the Grimms include The White and the Black Bride (AT 403), Sleeping Beauty (410), Kind and Unkind Girls (480), Snow White (709), and A Child of St. Mary (710). Pandur's version of each shows close proximity to the Grimm version, but each in different ways. The White and the Black Bride and Kind and Unkind Girls are abbreviated retellings of the contents, lacking personal touch. Sleeping Beauty is somewhat longer, with dialogues typical of the storyteller's featuring of formal conversations in the parlors of high society, as he overheard tea-party chats as the butler of a country gentleman. In A Child of St. Mary, on the other hand, after the girl's expulsion from heaven the life story of the prince from AT 450 (Little Brother and Little Sister) is inserted, only to make the two meet and prepare for the usual happy end. The most remarkable is the composition of Snow White, blending AT 709 and 883 quite innovatively. The evil stepmother is replaced by a Roman Catholic priest in whose care the father leaves the girl while he travels overseas on business. Also, twelve robbers replace the seven dwarves who are deeply moved by the fate of the innocent girl. When she dies they commit suicide next to her glass coffin in repentance.

I see here two kinds of influences by the Grimm tales. The close and succinct variants may have come from the schoolbook of Pandur's only daughter, a source too close and recent for creative manipulation. The other two stem from an earlier Grimm influence by way of popular chapbook prints, bearing all the marks of the narrator's usual way of internalization. In both cases, I suspect secondhand literary influence rather than reading.

These examples may give an idea of the continued viability of the *KHM* even beyond Germany and the rest of the Western world. It seems the messages these stories convey are of general validity, cutting across ideological systems. Lacking more focused research concerning the interaction of oral and literary tradition, storytellers and their repertoires are the best sources to consider. Once scholars record the total corpus of narrators, without ignoring, rejecting, or only grudgingly acknowledging materials their own sense of style would regard as inappropriate, the nature of folk narrative processes will be better understood. The four examples show diverse relationships to the booktales of the Grimms. Some are more direct, coming from first-hand reading, others show secondhand oral adaptation. Depending on personality, cultural context, temporal distance, and experience, there are many other possible variables. The literary influence, in a subtle way, may not only be discerned from single tales but from personal and communal repertoires, revealing the stylistic rules of narration in general.

It should be made clear that modern, particularly Western, urban society's profound involvement with the Grimm tales as "folktales" is not limited to the telling of, or listening to, formal narration. The presence of the tales may not even have to be manifested by passive knowledge of story plots. The spirit, philosophy, ideology, and behavioral patterns of the tales appeal to a much larger audience, beyond the telling context. The metaphoric uses of tale characters, images, sayings, situations, dialogues, miracles, transformations, and figurative speech formulas are generally known and appear as useful and meaningful tools in everyday life. The acts and even the total careers of tale heroes appear to be models for men and women to follow.[66] Thanks to the *KHM* and its new version, comprised of a selected set of tales normalized and "adapted" (*umfunktioniert*) by child psychologists, educators, writers,[67] and professional narrators, Sleeping Beauty, Rapunzel, Frog Prince, and Cinderella became assumed or ascribed personality types in the Western world. This might well be the case; and, as Bausinger claims, the new rational worldview drove primary tale communication from adult society into the nursery. But how could the booktales of the Grimms eclipse storytelling tradition when the earlier practice of booktale retelling did not? Bausinger stresses here the passing of face-to-face storytelling as an adult pastime, not the abandonment of oral tradition, which already in the eighteenth and nineteenth century was strongly contaminated with tales read from books.[68]

The strongest impact the Grimm tales made on modern civilization—
and I would not want to distinguish here the adult world from the
world of children—is outside formal storytelling in the traditional
sense. Modern society is aware of the power of tales and their symbolism.
For that reason educators and psychologists keep debating whether
tales are helpful or harmful to mental health. Currently, in addition to
Bettelheim's book,[69] there is a great proliferation of Jungian interpretation of the Grimm tales filling the shelves of German bookstores,
trying to resolve the puzzle of why the world of the magic tale still
keeps producing new means to persist.

Divorced from the book, tale particles assume a life of their own.
They become symbols for reference, capable of describing feelings,
arguing for right and wrong, and summarizing conditions in delicate
situations. Thus, within the context of modern society, tale motifs
have become commonly understood signifiers, formulas to cite, metaphors to substitute for lengthy explanations. The capability of tales to
break into meaningful units accounts for their practical exploitation in
today's consumer-oriented world. Commercial advertisements in print,
in radio broadcasts, and on television screens depend heavily on the
magic tale's promise of happiness to sell products and lure tourists.
Political cartoons feature topical events displaced in a satirical never-
never land; toys, games, costumes, and other paraphernalia of the
Märchen help indoctrinate children into the modern Grimm-*Märchen*
subculture. In Germany, all this goes hand in hand with the storybook plus cassette, or even video tapes. The method of merchandizing
Grimm resembles the selling of popular American movie characters
and events as toys and games. This type of adaptation may be characteristic of further ramification of the tale tradition and continued
fascination with its implications. After all, the objectified artistic land
of the tale offers fulfillment of hopes and desires to those who can
daydream and assume the roles of heroes and heroines, taking a
guided tour through the "fairy-tale woods" (*Märchenwald*)[70] and its
clearings, the avenues of danger and adventure, between good and
evil. As Kurt Ranke said, the tale hero is a wanderer between the
worlds.[71] Indeed, there is no better expression of hope in terms of
human creativity than the tale told, read, played, or gestured, and the
tale normalized and standardized by the current edition of the *KHM*.

Transformations of some popular Grimm tales and their adaptations for drama, ballet, opera, puppet play; for stage, movie, radio, and

television presentation; poetry, novel, short story, joke, and political cartoon are innumerable.[72] It would seem worthwhile to explore the literary fairy tale in its development as related to the Grimm collection from the mid-nineteenth century to our day, especially during the last decade, which has witnessed a growing interest among writers and artists in developing satires, travesties, fantasy tales, and even science fiction movies exploiting Grimmian formulas. Their success attests that the popular audience has internalized these formulas. But since the authors depart sharply from traditional folklore patterns, little if any return influence on folktale may be expected from them. For this reason, their work is beyond the scope of folkloristic consideration.

In the country of the Grimms, founding fathers of folklore and discoverers of the genre *Märchen,* the telling of *Märchen* seems to go far beyond any expectation. The Grimm corpus has become a shared national property, representative of what average people know as folktales which are to be studied, performed, and enjoyed in multiple forms, peddled, and sold in manifold packaging. The attitudes toward the tales change, but neither hostility nor support can alter the fact that they are alive and well in the cross fire of controversies. Opinions about the *Märchen* are expressed by everyone in the intellectual marketplace, and no one is neutral or indifferent. It is unlikely that the tales will cease to exist or be replaced; they permeate the landscape of the country wherever the Autobahn takes the traveler. The German ADAC provides drivers with a map to guide them through the world of the magic tale, the sites where Grimm heroes resided—from the modest night quarter of the Bremen City Musicians to Sababurg, the hunting castle of the Landgraf of Hessen, and the residence of Dornröschen. There are some two hundred "fairy-tale woods" (*Märchen-wälder*), parks or lands in Germany to enculturate children and adults seeking family recreation. These feature a repertoire primarily of Grimm tales, in this order of popularity: Hansel and Gretel, Cinderella, Snow White, Little Red Riding Hood, Sleeping Beauty, Brother and Sister, Frog King, Lucky Hans, Frau Holle, Tischlein Deck Dich, Rapunzel, and The Brave Little Tailor. Helga Stein asks: Is this a new form of tradition or transmission of folktales?[73] The question is timely, but an answer may be expected only after the function and influence of the fairy-tale gardens (*Märchengärten*) have been adequately explored.

In the festive atmosphere of the Grimm anniversary, Frau Dorothea

Viehmann, the *Märchenfrau* from Kassel, narrates again. This charming old lady, in her traditional costume and bonnet and with her
Niederzwehrn dialect, was reborn as if stepping out of the familiar
picture drawn by Ludwig Grimm. But there is one slight difference between Mrs. Viehmann and her current representative in Niederzwehrn.
The latter, unlike her predecessor, has a book in front of her from
which she reads her tales—a selection of Grimm *Märchen*. The present
Märchenfrau is Anni Keye, who is in her seventies; she is so impressed
by her act that even her husband, who drives her to storytelling appoint-
ments, is not sure if it is Dorothea or the Anni he married long ago.

The costumed *Märchenfrau* and her numerous companions in
Germany, and elsewhere in Western Europe, and maybe in the world,
become, so to speak, the symbols of folklore transmission. With the
printed book in their hands, they communicate their messages by
word of mouth. Perhaps they also appear on the film screen. Tradition
may live only because—not despite the fact that—it is carried and
supported by modern means of communication.

The *Märchenfrau* is a conscious cultivator of tradition. Ever since a
public appeal for an official "German fairy-tale road" (*deutsche Märchen-
strasse*) was made, she has been active in contributing to the program
of the Kassel station. Anni is regarded as an important contributor to
the Kassel club and group travel programs (as witnessed by the tourist
guide for 1985). The length of her tales ranges from three to fifteen
minutes: she goes on as long as the customers want to listen. And they
do, indeed! The enchantment of the *Märchen* is as much in demand as
before. As reported in *Heim und Welt* (Jan. 15, 1985), "today's fairy-
tale tellers have become fully integrated into mass tourism." Even
more important, according to a poll of the Sample-Institute, 94
percent of West Germans are familiar with the adventures of Hansel
and Gretel, 93 percent with Snow White, 91 percent with Little Red
Riding Hood, and 90 percent with the Grimm version of Sleeping
Beauty (*Abendpost*, Mar. 28, 1985).

Since the time of the Grimms, folklore has been regarded as the
treasury of the past, which must be rescued and preserved. Although
traditional folklorists have kept tolling the bell over the demise of the
folktale, its techniques of transmission and spread may speed up and
change, the formats of the stories may multiply with the introduction
of modern media, but the folklorization of the Grimm tales appears as
strong evidence for the persistence of the folktale.

Notes

1. Rudolf Schenda, "Einheitlich—urtümlich—noch heute: Probleme der volkskundlichen Befragung," in Klaus Geiger, Utz Jeggle and Gottfried Korff (eds.), *Abschied vom Volksleben* (Tübingen: Tübinger Vereinigung für Volkskunde, 1970), pp. 124–54.

2. Vilmos Voigt, *A folklór alkotások elemzése* (Analysis of folklore products) (Budapest: Akadémia, 1972).

3. Hermann Bausinger, "Kinder und Jugendliche im Spannungsfeld der Massenmedien: Die Wiederkehr des Märchens," *AJS Informationen,* Sept.–Oct., 1976, pp. 1–3.

4. Vilmos Voigt, "A néprajztudomány mai kérdései," *Kritika,* July, 1986.

5. Walter A. Berendsohn, *Grundformen volkstümlicher Erzählerkunst in den Kinder- und Hausmärchen der Brüder Grimm* (Wiesbaden: D. Martin Sändig, 1921); Johannes Bolte and Georg Polívka, *Anmerkungen zu den Kinder- und Hausmärchen der Brüder Grimm,* vol. 4 (rpt. Hildesheim: Georg Olms, 1963), pp. 467–75.

6. Albert Wesselski, *Versuch einer Theorie des Märchens* (Reichenberg: Sudetendeutscher Verlag Franz Kraus, 1931), p. 196.

7. Rudolf Schenda, "Märchen erzählen—Märchen verbreiten: Wandel in den Mitteilungsformen einer populären Gattung," in Klaus Doderer (ed.), *Über Märchen für Kinder von heute* (Weinheim and Basel: Beltz, 1983), pp. 28–30.

8. From the introduction to the 1819 edition.

9. "Wenn wir also hiermit ganz besonders die Märchen der Ammen und Kinder, die Abendgespräche und Spinnstubengeschichten gemeint haben, so wissen wir zweierlei recht wohl, dass es verachtete Namen und bisher unbeachtete Sachen sind, die noch in jedem einfach gebliebenen Menschengemüth von Jugend bis zum Tod gehaftet haben"; from the Grimms' appeal to all friends of German poetry and history, cited by Heinz Rölleke in *Die Märchen der Brüder Grimm* (Munich: Artemis, 1985), p. 65.

10. Ibid., pp. 63–69.

11. Kurt Ranke, *Die Welt der einfachen Formen* (Berlin: Walter de Gruyter, 1978), pp. 87–91.

12. Berendsohn, p. 11.

13. John M. Ellis, *One Fairy Story Too Many: The Brothers Grimm and Their Tales* (Chicago: University of Chicago Press, 1983); Heinz Rölleke, "John M. Ellis: One Fairy Story Too Many," *Fabula,* 25 (1984), 330–32.

14. Schenda, "Märchen erzählen," pp. 31–32.

15. Agnes Kovács, "Benedek Elek és a magyar néprajzkutatás" (Elek Benedek and Hungarian folklore research), *Ethnographia,* 72 (1961), 434.

16. Wayland D. Hand, "Die Märchen der Brüder Grimm in den Vereinigten Staaten," *Hessische Blätter,* 54 (1963), 525–44.

17. Kovács, p. 435.

18. Stith Thompson, "Fifty Years of Folktale Indexing," in Wayland D. Hand and G. O. Arlt (eds.), *Humaniora Essays in Literature, Folklore, Bibliography Honoring Archer Taylor on His Seventieth Birthday* (New York: Augustin, 1960), pp. 49–57.

19. N. J. Girardot, "Initiation and Meaning in the Tale of Snow White and the Seven Dwarfs," *Journal of American Folklore,* 90 (1977), 280.

20. Ibid., p. 279.

21. Steven Swann Jones, "The Structure of Snow White," *Fabula,* 24 (1983), 56–71.

22. Robert Darnton, *The Great Cat Massacre and Other Episodes in French Cultural History* (New York: Basic Books, 1984), p. 13.

23. Ibid., p. 16.

24. Ibid., pp. 50–51.

25. Rudolf Schenda, "Folkloristik und Sozialgeschichte," in Rolf Kloepfer et al. (eds.), *Erzählung und Erzählforschung im 20. Jahrhundert* (Stuttgart: Kohlhammer, 1981), pp. 489–530.

26. Hermann Bausinger, "Mündlich," *Folklore and Oral Communication: Narodna Umjetnost,* special issue, 1981, p. 14.

27. Wesselski, pp. 127–31, 156–57, 197.

28. Berendsohn, p. 24.

29. Alan Dundes, "Who Are the Folk?" in his *Interpreting Folklore* (Bloomington: Indiana University Press, 1980), pp. 1–19.

30. Linda Dégh and Andrew Vázsonyi, "The Hypothesis of Multi-Conduit Transmission in Folklore," in Dan Ben-Amos and Kenneth Goldstein (eds.), *Folklore: Performance and Communication* (The Hague: Mouton, 1975), pp. 207–54.

31. Rainer Wehse (ed.), *Märchenerzähler—Erzählgemeinschaft* (Kassel: Röth, 1983); *National Storytelling Journal 1984—*; Linda Dégh, "Frauenmärchen," in Kurt Ranke (ed.), *Enzyklopädie des Märchens* (Berlin: Walter de Gruyter, 1985), Bd. 5, Lieferung 1, pp. 211–20.

32. Linda Dégh, *Folktales and Society: Storytelling in a Hungarian Peasant Community* (Bloomington: Indiana University Press, 1969), pp. 146–58.

33. Kovács, pp. 430–43.

34. Dégh, *Folktales and Society,* pp. 153–54.

35. Ádám Sebestyén, *Bukovinai Székely népmesék* (Székely folktales from the Bucovina), 2 vols. (Szekszárd: Tolnamegyei Tanács V. B. Könyvtára, 1979–81), vol. 1.

36. *KHM* 4: Fürchten lernen; 21: Aschenputtel; 47: Machandelboom; 80: Vom Tode des Hühnchens; 129: Die vier kunstreichen Brüder.

37. Gyula Ortutay, "Jacob Grimm und die ungarische Folkloristik," *Deutsches Jahrbuch für Volkskunde,* 9 (1963), 181.

38. Wesselski, pp. 127–31.

39. Max Lüthi, "Die Herkunft des Grimmschen Rapunzelmärchens," *Fabula,* 3 (1959), 112–13.

40. Gottfried Henssen, *Überlieferung und Persönlichkeit: Die Erzählungen und Lieder des Egbert Gerrits* (Münster: Aschendorff, 1951), p. 16.

41. Vladimir Propp, "Märchen der Brüder Grimm im russischen Norden," *Deutsches Jahrbuch für Volkskunde,* 9 (1963), 104–12.

42. Felix Karlinger, " 'Schneeweißchen und Rosenrot' in Sardinien: Zur Übernahme eines Buchmärchens in die volkstümliche Erzähltradition," *Hessische Blätter,* 54 (1973), 585–93.

43. Laurits Bødker, "The Brave Tailor in Danish Tradition," in Winthorp Edson Richmond (ed.), *Studies in Folklore* (Bloomington: Indiana University Press, 1957), pp. 21-22.

44. Richard M. Dorson, "Print and American Folklore," *California Folklore Quarterly,* 4 (1945), 207.

45. Reidar Th. Christiansen, *European Folklore in America* (Oslo: Universitets-forlaget, 1962), p. 58.

46. Maud Karpeles, *Cecil Sharp: His Life and Works* (London: Routledge & Kegan Paul, 1967), pp. 140-71.

47. Marie Campbell, *Tales from the Cloud Walking Country* (Bloomington: Indiana University Press, 1958), p. 9.

48. Ibid., pp. 24-25.

49. Leonard Roberts, *Old Greasybeard: Tales from the Cumberland Gap* (Detroit: Folklore Associates, 1969), see annotations.

50. Kurt Ranke, "Der Einfluß der Grimmschen Kinder- und Hausmärchen," *Papers of the International Congress of European and Western Ethnology,* International Commission of Folk Arts and Folklore (CIAP) (Stockholm, 1955), pp. 126-35, esp. p. 132.

51. Ibid., p. 127.

52. Lutz Röhrich, "Argumente für und gegen das Märchen," in his *Sage und Märchen: Erzählforschung heute* (Freiburg: Herder, 1976), p. 21.

53. Sándor Kozocsa, "Grimmsche Märchen in Ungarn: Eine Bibliographie," *Hessische Blätter,* 9 (1963), 559-74, and Voigt, *A folklór alkotások elemzése,* pp. 336-38, list seventy-three collections and 220 editions in Hungary between 1861 and 1961. Similar listings are also offered in vol. 54 of the *Hessische Blätter:* "Dem Gedenken der Brüder Grimm am 100. Todestag von Jacob Grimm 20. September 1963" by H. Ikeda from Japan, K. Briggs from Great Britain, Wayland Hand from the United States, and Vladimir Propp from northern Russia.

54. Gyula Ortutay, "A szimpozion célja" (Goal of the Symposium), *A szájhagyo-manyozás törvényszerüségei,* Nemzetkösi szimpozion Budapesten 1969 május 28-30, ed. Vilmos Voigt (Budapest: Akadémia, 1974), p. 18.

55. Lauri Honko, "What Kind of Instruments for Folklore Protection?" *NIF Newsletter,* 13, nos. 1-2 (1985), 3-11.

56. József Faragó, "Alpine Storyteller Minya Kurcsi," in Linda Dégh (ed.), *Studies in East European Folk Narrative* (n.p.: American Folklore Society, 1978), pp. 559-618.

57. Dégh, *Folktales and Society,* pp. 74-76; József Faragó, *Kurcsi Minya havasi mesemondó* (Alpine storyteller Minya Kurcsi) (Bucharest: Irodalmi könyvkiadó, 1969).

58. This introductory cadence to a complex *Märchen* I recorded from fisher-man János Nagy is typical; see Gyula Ortutay, Linda Dégh, and Agnes Kovács, *Magyar népmesék,* 3 vols. (Budapest: Szépirodalmi könyvkiadó, 1960), vol. 2, p. 110.

59. Robert J. Adams, "Social Identity of a Japanese Storyteller" (Diss., Indiana University, 1972).

60. Ibid., p. 154.

61. Ibid., p. 147.

62. Hazel Wrigglesworth, "Folk Rhetoric in the Narration of Ilianan Monobo Folktales" (Diss., Indiana University, 1975).

63. Ibid., pp. 197–204.

64. Ibid., p. 203.

65. Linda Dégh, *Pandur Péter meséi* (Tales of Peter Pandur), 2 vols. (Budapest: Franklin, 1943).

66. Linda Dégh, "Zur Rezeption der Grimmschen Märchen in den USA," in Doderer (ed.), *Über Märchen für Kinder von heute,* pp. 122–26; Kay Stone, "Mißbrauchte Verzauberung: Aschenputtel als Weiblichkeitsideal in Nordamerika," in Doderer (ed.), *Über Märchen für Kinder von heute,* pp. 78–98.

67. Hermann Bausinger, *Volkskunde* (Darmstadt: Carl Habel, n.d.), p. 145.

68. Ibid., p. 146.

69. Bruno Bettelheim, *The Uses of Enchantment: The Meaning and Importance of Fairy Tales* (New York: Alfred A. Knopf, 1976).

70. The fascination of Germans with the forest as the mysterious dwelling of supernatural tale actors is delicately featured in Heine's childhood fantasy poem "Waldeinsamkeit"; see his *Sämtliche Werke,* ed. Ernst Elster (Leipzig and Vienna: Bibliographisches Institut, n.d.), vol. 1, pp. 391–95.

71. Kurt Ranke, "Betrachtungen zum Wesen und zur Funktion des Märchens," *Studium Generale,* 11 (1958), p. 656.

72. Listings and folkloristic evaluation of literary and artistic adaptations include Hand, "Die Märchen der Brüder Grimm"; Lutz Röhrich, *Märchen und Wirklichkeit,* 4th ed. (Wiesbaden; Franz Steiner, 1974); Röhrich, "Argumente für und gegen das Märchen"; Lutz Röhrich, "Der Froschkönig und ihre Wandlungen," *Fabula,* 20 (1979), 170–92; and Lutz Röhrich, "Metamorphosen des Märchens heute," in Doderer (ed.), *Märchen für Kinder von heute,* pp. 97–115; Dégh, "Zur Rezeption der Grimmschen Märchen"; Jan Uwe Rogge, "Märchen in den Medien: Über Möglichkeiten und Grenzen medialer Märchen-Adaption," in Doderer (ed.), *Märchen für Kinder von heute,* 1983; Wolfgang Mieder, *Grimms Märchen-modern: Prosa, Gedichte, Karikaturen* (Stuttgart: Reclam, 1979); Katalin Horn, "Märchenmotive und gezeichneter Witz: Einige Möglichkeiten der Adaptation," *Österreichische Zeitschrift für Volkskunde,* 37 (1983), 209–37.

73. Helga Stein, "Einige Bemerkungen über die Märchengärten," paper presented at the Congress of the International Society for Folk Narrative Research, Edinburgh, 1979.

DONALD WARD

New Misconceptions about Old Folktales: The Brothers Grimm

ONE OCCASIONALLY encounters the contention that the Brothers Grimm were guilty of manipulative deception when they added elements of cruelty to the tale of Cinderella that were not in their sources. The reference is typically to the bloody scene of the stepsisters cutting off their heels and toes in the attempt to make the slipper fit. I find this contention to be somewhat strange, for one merely needs to look up tale type 510 in the Aarne-Thompson index,[1] which leads one, in turn, to the monograph by Marian Roalfe Cox[2] that documents this motif in scores of variants disseminated from India to Iceland, so that it is immediately evident that the Grimms scarcely could have invented the motif. One could, of course, also consult a more recent monograph, *The Cinderella Cycle* by Anna Birgitta Rooth,[3] which on this particular point would lead one back to the earlier monograph by Cox.

In a recent essay by one of America's finest folklorists, Alan Dundes, one reads, too, that the Grimms were guilty of deception in portraying their main informant for the second volume of the *Kinder- und Hausmärchen* as a Hessian peasant woman. "Dorothea Viehmann," writes Dundes, "was an educated, literate, middle-class woman whose first language was French not German."[4] It is true enough that Katharina Dorothea Viehmann née Pierson (1755–1815) belonged to a fourth-generation Huguenot family. She probably knew French, but it is almost certain that her first language was German. She was of Huguenot descent only on her father's side. Her mother was Martha Gertrud Pierson née Spangenberg (1736–1804), a member of a long line of Hessian innkeepers. Frau Viehmann was brought up, as was her

91

German mother, in a village tavern in which German was necessarily one of the languages in use. Even in regard to the Huguenot side of the family, the French connection was somewhat tenuous. The paternal great-grandfather, who himself was born in Holland, had emigrated to Hesse in 1686, 128 years before the Grimm brothers met Frau Viehmann. More interesting still is the fact that he came to Hesse from Metz, a city in the Alsace-Lorraine, which had been a part of Germany until the year 1648 when France laid claim to the region in the confusion that reigned at the end of the Thirty Years' War. The city remained decidedly German for many years after the French takeover, so it is safe to assume that the great-grandfather had emigrated from a German city to Hesse just thirty-eight years after the French takeover. Because of this background it is almost certain that even the Huguenot side of Frau Viehmann's family had been as German as they were French. As stated, Frau Viehmann's mother came from a long line of Hessian innkeepers, and she, like her daughter, had grown up in an inn where they must have had ample opportunity to hear many tales told by imbibing guests. Indeed, a number of the tales the brothers collected from Dorothea Viehmann, some of which they chose not to include in the second volume, were of the *Schwank*-like variety that were (and are) told in taverns. The father, who belonged to the Huguenot branch of the family, was named Johann Friedrich Isaak Pierson (1734–98). The thoroughly German names would seem to indicate that even he was ethnically more German than French, although the German names may have merely reflected bureaucratic necessity. The claim, moreover, that Frau Viehmann was "middle class" is also open to question. Frau Viehmann was married to the tailor Nikolaus Viehmann (1755–1825), who had a small shop in the village of Niederzwehren, at that time a farming village. From what we know, the tailoring enterprise was not very successful and the Viehmanns lived in poverty. Frau Viehmann earned additional income by growing vegetables on their small farm, and she carted her wares daily into Kassel, where she sold them door to door.

From all of this information it is evident that Dundes was mistaken in his assessment of the identity of the Grimm informant. How did he arrive at this mistaken information? Dundes, as well as some of the scholars I referred to at the beginning of this essay, cite the same source for their inferences, namely, the recent work by John Ellis, *One Fairy Story Too Many: The Brothers Grimm and Their Tales*.[5] It is a work that is going to mislead many a scholar unless the situation is clarified in emphatic terms.

The most unfortunate aspect of the work is that it is virtually the only thorough investigation of the Grimms' methods of collecting, editing, and publishing the tales that is available in English, and thus scholars who do not read German will depend on it for their information on the topic. The work is clearly intended to be provocative, as the very title recalls the exposé of Field Marshal Montgomery's flawed strategy in World War II, *A Bridge Too Far.* In my opinion, it was a mistake to choose for a work that purports to be serious scholarship a title that is reminiscent of a journalistic exposé; but the choice is chiefly a matter of taste, and it is not in the title of this work that the problem lies. Nevertheless, the provocative title does indicate a zeal on the part of the author to produce a sensational exposé, a task he accomplishes with a vengeance. If it was Ellis's goal to leave his readers standing aghast at his "revelations," then it can be asserted that he was eminently successful in achieving this. The "fairy story too many" is the Grimm collection of *Kinder- und Hausmärchen* (hereafter referred to as KHM) itself. It is, according to Ellis, in its claim to be something it is not, as wildly fanciful as the most imaginative of fairy tales.

The most valuable contribution of this book is that it makes available to English readers a wealth of scholarship on the Brothers Grimm that has gone virtually unnoticed in the U.S. for years. Indeed, virtually all of Ellis's material is based upon the research of others. He apparently did not engage in any kind of primary research, did not consult archival materials nor manuscripts or letters. Even though Ellis acknowledges his secondary sources in footnotes, he often does so as a kind of afterthought, giving at least the impression that much of the research is his own. This practice is most disturbing when Ellis compares the manuscript materials with subsequent editions, something he could not have done without the splendid synoptic edition of Heinz Rölleke. Indeed, Rölleke is the author upon whose research Ellis relies throughout his book, a fact that does not, however, preclude him from criticizing this scholar from whose works he draws upon so liberally. The only truly original contribution Ellis has to offer is his tone of indignation at the alleged "fraud and forgery"[6] perpetrated by the Grimms. Alas, it is in this original part of his work where Ellis goes far astray.

Ellis places great stress upon the programmatic statement included in the Grimms' prologue to the first edition of KHM. In it the brothers state their goals in the idealized and effluent expressions so characteristic of the Romantic Age. They claim to have collected the material from the simple people of Hesse and maintain that the stories are the survivals of ancient German myth. Moreover, they insist that they treated their sources with all the reverence they deserved, and that they had tried to collect the tales as faithfully as possible: "No particular has been added through our own poetic recreation, or improved or altered, because we should have shrunk from augmenting tales that were so rich in themselves."[7] Ellis then attempts to establish that the tales were neither purely German nor collected from the simple folk. He furthermore argues that the tales were thoroughly altered both in content and in form during the many redactions. Most of his inferences here are valid enough, but none of this is in any way new.

Ellis places special importance on the fact that, by the time the second edition of KHM appeared in 1819, the brothers had retreated from their original plan and now freely admitted the fact "that the expression [of the tales] largely originates with us."[8] In subsequent editions, Wilhelm Grimm even carries this admission further, stating that they were responsible for both "the expression and the execution of the individual tales."[9] These statements are nothing less than an honest admission that the brothers, or at least Wilhelm Grimm, had abandoned the original plan of not "augmenting" the tales in any way as stated in the prologue to the first volume. But with an indignation that defies understanding, Ellis sees these admissions as evidence of "fraud and deception" on the part of the Grimms. It may well be that the original program for publishing the tales as stated in the first volume of the first edition was somewhat misleading, but the open admission of a revision of these standards in subsequent editions was impeccably honest. Ellis, in his zeal to create an exposé, not only distorted the situation, he either overlooked or suppressed information that explains why it was necessary for the Grimms to change their plans. Important for an understanding of Wilhelm Grimm's editing methods is the degree to which the second edition of the KHM of 1819 was a brand-new work. A total of thirty-four tales from the first edition of 1812–15 had been deleted from the collection, including both "Puss-in-Boots" and "Bluebeard" (because they were obviously derivative from Perrault). Moreover, forty-five new tales which the brothers had located in intervening years were added to the collection and eighteen tales had undergone substantial revision on the basis of more complete variants that they had since encountered.

Ellis also seems to have forgotten or ignored the fact that the Grimms were working in an era not only before the availability of recording devices, but also even before shorthand notation had been invented, and were thus forced in many cases to work with fragmentary notes. It is also known that many of the tales they collected were found in fragmented form, and that these either had to be abandoned altogether or expanded on the basis of other materials. In a communication that accompanied some tales he had sent to his mentor, Carl von Savigny, in 1808, for example, Jacob Grimm commented specifically that the beginnings of tales were most appealing because that was the part the narrators remembered best, and that the endings, by contrast, frequently disintegrated into incomprehensible gibberish.[10] It is apparent that, already in 1808, the Grimms were working with a dying oral tradition.

All of these factors occasioned a change of plans for the Grimms. They, and especially Wilhelm, who from the second edition on assumed primary responsibility for the KHM, abandoned the hope of presenting the tales in pure form exactly as they had been found. He said as much in the prologue to the second edition and, as has already been pointed out, he intensified this admission in subsequent editions. Had Wilhelm Grimm not revised and restored the tales, no one other than a handful of philologists and narrative researchers would have heard of them today.

Wilhelm, now more than ever, intended the book as a collection of *Kindermärchen;* and he outlined this goal in the prologue to the second edition, stating further that "we have thus eliminated in this edition any expression that is not suitable for childhood."[11] One could well argue that taking such liberties with the material is not in keeping with the rigorous practices of narrative research. To accuse the Grimms of not living up to the rigorous demands of the discipline is an easy trap to fall into. So many later scholars have championed the Grimms as the founders of the study of folklore and of folk narrative research that it is easy enough for one to believe that they had indeed created a rigorous discipline at that time. Ellis not only falls victim to this trap, he falls in head over heels. Throughout the work he criticizes the Grimms for not adhering to the rigorous demands of folkloristic research and the principles of critical text-editing, apparently unaware that the academic world had yet to develop any methods in these areas at that time. At one point Ellis calls attention to the Grimms' sources and remarks that "the overwhelming predominance of references to the Hessian district . . . as the sources of the tales might by itself have raised doubts as to their seriousness as folklorists."[12] How could one harbor doubts as to their "seriousness as folklorists" when there existed at that time not the semblance of a field of folkloristic study? In short, Ellis criticizes the Grimms for not adhering to the rigorous demands of scholarship that in that day did not exist!

Ellis also exaggerates the influence that the Perrault collection had on the Grimm tales, accusing the Grimms of hiding the fact that many of their informants, Dorothea Viehmann among them, were educated men and women of Huguenot-French background, all of whom knew their Perrault quite well. In so doing, he conveniently ignores, or even suppresses, the fact that there are all together eight narratives in the Perrault collection, only seven of which qualify as *Märchen*. The Grimms, by contrast, worked with a corpus of over 250 tales (including those that were deleted, others that were not published, and others that were variants of the published tales). Thus, even if the Grimm variants to these seven tales were directly attributable to the Perrault collection, this would account for only a small fraction of their total.[13] Moreover, only two or three of the nearly fifty tales that Frau Viehmann told the brothers can be seen as related to the Perrault stories. Many of the stories she contributed are relatively coarse *Schwänke* that she obviously had heard in the family tavern.

Ellis also takes the Grimms to task frequently for not identifying their sources—Frau Viehmann being the exception. But Ellis himself completely ignores the existence of known sources for the KHM who certainly could qualify as members of the "folk" (that this designation is itself highly problematic, and that its use is avoided by most scholars of narrative today is another fact of which Ellis is apparently unaware). There was, for example, the retired Sergeant of the Dragoons, Friedrich Krause,[14] the shepherd of Köteberg, the rag-collector of Eichsfeld, the "Märchen-Frau" of Marburg (Brentano also had collected narratives from the latter), among others, all of whom are never mentioned by Ellis. Moreover, he makes no reference to the so-called *Bökendorfer Märchenkreis,* which included members of the Haxthausen and Droste-Hülshoff families, who, although among the educated and middle-class acquaintances of the brothers, nevertheless provided stories in Low German dialect that were obviously from oral tradition.

Ellis also takes the Grimms to task for not revealing the identity of each and every informant, and he attacks Heinz Rölleke for making the apology that the Grimms were silent about the identity of their informants because "they wanted to give the impression that the collective origin of the fairy tales . . . required as it were a collective tradition."[15] Ellis characterizes this explanation as "a highly unconvincing argument." First, it must be pointed out that, at that time, there was absolutely no precedent for identifying sources. Who was around then to demand of the Grimms that they provide information about where they acquired their tales when no such demands had ever been voiced or written before? Secondly, if Ellis had been aware of the Grimms' many writings regarding the bearers of tradition, then he would have known that Rölleke's argument is in no way "highly unconvincing." It is based on a thorough familiarity with the thinking of the Grimms on this issue as it has been expressed in many of their writings.

Ellis also attacks Rölleke on another issue. Rölleke had once "warned against conclusions that are too extreme," stating that "one cannot, just from the fact that some of the main contributors were of Huguenot origin, simply conclude that the Grimms' Fairy Tales originate in France."[16] Ellis accuses Rölleke of using here "a trick of argument." He asserts that the question is not whether the tales are essentially "all French but whether they are essentially all German. If we keep our eyes on the real issue, rather than on the red herring which substitutes for it here, we shall still have to go on being disturbed by the fact that there is very considerable French presence and influence in a collection which the Grimms tried to pass off as German through and through, knowing that not to be the case."[17] If it were really true that the Brothers Grimm had tried to "pass off" the collection "as German through and through," Ellis might have a point. The fact is, however, that it is Ellis, and not Rölleke, who is on shaky ground because of his lack of knowledge about the Grimms' notions regarding the provenience of *Märchen.* It is true that in their prologue to the first volume of the first edition, they voiced pride in the German nature of the collection.[18] I do not think an apology is needed for the Grimms' national pride, though, for in 1812 Hesse was still under French occupation, and they clearly felt the need to stress the German component of the work. The significant point here is that they altered their viewpoint considerably by 1819, when the second edition appeared.

It was, incidentally, the same year that the first volume of Jacob Grimm's *Deutsche Grammatik* appeared. Much had happened in the intervening years: The War of Liberation had been successful, and the Napoleonic occupation of the homeland had ended. Rasmus Rask had also published his *Untersuchung über den Ursprung der alten nordischen oder isländischen Sprache* in 1818, in which he made the first systematic phonology of the Germanic languages showing their relationship to other Indo-European languages. He thus posited the existence of a proto-Indo-European language and thereby anticipated some of the findings Jacob Grimm was to make independently in his *Deutsche Grammatik*. Moreover, scholars from over much of Europe and Asia, inspired by the work of the Grimms, began to discover narrative traditions that were clearly related to the Grimm corpus.

The situation that the Grimms had suspected earlier that led them to avoid the word *deutsch* in the title of the KHM (cf. *Deutsche Sagen, Deutsche Mythologie, Deutsche Rechtsaltertümer, Deutsche Grammatik,* and *Deutsche Heldensage*) was now beginning to emerge with clarity. It is to the credit of the Grimms that they fully acknowledged, in the prologue to the second edition, that the *Märchen* were by no means exclusively of German provenience:

> Not merely do we encounter these tales in the diverse regions where German is spoken, but also among related Nordic and English peoples. Especially striking is their similarity with Serbian tales, for no one could fall victim to the notion that the tales could have been transplanted into a remote Hessian village by Serbians, any more than the other way around. Finally, there are agreements in individual traits and expressions as well as in the plots of complete tales with oriental (Persian and Indic) tales. The relationship that emerges in the languages of all these peoples and which Rask has recently proven with scholarly acuity is thus repeated precisely in their traditional poetry, which is nothing more than a higher and freer language of man.[19]

The Grimms thus considered the *Märchen* to be an Indo-European inheritance—an argument Wilhelm Grimm repeated in both the 1850 and 1857 editions of the KHM—and he certainly gave up the notion of a "purely German" nature of the collection. Ellis, however, ignores all this information. By concentrating on remarks that were made in the first edition during the French occupation of Hesse, he creates his own windmill that, for him, represents *the* programmatic methods of the Grimms, and that he then attacks with Quixotic self-righteousness.

There is certainly much more that can be said about the methods of the Brothers Grimm. In spite of scores of valuable studies by German scholars in recent years, there remains much work in the way of a truly critical analysis of the sources used by the Grimms, not merely for the KHM but for many of their works. In regard to the *Deutsche Sagen,* for example, I have noted that the Grimms had a proclivity for labeling a legend *mündlich* (oral) in cases in which they had clearly acquired the text from a written source.[20]

If we look objectively at the methods of the Grimms in the context of Western intellectual history, we find the same situation that can be encountered again and again in the history of scholarship. Investigators who are on the frontier of a new wave of ideas let their judgment be dominated by their enthusiasm for the importance of the new mode of thought. This situation was intensified in the case of the Grimms by the great political and social turmoil that was occasioned by the Napoleonic wars. The problem has also been exacerbated by those who virtually deified the Grimms. Such worship, in turn, led subsequent generations into a near frenzy of demythologizing the Grimms and their work. Neither group of scholars has served the Grimms well. An honest and objective assessment is still needed for a genuine appreciation of the contributions of the Grimms to our understanding of human creativity.

Notes

1. Stith Thompson, *The Types of the Folktale: A Classification and Bibliography: Antti Aarne's Verzeichnis der Märchentypen, Translated and Enlarged by Stith Thompson,* FFC 184 (Helsinki: Suomalainen Tiedeakatemia, 1961).

2. Marian Roalfe Cox, *Cinderella: Three Hundred and Forty-Five Variants of Cinderella, Catskin, and Cap o'Rushes,* Publications of the Folk-Lore Society, 31 (London: The Folklore Society, 1893).

3. Anna Birgitta Rooth, *The Cinderella Cycle* (Lund: C. W. K. Gleerup, 1951).

4. Alan Dundes, "Nationalistic Inferiority Complexes and the Fabrication of Fakelore: A Reconsideration of Ossian, the *Kinder- und Hausmärchen,* the *Kalevala,* and Paul Bunyan," *Journal of Folklore Research,* 22 (1985), 5–18; see esp. pp. 8–9.

5. John M. Ellis, *One Fairy Story Too Many: The Brothers Grimm and Their Tales* (Chicago: University of Chicago Press, 1983).

6. Ibid., p. 103.

7. Ellis's translation, pp. 13–14.

8. Ellis's translation, p. 17.

9. Ellis's translation, p. 19.

10. Dieter Hennig and Bernhard Lauer (eds.), *Die Brüder Grimm: Dokumente ihres Lebens und Wirkens* (Kassel: Weber & Weidemeyer, 1985), p. 537.

11. "Vorrede" to the second edition; quoted from Jacob Grimm and Wilhelm Grimm, *Kinder- und Hausmärchen, nach der zweiten vermehrten und verbesserten Auflage von 1819,* ed. Heinz Rölleke, 2 vols. (Cologne: Eugen Diederichs, 1982), II, 542.

12. Ellis, p. 27.

13. See the essay by Heinz Rölleke in this volume for a more detailed discussion of the repertoires of the Huguenot informants.

14. See the contribution by Gonthier-Louis Fink in this volume for a discussion of this informant and of the tales he contributed.

15. Ellis, p. 28.

16. Quoted from Ellis's translation, p. 107.

17. Ellis, p. 107.

18. "Vorrede" to the first edition of *Kinder- und Hausmärchen* (Berlin: Reimer, 1812); quoted from Wilhelm Grimm, *Kleinere Schriften,* ed. Gustav Hinrichs (Berlin: F. Dümmler, 1881–87), I, 332.

19. "Einleitung: Über das Wesen der Märchen," in *Kinder- und Hausmärchen,* 2d ed., 2 vols. (Berlin: Reimer, 1819), I; quoted from Wilhelm Grimm, *Kleinere Schriften,* I, 337f. (my own translation).

20. Rudolf Schenda, of the University of Zurich, has lately been investigating the sources of the Swiss narratives that appeared in the Grimms' *Deutsche Sagen* and has noted a proclivity on the part of the brothers for attributing oral sources to legends of diverse origins. See for example Rudolf Schenda, "Jacob und Wilhelm Grimm: Deutsche Sagen Nr. 103, 298, 337, 340, 350, 357 und 514: Bemerkungen zu den literarischen Quellen von sieben Schweizer Sagen," *Schweizerisches Archiv für Volkskunde,* 81 (1985), 196–206.

HEINZ RÖLLEKE

New Results of Research on
Grimms' Fairy Tales

IN CONTRAST to all other German literary classics, the assumptions, origins, environment, and above all the intentions of the greatest best-seller of all times—I mean *Grimms' Fairy Tales*—remain still today insufficiently investigated, and even less well known. On the one hand, this is because things that are very familiar, phenomena that we have known intimately all our lives, seldom seem worth questioning—and *Grimms' Fairy Tales* belong to the unquestioned intellectual baggage of almost every German-speaking person. On the other hand, major difficulties of both methodological and factual nature stand in the way of the investigation and presentation of the above-mentioned problems.

Methodologically, *Grimms' Fairy Tales* do not reflect the intentions of a single author, as literary masterworks otherwise do, but the highly divergent purposes of two imitative collectors and revisers and about forty different contributors, as well as thirty different published or manuscript sources spanning six centuries and almost all of the German-speaking areas. Factually, a serious and comprehensive philological investigation of *Grimms' Fairy Tales* would have to consist of some 240 individual studies, since that many texts play a part in the printing history and success story of this work. There were 211 texts in the edition of 1857, the last during the Grimms' lifetime, and thirty texts that were eliminated along the way in the course of the previous editions, not to mention numerous parallel versions, about which the Grimms reported in their scholarly commentary on the stories. For each text, one would need to describe its history before the Grimms; to uncover the form in which the Grimms became familiar with the tale, through hearing or reading it; and to document and interpret the changes made, whether as a result of a misunderstanding, for reasons of stylistic improvement, motivation, embellishment, or abridgement, or above all as the result of manifold contamination. And this must be done not only for the first edition of 1812–15, but for all seventeen editions of the collection (seven of the full version, and ten of the short version), taking into account, of course, the manuscript material in the form of inscribed notations and textual changes.

Since we lack this comprehensive presentation, all wholesale judgments, to which this work like hardly any other in world literature has been subjected, must remain unprovable for the present and for the foreseeable future. One does not find, either, in direct testimony or statements by the Grimm brothers or their contributors, so much as a hint that would render permissible such deductive conclusions. The Grimm brothers carefully destroyed the texts they had evaluated and employed, both their own manuscripts and those by others, whether or not they were copied from written texts or were written down from oral narration. If Clemens Brentano's gifted carelessness had not resulted in his failure to return the sheaf of papers with the tales that the Grimms sent him in 1810, and these manuscripts had not thereby been preserved, the riddles would be still greater. In connection with preparing a historical-critical edition of these materials, with commentary, in 1975,[1] I succeeded in achieving preliminary results that made it possible to correct, in part, the mistakes and misunderstandings that had continued to be passed on. I must take this opportunity to emphasize expressly that this represents only the beginning, not the end, of the necessary process of questioning and investigating.

In this short review of the present situation, I must restrict myself to the subject of the Grimms' contributors as well as the Grimms' establishing of their texts and the changes they made. I hope also to be able to clarify the related problems with several significant examples.

As is well known, in their published citations of sources for the individual tales, the Grimms did not name any of their contributors, and limited themselves instead to extremely vague information, like "orally in Hessia," "from the area of the Main River," "from Westphalia," and so on. In doing this, they were alluding to the anonymous spirit of the folk to which they attributed the invention and transmission of the tales.

They made two exceptions, which are therefore especially noteworthy. Outside the framework of the commentaries on the individual tales, namely in various prefaces, the names von Haxthausen and Dorothea Viehmann occur. The aristocratic Westphalian family von Haxthausen (among the members of which, in this context, the sisters von Droste-Hülshoff must be reckoned) had to be named because they constituted a branch office of the Grimms' fairy-tale collecting enterprise, so to speak. Almost one-third of the complete corpus of tales derives from the Haxthausens. They collected tales in their environs as the Grimms did in Kassel, and sent in the products of their labors. I will return to their role, briefly, in another context later.

Dorothea Viehmann, however, was recognizably transformed by the Grimms into the ideal type of a teller of tales. As such, she was supposed to determine the image of the circle of contributors that the readers were to carry away with them—and in the most literal sense, for her portrait, drawn by their brother Ludwig Emil Grimm, adorned the second volume of the tales beginning with the second edition of 1819. How, then, is this ideal contributor—from whom, indeed, thirty of the Grimms' tales derive—presented to the reader? I quote from the preface to the first edition of the second volume (1815): "One of those happy coincidences, however, was the acquaintance with a *peasant woman* from the *village* of Zwehrn near Kassel, through whom we received a considerable part of the tales communicated here, which are therefore *genuinely Hessian* tales. This woman, still hale and hearty and not much over fifty years *old,* is called the Viehmann woman [*die Viehmännin*]... and was probably beautiful when she was young. She retains these old legends firmly in her memory..., narrates them deliberately, surely, and in an uncommonly lively way ... so that with a little practice one can *write them down* as she is telling them. *Some things* have in this way been *retained literally,* and in their genuineness will not fail to be recognized" (italics mine).[2]

The passage cited here was changed only little in the second edition of 1819, but the changes were quite significant. The reference to the "genuinely Hessian tales" has disappeared and not been replaced. The key words "peasant woman" from a "village," "old," and so forth remain unchanged, however. In the Grimms' image of this contributor, these were the words that mattered, and these words have indeed determined the general image, and even the scholarly view, of the origin of the Grimms' collection to the present day. One thinks of old, simple women from the countryside who remember such stories, which have come down to them from generation to generation reaching back to time immemorial. Preferably, one envisions them as illiterate, unafflicted by any touch of literary education or equivalent fruits of reading. And if such people have always lived in the same spot, then the guarantee that their storytelling is unadulterated and unspoiled is still stronger.

But what are the facts? Frau Viehmann was the wife of a tailor. She was not as old as one usually imagines a grandmotherly storyteller to be. She was skilled in handling people—after all, twice a week she walked to Kassel in order to sell produce from her garden to her customers there, including the Grimm brothers, who, with their proverbial shyness, never went themselves to the storytellers but always waited until the latter came, or were sent, to them. That was so in the case of Frau Viehmann, too. Who sent her to them? The family of the French preacher Ramus in Kassel, with whom the Grimms were most closely acquainted. Why? Frau Viehmann was descended from Huguenot immigrants, was born a Pierson (which the decidedly German name "Viehmann" permitted one to forget entirely), and from childhood on she had spoken French as well as German.

Two things thereby become clear. First, the hitherto much-debated influence of French fairy-tale collections (Charles Perrault, Marie d'Aulnoy, *Bibliothèque bleue,* etc.) on Frau Viehmann's repertoire may be effortlessly explained as resulting from her cultural origins. Through oral tradition in her family or through French books the family possessed, Frau Viehmann-Pierson received a part of her treasure of tales. Second, the Grimms' quiet elimination of the reference to the supposedly "genuinely Hessian" character of their stories can only be explained by the fact that the brothers had recognized these connections in the meantime or could no longer ignore them publicly. They never pointed out the connections anywhere, but instead remained silent about them. At the same time, they never made directly false statements about this matter that they found so delicate (the subject was a ticklish one in view of the collection's patriotic intent and its supposed testimony to the existence of "purely primeval German myth"). The same language is spoken in the book's title, after all. In contrast to all similarly oriented undertakings of that period (*Des Knaben Wunderhorn: Alte deutsche Lieder, Die teutschen Volksbücher, Deutsche Sagen, Deutsche Grammatik, Deutsche Mythologie,* etc.), in the title of this collection of tales the word "German" (*Deutsch*) is significantly absent. The Grimms were aware of the internationality of this genre, and ultimately of their contributors as well. Here, too, one finds concealment, but not false representations.

But let us return to Frau Viehmann. If one was inclined at first—along with the Grimms, or even in opposition to them—to consider their repertoire primevally Hessian or at least primevally German, then after the discoveries about Frau Viehmann, with customary German radicalism, people wheeled about and charged off toward the opposite extreme. Now all of the texts deriving from Frau Viehmann were considered, and continue to be considered (above all, among American Germanists), to be French, which is of course sheer nonsense. In fact, only about one-third of her repertoire shows direct or indirect French influence. The other two-thirds she probably appropriated in her youth from carters stopping for the night and servants at the Knallhütte tavern, as befitted the inquisitive little daughter of an innkeeper. Among these tales, significantly, stories of an anecdotal, coarse nature with almost exclusively male heroes dominate.

In concluding these comments about Frau Viehmann, I wish to make only one final observation in passing. In her whole repertoire, there is not a single witch or woman versed in magic, such as populate over half of the Grimms' texts. On this point, further investigation is needed. There are still many observations to be made and new results to be achieved.

When the "genuinely Hessian" aura of Frau Viehmann became no longer tenable, or at least began to pale, in those circles which wanted, at all costs, to have their tales traced to old, unspoiled contributors, people recalled another figure with the homey name "Old Marie." In 1890 Herman Grimm, Wilhelm's son, had attributed to her the most important tales of all. And this old woman was indeed really an unspoiled, entirely Hessian nursemaid as in the book of fairy tales. She was the housekeeper in the Wild family's pharmacy, that is, in the house next to that in which the Grimm brothers lived. People believed in her role all the more firmly and attributed to her the not-inconsiderable repertoire of the young Wild siblings, who were the very first contributors. Her pedigree was perfect for the German fairy-tale tradition. She did not know any French, and she never lived anywhere else but Kassel.

In this matter, though, people should have asked themselves much earlier why the Grimm brothers did not accordingly make a good deal of this much "less questionable" storyteller, and indeed why the Grimms never mentioned this fine specimen of native fairy-tale knowledge a single time. The answer is shockingly simple. She did not contribute any of the tales.

Herman Grimm, out of bias and ignorance of the facts, simply put "Old Marie" in the place of a young—and by the way very pretty— Marie. The person in question was not Marie Clar, born in 1747 near Kassel, but Marie Hassenpflug, born in 1788 into a Huguenot family named Droume from the Dauphine in France. In view of this discovery, the literal agreement between many passages of the Grimm brothers' stories (above all, "Little Red-Cap," "Little Thorn-Rose," "Puss in Boots") with those of Charles Perrault is no longer puzzling; it is obvious. The highly educated and well-placed Hassenpflug family lived entirely in and through French culture and French literature. Yet here, too, one must warn against drawing hasty and distorted con- clusions, such as Professor Ellis has done in his recent book, *One Fairy Story Too Many*,[3] namely that the whole repertoire of the Hassenpflugs was drawn from Perrault (in addition to Marie, who had hitherto been unknown, both Jeannette and Amalia Hassenpflug also contributed stories). That would have been indeed too much like a fairy tale. The twelve Perrault texts would have had to make forty. No, in this case it is much as with Frau Viehmann. There are tales in the Hassenpflug repertoire that they remembered from their childhood spent in Hanau on the Main river, and these are largely influenced by French stories. But there are also tales that they learned after the family's move to Kassel, and these are owing to German narrative tradition. Moreover, the Grimms made this distinction quite neatly, once again without saying so directly. They classified the former group as "from the areas around the Main," and the latter as "from Hessia."

With the more exact characterization of Dorothea Viehmann-Pierson on the one hand, and the rejuvenation of Old Marie on the other, the field of direct contributors to the Grimm collection has gained uni- form contours (as it does too, by the way, for the collection of legends, which was completed only later). We are dealing almost exclusively with people from the—well-placed—middle classes. With the excep- tion of Frau Viehmann, they are all very young ladies (between fifteen and twenty years old), and they have an excellent command of French or are from families that come from France (the Wild family was from Switzerland). Therewith, the international "admixture" of the Grimms' texts is explicable and understandable. We should be happy about this phenomenon, as was Wilhelm Grimm himself, by the way, when he wrote, as early as 1811: "and thus it seems to become ever clearer that the countries have influenced one another, and what they have communicated to one another. . . . Once we have recognized this completely, we may dare to trace the thread that old Fable has spun . . . and drawn forth throughout the world. How would it otherwise be possible, without this research into its wanderings among peoples, to understand the life of poetry, its origins, and its growth?"[4]

One further word about class distinctions is in order here. From the fact that the Grimms' "immediate sources" were without exception well-placed members of the middle class or the aristocracy, one should in no way conclude that the stories were transmitted only in these circles and have nothing to say about the common folk, whether in their context or the manner of their transmission. In all demonstrable cases, when they did not get them from books, the eloquent narrators whose tales the Grimms adapted drew their inspiration from the oral tradition of the simplest people: domestic servants, peasants, herders, and carters. And that is also probably the level of society in which these stories were taken up and passed on. It is only that, in view of our new knowledge about the creation of the Grimms' collection, the manifold filtering to which these tales were subjected must be considered and taken into account.

First of all, under the influence of Clemens Brentano and the model versions produced by Philipp Otto Runge, the Grimms were from the beginning only interested in texts that were well told, artistically appealing, and free of obscenity and class hatred. Therefore, they necessarily came into contact only with contributors who were eloquent, educated, and familiar with the extremely artistic French fairy-tale tradition.

Second, these contributors, for their part, passed on to the Grimms only those texts that they considered appropriate in view of the brothers' criteria.

Third, the servants, carters, and so on who confided their texts to the Grimms' contributors were undoubtedly very careful not to present to their masters texts that were obscene or expressed class hatred or resentment.

Thus, after self-censorship by the actual tellers, there followed a process of selection and slight reworking of the texts by the contributors (as is especially demonstrable in the Westphalian texts provided by Haxthausen), and thereupon there was further selection and, in some cases, thorough reworking by the Brothers Grimm. Then these texts were published, in part, and the published texts underwent more or less major revision from one edition to the next. A large number of folktale scholars who insist upon the literal fidelity of the Grimms' transmission have also neglected to draw the appropriate conclusion from what remained unsaid in the Grimms' preface quoted above, or rather, from what was stated in the negative there. The express reference to the fact that they had partially written down Frau Viehmann's words verbatim makes clear that as a rule they did not proceed that way.

Let us take a look at the Grimms' statement about the origins of a sequence of six arbitrarily chosen tales: KHM 11, "from 2 tales from the Main River area"; KHM 12, "from Schulz . . . too prolix"; KHM 13, "In conformity with two tales, both from Hessia, which complement each other"; KHM 14, "from a tale from the principality of Corvey, but it is preserved from a Hessian story that . . . "; KHM 15, "from differing tales from Hessia"; KHM 16, "from two tales"; etc. Thus, one sees how often and how extensively reworking occurred. Scholarship on the Grimms and on folktale has not yet taken this state of affairs seriously enough, and has not taken it into account with sufficient exactitude.

If we want to find out more about the stages in the development of the Grimms' texts we cannot start, as we have previously, with theories about the origin of texts and about hypothetical original versions, but must begin instead the other way around, with the last attested texts (in the last edition of the Grimms' collection during their lifetime), and try to uncover one layer of the text's development after the other. Then, we can hope to reach the core of the story, around which such numerous revisions have been undertaken.

Thus, it has been shown, for example, that the opening theme of the famous story of Hansel and Gretel about the "famine" that afflicted the country was an addition introduced by Wilhelm Grimm in the fifth edition (1843). When scholarly critics like Helmut Brackert make this theme the starting point for their interpretation and argue that social conditions and problems of earliest times have been preserved therein, they are definitely on the wrong track.[5] Or when Eugen Drewermann sees in "Snow-White and Rose-Red" (KHM 161) ancient wisdom that has been stored and transmitted,[6] he purely and simply fails to recognize that this is an artistic fairy tale whose core was invented by Caroline Stahl in 1819, and whose poetic development and embellishment was added by Wilhelm Grimm in 1837.[7]

But not only such weighty textual changes (of which there are more than the reader imagines) are the subject of debate. In 1850, Wilhelm Grimm, for once, uncharacteristically commented upon one detail in his method, a point that Grimm scholars so far have not investigated: "The sixth edition of *Grimms' Fairy Tales,* too, . . . has been improved and perfected with regard to particulars. I have constantly taken pains to introduce folk sayings and curious figures of speech, to which I am always listening attentively."[8] Even a cursory comparison of earlier and later versions of the Grimms' stories effortlessly provides dozens of examples of passages about which one can say, by way of exception, that they come from Wilhelm Grimm and not from his contributors: "All good things come in threes" (KHM 2); "Whoever begins a thing must go on with it" (KHM 15); "I will show mercy instead of passing sentence" (KHM 36); "When the going gets rough, one gets going" (KHM 52); "Out there where the fox and the hare bid each other goodnight" (KHM 55); "You will learn by suffering harm" (KHM 64); "A good beginning is half the battle" (KHM 114).[9]

Here literary scholars—and with them the interpreters, too—stand for once on firm ground. This terrain should be measured and surveyed further. Much new information, and probably decisive results, would then be added to our new, still very scant knowledge about *Grimms' Fairy Tales.*

We do not have to fear that in carrying out these investigations we will be detracting from the magical charm of this work. We will not lose anything but unfounded, camouflaging myths or a few chauvinistic emphases. We will gain insight, instead, into a multifaceted and fascinating phenomenon, namely, under which presuppositions and circumstances this work managed to become what it is: the most often translated, most often published, and best-known German-language work of all time.

"Everything that mankind investigates in detail is miraculous."[10] Jacob Grimm said that, and so do I.

Notes

This essay appeared in German in *Jacob und Wilhelm Grimm: Vorträge und Ansprachen,* Göttinger Universitätsreden (Göttingen: Vandenhoeck & Ruprecht, 1986), pp. 39–48. The English translation is by James M. McGlathery.

1. Heinz Rölleke (ed.), *Die älteste Märchensammlung der Brüder Grimm: Synopse der handschriftlichen Urfassung von 1810 und der Erstdrucke von 1812* (Cologny-Genève: Fondation Martin Bodmer, 1975).

2. Jacob Grimm and Wilhelm Grimm, *Kinder- und Hausmärchen: Gesammelt durch die Brüder Grimm. Vergrößerter Nachdruck der zweibändigen Erstausgabe von 1812 und 1815 nach dem Handexemplar des Brüder Grimm-Museums Kassel mit sämtlichen handschriftlichen Korrekturen und Nachträgen der Brüder Grimm sowie einem Ergänzungsheft, Transkriptionen und Kommentaren,* ed. Heinz Rölleke (with Ulrike Marquardt), 3 vols. (Göttingen: Vandenhoeck & Ruprecht, 1986), II, iv–v: "Einer jener guten Zufälle aber war die Bekanntschaft mit einer *Bäuerin* aus dem nah bei Kassel gelegenen *Dorfe* Zwehrn, durch welche wir einen ansehnlichen Theil der hier mitgetheilten, darum *ächt hessischen* Märchen... erhalten haben. Diese Frau, noch rüstig und nicht viel über fünfzig Jahre *alt,* heißt Viehmännin... und ist wahrscheinlich in ihrer Jugend schön gewesen. Sie bewahrt diese alte Sagen fest in dem *Gedächtniß...* erzählt sie bedächtig, sicher und ungemein lebendig... so daß man ihr mit einiger Übung *nachschreiben* kann. *Manches* ist auf diese Weise *wörtlich beibehalten,* und wird in seiner Wahrheit nicht zu verkennen sein" (italics mine).

3. John M. Ellis, *One Fairy Story Too Many: The Brothers Grimm and Their Tales* (Chicago: University of Chicago Press, 1983).

4. Wilhelm Grimm (trans.), *Altdänische Heldenlieder, Balladen und Märchen* (Heidelberg: Zimmer und Mohr, 1811), p. v: "und so scheint es immer deutlicher zu werden, wie die Völker aufeinander gewirkt, was sie gegenseitig sich mitgetheilt.... Haben wir dieses vollständig erkannt, dann dürfen wir es wagen, dem Faden nachzugehen, welche die alte Fabel gesponnen und... durch die Welt gezogen. Wie wäre es aber möglich, ohne dies Forschen nach ihren Völkerwanderungen das Leben der Poesie, ihre Entstehung und ihr Wachstum, zu begreifen?"

5. Helmut Brackert (ed.), *Und wenn sie nicht gestorben sind...: Perspektiven auf das Märchen,* edition suhrkamp, 973 (Frankfurt a.M.: Suhrkamp, 1980), p. 237.

6. Eugen Drewermann, *Schneeweißchen und Rosenrot* (Olten and Freiburg im Breisgau: Walter 1983).

7. See Heinz Rölleke, "Schneeweißchen und Rosenroth: Rätsel um ein Grimmsches Märchen," in Rölleke, *Wo das Wünschen noch geholfen hat* (Bonn: Bouvier, 1985), pp. 191–206, and Rölleke, "KHM 161 in der Grimmschen Urfassung," *Fabula,* 27 (1986), 265–87.

8. Jacob Grimm and Wilhelm Grimm, *Kinder- und Hausmärchen: Ausgabe letzter Hand mit den Originalanmerkungen der Brüder Grimm, mit einem Anhang sämtlicher, nicht in allen Auflagen veröffentlichten Märchen,* ed. Heinz Rölleke, 3 vols. (Stuttgart: Philipp Reclam, 1980), I, 27: "Auch die 6. [Märchen-] Ausgabe ... ist im einzelnen verbessert oder vervollständigt worden. Fortwährend bin ich bemüht gewesen, Sprüche und eigentümliche Redensarten des Volks, auf die ich immer horche, einzutragen."

9. Ibid.: "Aller guten Dinge sind drei" (I, 34); "Wer A sagt, muß auch B sagen" (I, 102); "Ich will Gnade für Recht ergehen lassen" (I, 203–4); "die Not macht

Beine" (I, 234); "wo Fuchs und Hase sich gute Nacht sagen" (I, 287); "durch Schaden wirst du klug werden" (I, 347); "Frisch gewagt ist halb gewonnen" (II, 147).

10. In a letter to the Haxthausens of 10 September 1822 in Alexander Reifferscheid (ed.), *Freundesbriefe von Wilhelm und Jacob Grimm* (Heilbronn, 1878), p. 88: "Alles was der Mensch genau betrachtet, ist wunderbar."

WOLFGANG MIEDER

"Ever Eager to Incorporate Folk Proverbs": Wilhelm Grimm's Proverbial Additions in the Fairy Tales

ANYONE ACQUAINTED with the voluminous works of the Brothers Grimm is most likely aware of Wilhelm Grimm's interest in proverbs and proverbial expressions, particularly evident in his publications on the medieval *Bescheidenheit* of Freidank. In his own edition of this collection of gnomic verses, entitled *Vridankes Bescheidenheit* (1834), he listed numerous Middle High German proverbs as parallels and also expressed the desire to assemble a medieval proverb collection. Although this plan unfortunately never materialized, he often utilized proverbial materials in his writings as explanatory annotations. It also was primarily his interest in all expressions of folk speech that led him to incorporate new proverbial texts into later editions of the *Kinder- und Hausmärchen.* Yet his brother Jacob Grimm also showed a considerable scholarly interest in proverbs in his philological and historical studies, where they served him as early and convincing references to folk wisdom.

The two brothers knew or possessed such significant proverb collections as Johann Agricola's *Sybenhundert und fünfftzig Teütscher Sprichwörter* (1534); Sebastian Franck's *Sprichwörter, Schöne, Weise, Herrliche Klugreden und Hoffsprüch* (1541); Eucharius Eyering's *Proverbiorum Copia* (1601–3); Friedrich Petri's *Der Teutschen Weißheit* (1604–5); Christoph Lehmann's *Florilegium Politicum* (1630); and Johann Michael Sailer's *Die Weisheit auf der Gasse* (1810); among others. These works were repeatedly cited as references, and of course Jacob Grimm also used Johann Friedrich Eisenhart's *Grundsätze der deutschen Rechte in Sprüchwörtern* (Basic Prin-

112

ciples of German Law in Proverbs) (1759 and 1792) for his publications on legal history. It should be no surprise then that proverbs, proverbial expressions, proverbial comparisons, and twin formulas play a major role in the entire corpus of the Brothers Grimm.

The Grimms frequently used such expressions in their many letters and at times they also appear as part of their scholarly style in their articles and books. In their editions of Middle and Early New High German literary works, they often comment on the meaning of old proverbs in their annotations that help to decode difficult passages. In the volumes of their so-called *Kleinere Schriften* (Minor Writings), both brothers repeatedly cite proverbial materials. Jacob Grimm's seminal essay "Von der Poesie im Recht" (1815) and Wilhelm's article on "Die mythische Bedeutung des Wolfes" (1856) contain so many proverbs and proverbial expressions that we can consider them significant paroemiological studies in themselves. Other essays exhibit similar preoccupation with proverbial language, clearly showing that the Grimms considered the traditional folk speech of great value for their etymological, philological, historical, cultural, folkloric, and literary studies.

If Wilhelm Grimm was without doubt the expert on medieval proverbs, his brother Jacob was extremely knowledgeable about legal proverbs. In his famous *Deutsche Rechtsaltertümer* (1828), he gives detailed explanations of dozens of such proverbs, and he also finds much use for proverbial materials in his *Deutsche Mythologie* (1835). Often these small proverb studies within larger chapters are so enlightening that Lutz Röhrich, for example, in his *Lexikon der sprichwörtlichen Redensarten* ([Encyclopedia of Proverbial Expressions] 1973), has quoted liberally from these works. But the brothers also made great use of proverbs and proverbial expressions in their more philological and linguistic publications. Jacob's large *Deutsche Grammatik* (1819–37) contains in a scattered fashion an early stylistic study of the proverb, and the first four volumes of the *Deutsches Wörterbuch* (1854–63) are a rich storehouse of proverbs and other folk expressions. Wilhelm, especially, amassed proverbial texts to such a degree that we can discover small "proverb collections" under some of the entries. But this unsurpassed dictionary not only lists proverbial texts; the Grimms also cite them for etymological, semantic, and cultural-historical explanations. Obviously this is done in a much more compact fashion than in the works already mentioned and in Jacob's *Geschichte der deutschen Sprache* (1848). Yet the first four volumes of their dictionary alone (i.e., those volumes the Grimms edited themselves) doubtlessly contain one of the largest proverb collections of the German language.[1]

Of special interest, however, is how Wilhelm Grimm incorporated ever more proverbs and proverbial expressions in the successive editions of the *Kinder- und Hausmärchen*. Even though scholars have made some reference to the proverbial content of the tales, no systematic study of all texts of the seven editions between 1812/1815 and 1857 exists, and this task is also too large for us to accomplish here. Heinz Rölleke rightfully emphasizes in his three-volume reissue of the seventh edition (1857) of the *Kinder- und Hausmärchen* (1980) that a complete critical historical edition should provide identification of proverbial expressions and quotations.[2] The call for such an investigation is not new. Already in 1939 Archer Taylor pointed out that a "collection of the proverbs in the *Household Tales* of the Brothers might be made. In this particular case there are two questions to be answered. Will the comparison of several texts of a tale show that the proverb appearing in the tale really forms part of the tale? In other words, what, if any, is the role of the proverb in traditional narrative? A second question is: In what editions of the *Household Tales* do the proverbs appear? That is to say, can we show that Wilhelm Grimm added to the number of proverbs in the *Tales* during the many revisions which they underwent?"[3] A few proverbial texts were indeed culled from the Grimm collection by Johannes Bolte and Georg Polívka in the fourth volume of their *Anmerkungen zu den Kinder- und Hausmärchen* in order to show elements of folk speech in the fairy tales:

> The decorative language does not consist of poetic images drawn from literary speech but rather of sensual expressions taken from the common folk—expressions that are used in place of abstract words. . . .
>
> Alliterating twin formulas (house and home, chests and crates, *schlecht und recht*), onomatopeia (*ritsch ratsch*), proverbial comparisons (happy as a lark, a face like three rainy days), proverbial expressions (he made short work of it, I have to praise you to the skies), and proverbs (all good things come in threes, well begun is half done, birds of a feather flock together) provide a cozy atmosphere.[4]

Such short remarks have also been made by Kurt Schmidt and Friedrich Panzer,[5] but of particular interest are Lutz Röhrich's comments about how certain fairy-tale titles, names, and motifs have become proverbial due to the great popularity of the Grimm tales. As examples he cites "suffer like Cinderella" (*ein Aschenputteldasein fristen,* KHM 21), "live in the land of milk and honey" (*ein Schlaraffenleben führen,* KHM 158), "have everything fall into one's lap" (*sich die gebratenen Tauben in den Mund fliegen lassen,* KHM 158), "Table, set thyself!" (*Tischlein deck dich,* KHM 36), and so on.[6]

Röhrich also points out that in addition to such proverbial fairy-tale reminiscences there are also actual fairy tales "that are intended to affirm and demonstrate the truth of proverbial expressions and proverbs,"[7] as for example the fairy tale with the title "The Sun Will Bring It to Light" (KHM 115). Here the German proverb *Die Sonne bringt es an den Tag* given in the title is in fact explained through the narrative. The proverb acts as the primary text and the narrative plays a secondary, etiological role. The shortest example of such a proverbial narrative in the Grimm collection is "The Nail" (KHM 184), which exemplifies the proverb "haste makes waste" (*Eile mit Weile*) in less than a page.

There is no doubt about the fact that Wilhelm Grimm was cognizant of the proverbial character of these fairy-tale texts. In his own detailed notes to his fairy-tale collection he explains that the tale "The Sun Will Bring It to Light" obviously also exemplifies the proverb *Es wird nichts so fein gesponnen, es kommt endlich an die Sonnen* (literally: "Nothing is so finely spun that it won't come to light") and even traces it back to medieval documents.[8] And in his annotations to "The Nail" Wilhelm quotes a lengthy Middle High German proverb he had found during his work on the edition of Freidank's *Bescheidenheit.*[9] Of interest are also his lengthy explanations for the Cinderella tale (KHM 21) whose title has become proverbial; he even found the name Aschenputtel already mentioned in the proverb collections of Agricola and Eyering.[10] Other such explanations that Wilhelm Grimm includes for the proverbial expressions are *wo wird der seine Feder hinblasen* (literally: "whither will he blow his feather," KHM 63), *der Schwabe muß allezeit das Leberle gefressen haben* (literally: "Swabians always have to have eaten the liver," KHM 81), and *wenn der Wolf (Fuchs) die Gänse beten lehrt, frißt er sie zum Lehrgeld* (literally: "when the wolf—or fox—teaches the geese to pray, he gets his tuition by devouring them," KHM 86).[11] We can see that Wilhelm recognized the relationship between folk narratives—especially fairy tales—and proverbs or proverbial expressions. Little wonder then that he later felt justified in adding proverbial materials to fairy-tale texts, since they belong to their obvious proverbial style.

Yet these fairy tales based on proverbs, the fairy-tale reminiscences in proverbs and proverbial expressions, and the paroemiological explanations by Wilhelm Grimm do not reveal which role this fairy-tale collector and scholar with his deep interest in folk speech played as far as the proverbial style of so many fairy tales is concerned. All the examples given thus far were consciously chosen for the fact that the proverb or proverbial expression was *not* added by Wilhelm in one of the later editions. They do show, however, that proverbial texts definitely are part of the traditional fairy-tale style. And when Wilhelm added proverbial materials in later editions, he did so with the justification that he imitated the folk speech that belongs to fairy tales. Heinz Rölleke has voiced similar conclusions: "Be that as it may, with his revisions and expansions and his preferential and often admitted attention to popular expressions and metaphors, Wilhelm Grimm found a fairy-tale tone and brought it to such stylistic perfection that his procedure is sufficiently justified simply by the success of that tone."[12]

What significance does Wilhelm Grimm have for the proverbial style of the *Kinder- und Hausmärchen* and what motivated him to make these stylistic changes at all? We have seen that he had great interest in traditional proverbs and expressions. From letters dating from 1811 and 1813 to Paul Wigand we learn that Wilhelm as a young man "picked up telling proverbial expressions from other people," and "he looked to the speech of the common people in order to assure himself as to their type and manner of speaking, and wove such proverbial expressions, proverbial comparisons, and proverbs into the texts of the tales."[13] His love for certain "words and proverbial expressions" that "belong to the language and must not be omitted from its study and synopsis"[14] had also already been mentioned by Wilhelm Grimm to Karl von Savigny in a letter of December 12, 1814, in connection with his work on the second volume of the fairy-tale collection. And in an 1826 review of an English collection of *Fairy Legends and Traditions of the South of Ireland* (1825) he wrote the following, which once again proves that proverbial language belongs to the style of fairy tales and that Wilhelm had a special interest in it: "They [fairy tales] depict, namely, in a completely faithful way, the domestic condition, mode of thinking, way of life, and mores of a not very familiar country. The Irish will recognize the scenes depicted, the individual features, the proverbial expressions, popular jests and metaphors, and untranslatable 'bulls' more readily and with special enjoyment, but even foreigners can be expected to sense and cherish them."[15]

Such proverbial discoveries in the fairy tales of other nationalities surely strengthened Wilhelm's conviction that he could integrate into "his" fairy-tale texts some proverbs and proverbial expressions now and then without thereby jeopardizing the general authenticity of the texts. He also received much support from his wife Dortchen, who shared his interest in proverbs and who, according to Bolte and Polívka, added such folk expressions as the following ones in the margins of her husband's own copy of the second edition of the *Kinder- und Hausmärchen* (1819):

> e.g., *geschäftig wie eine Maus im Kindbett* (literally: busy like a mouse in childbed), *ein Erbsenzähler* (literally: a pea-counter), *ein Trübetrost* (foul-weather friend), *laß dich heimgeigen* (literally: go fiddle yourself home), *die Petersilie war ihm verhagelt* (he has come a cropper), *davon wächst mir kein Speck in die Küche* (literally: that won't put any bacon on my table), *der hat auch Werg am Rocken hängen* (he's got his finger in the pie, too), *das geht so gut, als wenn einen der Storch laust* (literally: that works as well as when a stork picks your lice), *de hat en Mul am Kope* (literally: he's got a mill turning in his head), *de macht mich rechts und links* (he puts me in the know).[16]

She also was an active collaborator of the family friend Karl Simrock, to whom she sent examples for his popular proverb collection *Die Deutschen Sprichwörter* ([German Proverbs] 1846), and she used many folk expressions in her letters as well.[17] To a certain degree his wife's natural folk speech must have influenced Wilhelm Grimm and contributed to his preoccupation with proverbial materials.

Most likely Wilhelm Grimm heard his wife utter several proverbs a day, and who knows how often one of "her" proverbs or one of "her" proverbial expressions rang in his ears when he integrated an additional proverbial text into a fairy tale. Dortchen Grimm must have been an influence on her husband and therefore on the proverbial style of the later fairy-tale editions, for Wilhelm was always on the lookout for traditional verses, proverbs, and expressions, as he himself states in an extremely important paragraph in his introduction to the sixth edition of the *Kinder- und Hausmärchen* in 1850:

The sixth edition, too, has been enlarged by the addition of new tales and improved or added to regarding particulars. I have been ever eager to incorporate folk proverbs and unique proverbial expressions, which I am always listening for; and I want to cite an example, because it needs to be explained. Farmers, when they want to express their contentment with something, say, "das muß ich über den grünen Klee loben" [I have to praise that to the skies; literally: I have to praise that higher than green clover], and they take the image from the thick, fresh green fields of clover, as being a picture that pleases the heart. German poets in olden times had praised this picture too, and in the same sense.[18]

Wilhelm Grimm integrated this proverbial expression "jdn. etwas über den grünen Klee loben" (i.e., to praise someone [something] to the skies) into the fairy tale "The Four Talented Brothers" (KHM 129), that had appeared for the first time in the second edition of 1819. There a paragraph starts with " 'Yes,' the old man said to his sons, 'you have made good use of your time and have learned an honest trade.' "[19] Beginning with the sixth edition of 1850 this reads: " 'Yes,' the old man said to his sons, 'I must praise you to the skies, you have used your time well and have learned an honest trade.' "[20] This is but a small proverbial addition that gives this sentence the picturesque and folk speech flavor that Wilhelm was convinced belonged to the metaphorical fairy-tale language.

But how did Wilhelm Grimm integrate proverbs and proverbial expressions into the fairy tales, what are the texts, and which stylistic as well as semantic functions do they serve? We will limit ourselves to just a few examples, and must first stress one more time that many fairy tales contained proverbial materials right from the original edition of 1812/1815 and even in the still earlier manuscript of 1810. It would be a mistake to ascribe all proverbial matters in the *Kinder- und Hausmärchen* to Wilhelm Grimm, for as we have already seen, proverbs and proverbial expressions as part of folk speech belong to the traditional fairy-tale style. We will cite examples primarily from the first (1812/1815), the second (1819), and the seventh (1857) editions and will refer to the manuscript of 1810 only where necessary. References will also be made once to the fifth edition (1843) as well. (The KHM-numbers correspond to the seventh and last edition, which Wilhelm Grimm prepared himself.)

Such fairy tales as "The Sparrow and Its Four Children" (KHM 157) and "The Three Sisters" (KHM 16) contain a number of proverbs and proverbial expressions already in the 1812 edition, and Wilhelm made no changes or additions in any of the subsequent editions. The same holds true for "Clever Else" (KHM 34) and "The Wolf and the Fox" (KHM 73), which included their proverbial texts right from their first appearance in the second edition of 1819. Some of the expressions cited are, for example, "Kaufleut, geschwinde Leut" (the buyer beware; literally: merchants are swift people), "Hofbuben, böse Buben" (courtiers are knaves and villains), "in Saus and Braus leben" (to live riotously), "über Stock and Stein" (up hill and down dale), "zittern wie Espenlaub" (tremble like a leaf), and "Man muß das Beil nicht so weit werfen, daß man es nicht wiederholen kann" (one's grasp should not exceed one's reach). It is, of course, not absolutely certain that Wilhelm or even Jacob Grimm did not add one or the other expression before sending the texts to the printer. Where the proverbial material already appears in the first edition of 1812/1815 (these texts were not part of the manuscript of 1810), we may doubt that this was the case since we will be able to show that Wilhelm Grimm made such additions primarily for the second edition (1819) and for some of the later ones.

We also do not know whether Wilhelm had anything to do with the many proverbs in the fairy tale that is richest in them. We know that this story, "The Two Wanderers" (KHM 107), came into his possession on December 4, 1842, in Berlin from a student by the name of Mein. Wilhelm Grimm says nothing about the richness of proverbs in this tale in his annotations, and we do not know of the existence of a handwritten version. It is our conjecture that he received this "proverb fairy tale" pretty much as it appeared in the fifth edition of 1843 (never to be changed until 1857). Perhaps he added such proverbial comparisons as "still wie in einer Kirche" (quiet as in a church) and "schnell wie der Blitz" (quick as lightning) or proverbial expressions like "die Kirschen hängen ihm zu hoch" (that prize is beyond his reach), "sich keine grauen Haare wachsen lassen" (not take a thing too much to heart), and "das große Los gewinnen" (to win the first prize), but the many proverbs appear to belong from the outset to this didactic fairy tale as expressions of traditional wisdom. Two proverbs act as the frame to this didactic narrative: at the beginning stands "Berg und Tal begegnen sich nicht, wohl aber die Menschenkinder, zumal gut und böse" (literally: hill and dale do not meet, but people do, sometimes good ones and bad; cf. strange bedfellows).

This proverb is a metaphorical reference to the two main characters in the tale, a good tailor and an evil shoemaker. When the tailor gets his princess as a final reward, he uses a proverbial expression and a proverb to express the optimistic worldview held by the fairy-tale hero: " 'It's just as if,' the tailor said, 'I had won the first prize. My mother was right when she used to say that whoever trusts in God and is lucky won't lack for anything.' " (" 'Es ist mir geradeso,' sprach der Schneider, 'als wenn ich das große Los gewonnen hätte. Meine Mutter hatte doch recht, die sagte immer, wer auf Gott vertraut und nur Glück hat, dem kann's nicht fehlen.' ") Eight additional proverbs, such as "je größer der Schelm, je größer das Glück" (the bigger scoundrel one is, the better one's luck), "leicht verdient und leicht vertan" (easy come, easy go), "man muß weiter denken, als man geht" (you have to think ahead), "die Vögel, die morgens zu früh singen, die stößt abends der Habicht" (don't crow too soon), "essen, soviel man mag, und leiden, was man muß" (literally: eat what you can, and suffer what you must), "drei Schüsseln leer und auf der vierten nichts" (literally: three bowls empty and nothing in the fourth), "wer aber andern eine Grube gräbt, fällt selbst hinein (the biter will be bitten), and "ein Schelm gibt mehr als er hat" (rogues promise more than they can deliver), characterize the worldview of the two opponents and reduce their thought processes to a proverbial philosophy of the common man (*Popularphilosophie*),[21] as Wilhelm Grimm once called proverbs. The proverbs belong to the narrative structure of the fairy tale and accompany the narrative flow with familiar bits of wisdom. In view of the large "proverb collection" in this fairy tale, it is doubtful that Wilhelm would have added still more proverbs to it before its first publication in the fifth edition (1843).[22] The uniqueness of the tale also speaks against Wilhelm's tinkering with this narrative, for in the cases where we can prove that he added proverbial materials, it is always a matter of isolated, not large, additions.

But let us now turn to cases where Wilhelm Grimm is definitely at work as a proverbial stylist. It will become clear how he tried to imitate the popular fairy-tale style with such occasional additions. We start with an example from the fairy tale "The Magical Tablecloth, the Gold-Ass, and the Cudgel" (KHM 36) that will show that he continued to work on the proper integration of the proverb until he found the fairy-tale style he wanted:

1812: The innkeeper was curious, told himself that all good things would come in threes, and wanted to fetch this third treasure that same night.

1819: The innkeeper pricked up his ears and thought, what can this be? All good things come in threes, and by rights I should have this one as well.

1857: The innkeeper pricked up his ears: "What in the world can that be?" he thought to himself. "The sack surely is filled with nothing but jewels. I should have this one, too, for all good things come in threes."[23]

We can see that Wilhelm Grimm intentionally changed the proverb from its syntactically awkward wording "all good things would come in threes" ("aller guten dinge wären drei") to the usual statement "all good things come in threes" ("aller guten Dinge sind drei"). In the seventh edition he even introduces the proverb with the conjunction "for," which as a short introductory formula emphasizes this bit of proverbial wisdom. Furthermore he adds the proverbial expression "to prick up one's ears" ("die Ohren spitzen" [1819 edition]) and the colloquial interjection "what in the world" ("was in aller Welt"; [1857 edition]) that help to clarify the short statement of the first edition (1812) through popular folk speech. Even though he may have found the actual proverb already in his source, he changed its subjunctive form to the normal text and surrounded it with additional proverbial material. These are conscious stylistic variations in accordance with the fairy-tale style that he had recognized in other such tales. This is not a matter of his inventing a new fairy-tale style, but rather of adjusting his source to normal fairy-tale language.

With our second example of the fairy tale "The Golden Goose" (KHM 64), which has survived in its original wording in Jacob Grimm's handwriting from 1810, we can show that Wilhelm added proverbial materials primarily starting with the second edition of 1819. Here we deal with the well-known proverb "we learn by experience" ("aus Schaden wird man klug") and the equally current proverbial expression "why, that's just a drop in the bucket" ("das ist ja nur ein Tropfen auf den heißen Stein"), which both appear for the first time in the 1819 edition. This should not be too surprising, for the two brothers still worked rather more together on the 1812 edition, and it is known that Jacob insisted more rigorously on textual authenticity.

Notice, though, that some changes were nevertheless made from the 1810 manuscript to its first printing in 1812. There is thus no doubt that Jacob also sanctioned authorial intrusions in the texts:

1810: The third [son] goes now into [the] forest and gives his bread to the little man.

1812: Finally, the simpleton went out; the little man asked him for a piece of cake, just as he had done with the others.

1819: Then the simpleton said, too, "Father, I want to go out and cut wood." Answered his father: "Your brothers have done themselves harm. You leave it completely alone; you don't understand anything about it." The simpleton though begged that he might allow it; then he finally said, "Just go on and do it then; you'll learn by experience." But his mother gave him a cake that had been baked in the ashes with water and a bottle of sour beer. When he came into the forest, the old gray man met him likewise, greeted him, and said, "Give me a piece of your cake and a drink from your bottle; I'm so hungry and thirsty."

1857: Then the simpleton said, "Father, let me go out for once and chop wood." Answered his father: "Your brothers have done themselves harm at it. Keep yourself away from it; you don't understand anything about it." The simpleton though begged so long that he finally said, "Just go on then, you'll learn by experience." His mother gave him a cake that had been baked in the ashes with water and a bottle of sour beer. When he came into the forest the little old gray man met him likewise, greeted him, and said, "Give me a piece of your cake and a drink from your bottle; I'm so hungry and thirsty."[24]

What also becomes clear from contrasting these four parallel texts is that Wilhelm Grimm certainly got carried away in expanding the concise original narrative. Once he speaks of the "damage" (*Schaden*) that the two brothers of the fairy tale have experienced, the proverb "we learn by experience" ("durch Schaden wird man klug") is added almost automatically by association. The same associative phenomenon probably explains the additional integration of the proverbial expression "that's only a drop in the bucket" later in this fairy tale. Notice, however, that this expression was already included in the first edition (1812) and that this change therefore may have had Jacob's approval.

1810: And he asked him [the man]: why are you so sad—oh, I'm so thirsty and can never get enough to drink—.

1812: The simpleton asked what he was taking so much to heart.

"Oh! I am so thirsty, and can't get enough to drink; I've emptied a barrel of wine, to be sure, but what is a drop in the bucket?"

1819: The simpleton asked what he was taking so much to heart. "Oh!" he answered, "I'm so thirsty that I can't get enough to drink; I've emptied a barrel of wine, to be sure, but what is a drop in a bucket?"

1857: The simpleton asked, what he was taking so much to heart. "Oh!" he answered, "I'm so thirsty, and can't get enough to drink; I've emptied a barrel of wine, to be sure, but what is a drop in a bucket?"[25]

Some small editorial changes were performed even for the 1857 edition, but this text basically remained the same after 1812. What we see from the two proverbial examples in this fairy tale is that once they have been integrated they will stubbornly be maintained in all subsequent editions. This is another indication of how strongly Wilhelm Grimm felt that proverbial materials belong to the traditional fairy-tale style.

Even though our next example appears to be an almost negligible change, I include it nevertheless to show the difficulty of discovering which proverbial texts may already have existed in Wilhelm's sources and which were clearly added by him. "The Bremen Town Musicians" (KHM 27) contains several proverbs and proverbial expressions in its first printing in the second edition of 1819: "the donkey noticed that an unfavorable wind was blowing" ("der Esel merkte, daß kein guter Wind wehte"), "who can be jolly when his neck is in the noose" ("wer kann da lustig sein, wenn's einem an den Kragen geht"), "but good advice is in great demand here" ("aber nun ist guter Rat teuer"), "your shrieking cuts to the quick" ("du schreist einem durch Mark und Bein"), and "we shouldn't have let ourselves be frightened out of our wits" ("wir hätten uns doch nicht sollen ins Bockshorn jagen lassen").[26] Only the descriptive part of the sentence, "It wasn't long before he came upon a cat sitting on the road and making a very sad face" ("Es dauerte nicht lange, so saß da eine Katze auf dem Weg und machte ein gar trübselig Gesicht") was changed by Wilhelm Grimm for the 1857 edition by adding a proverbial simile: "It wasn't long before he came upon a cat sitting beside the road and making a face like three days of rainy weather" ("Es dauerte nicht lange, so saß da eine Katze an dem Weg und machte ein Gesicht wie drei Tage Regenwetter").[27] This small textual change appears to us quite appropriate, for it increases the metaphorical richness of this animal fairy tale. Whether some of the other proverbial expressions were added to the text by Wilhelm prior to its publication in 1819 could only be determined through a comparison of the two original narratives from the area of Paderborn and another variant from Zwehrn that, according to Wilhelm's annotations, helped to make up this composite fairy tale.[28] But these three narratives have not survived, and as far as we know we do not have Wilhelm's manuscript for the 1819 edition either. Also, the relatively long verse variant in Georg Rollenhagen's *Froschmeuseler* (1571) that Wilhelm Grimm cites in his notes is of no help in this matter. The three proverbs and proverbial expressions "all in good time" (*käm Zeit, käm Rath und ferner That*), "standing on ceremony won't help us here" (*es nützt uns hie kein Federlesen*), and "as though the house were tumbling down" (*als fiel das Haus über einen Haufen*) were *not* used in his composite version of the story.[29] They would easily have fit into this fairy tale, but for whatever reason he chose not to include them. All of this shows that we can investigate the proverbs and proverbial expressions that Wilhelm (and for the first edition perhaps also Jacob) added after the manuscript of 1810 and after the 1812/1815 edition, but what happened with many of the fairy tales prior to their first appearance in the *Kinder- und Hausmärchen* needs to be studied for each individual story. In order to answer this question, all variants of each fairy tale that Wilhelm Grimm mentions in his annotations would have to be painstakingly compared with their first publication by the Grimms. The variants from oral sources we will, of course, never locate, and even those that appear in early literary sources or in manuscripts perhaps still to be located in the Grimm archives would not present us with a complete picture. Yet continued detailed textual research like that by Heinz Rölleke will obviously help clarify the status of some of the proverbial materials that are present already in the given tale's first publication in the *Kinder- und Hausmärchen.*

We close our analysis with two proverb examples that appear only after the second edition of 1819, i.e., they were clearly and consciously added by Wilhelm Grimm since by this time his brother Jacob was no longer involved in the preparation of new editions of the *Kinder- und Hausmärchen.* In the fairy tale "The Clever Little Tailor" (KHM 114) Wilhelm Grimm probably added the popular proverb "Well begun is half done" ("frisch gewagt ist halb gewonnen") in order to express the optimism of the courageous tailor more convincingly through effective folk speech:

> 1819: The little tailor said cheerfully, "I'll yet accomplish that too."
> 1857: The little tailor did not let himself be frightened off, was completely cheerful, and said, "Well begun is half done."[30]

Finally, let us consider an important short paragraph in "Hansel and Gretel" (KHM 15) in which the differing texts from the manuscript of 1810 to the seventh edition of 1857 show how Wilhelm Grimm tried again and again to utilize folk speech in presenting the second plan of the mother (later the stepmother) and the father to abandon the children in the forest. He finally found the proverb "he who has begun a thing must go on with it" ("wer A sagt, muß auch B sagen") to justify the father's help with this evil deed. As Wilhelm thought more and more about children as listeners or readers of the fairy tales, he probably also was pleased about the didactic tendency of this proverb:

> 1810: Soon thereafter, they once again had nothing to eat, and the little brother heard again one evening in bed how their mother was telling their father that he should take the children out into the big forest. Then his little sister began to cry very hard, and the little brother got up again and wanted to go look for little stones. But when he got to the door, it had been locked by their mother; then the little brother began to be sad and was unable to comfort his little sister.
> 1812: Not long afterwards, there was again nothing in the house to eat; and Hansel and Gretel heard their mother say to their father one evening, "the children found their way back once, and then I let it go at that, but now there again is nothing but half a loaf of bread in the house; you must lead them out deeper into the forest so that they can't come home again, otherwise there's no help for us anymore." It weighed heavily on the father's mind, and he thought, it would be better after all if you shared the last morsel with your children. But since he had already done it once he could not say no. Hansel and Gretel heard their parents' conversation. Hansel got up and wanted to go pick up pebbles again, but when he got to the door their mother had locked it shut. But he comforted Gretel and said, "just go on back to sleep, Gretel, the dear God will find a way to help us."

We see that the manuscript of 1810 and the first edition of 1812 do not contain any proverbial materials. The most significant stylistic change between these two versions consists of the move from indirect to direct speech, the detailed account of the impoverished home, the precise description of the bread, the stones, and so on, as well as the substitution of the names Hansel and Gretel for the diminutives little brother (*Brüderchen*) and little sister (*Schwesterchen*). The text of the 1819 edition is basically identical, but the fifth edition of 1843 does include the proverbial expression "the dance is over" ("das Lied hat ein Ende") and the proverb "he who has begun a thing must go on with it" ("wer A sagt, muß auch B sagen"):

> 1843: Not long afterwards, need was everywhere apparent in the house; and the children heard how the [step]mother said to their father one night, "everything has been eaten up; we don't even have half a loaf of bread left; after that the dance is over. The children have to leave; we'll lead them deeper into the forest, so that they won't find the way back out. Otherwise, there's no hope for us." It weighed heavily on their father's mind, and he thought, "It would be better if you shared the last morsel with your children." But his wife wouldn't listen to anything he said, scolded him, and reproached him. Whoever has begun a thing must go on with it, and because he had given in the first time, he had to do so a second time, too.

The statement, too, that "need was everywhere apparent in the house" ("wieder Noth in allen Ecken [war]") is proverbial because it most likely is a short version of the twin formula "everywhere and anywhere" (an allen Ecken und Enden). This truncated alliterative formula and the expression "after that the dance is over" ("hernach hat das Lied ein Ende") drastically express the despair in this house because their metaphorical and acoustic language emphasizes the hopelessness of the situation and the parents' process of rationalization. The proverb "whoever has begun a thing must go on with it" ("wer A sagt, muß auch B sagen") serves to convince the father to participate in the dreadful deed of leaving the children to their fate in the woods. He cannot stand up against the proverbial and therefore "justified" argument of his wife since he had already taken part once before in abandoning the children in the forest. Wilhelm Grimm presents this conflict in a most convincing fashion; and he himself obviously was satisfied with these changes, for he retained this text of 1843 unaltered through his last edition of 1857.[31]

In regard to the style of those fairy tales to which Wilhelm Grimm did not add proverbial expressions, twin formulas, or proverbs, we can also judge his procedure favorably. For him the addition of proverbs was an attempt to conform certain fairy tales to a style that reflects folk speech, and they most surely were not conscious falsifications of the texts. We must take issue with John M. Ellis, who recently accused the Brothers Grimm of "deliberate deception" because of their textual changes,[32] arguing that "the Grimms appear to have been guilty of a pervasive habit of tinkering idly and uninhibitedly with the language of the texts."[33] As far as Wilhelm Grimm's proverbial additions to the fairy tales are concerned, it seems clear that he had no intention to deceive anybody. Nor did he undertake such changes without thought or in a lighthearted fashion, but rather always with the deliberate care and desire to re-create the traditional fairy-tale style. Especially in the case of those fairy tales the Grimms (primarily Wilhelm) had to consolidate from a number of variants into a composite tale, this method was perfectly reasonable. That such fairy tales belong today to some of the most popular stories of the *Kinder- und Hausmärchen* is, after all, undeniable proof of how successful Wilhelm Grimm was with this process. And we repeat one more time Wilhelm's perfectly honest statement concerning his integration of proverbs and proverbial expressions in the introduction to the sixth edition of 1850, which expresses his conviction of the appropriateness of his proverbial alterations and which is certainly free of any deception: "In the sixth edition, too, new tales have been added and individual improvements made. I have been ever eager to incorporate folk proverbs and unique proverbial expressions, which I am always listening for; and I want to cite an example."[34] Wilhelm Grimm thus cannot be accused of conscious deception as far as his proverbial additions to the fairy tales are concerned. Proverbs and proverbial expressions belong intrinsically to the fairy-tale style,[35] and it was not due solely to Wilhelm Grimm that they have become a stylistic characteristic of the stories in the *Kinder- und Hausmärchen*, or *Grimms' Fairy Tales*, as they came to be known in English.

Notes

The present article is a shortened English version of " 'Das muß ich über den grünen Klee loben': Wilhelm Grimms Sprichwörter und Redensarten in den Märchen," in Wolfgang Mieder, *"Findet, so werdet ihr suchen!": Die Brüder Grimm und das Sprichwort* (Berne: Peter Lang, 1986), chap. 12, pp. 115–41.

1. For more detail concerning these introductory comments, see Mieder, "Findet," pp. 115-41.

2. See Heinz Rölleke (ed.), *Kinder- und Hausmärchen: Ausgabe letzter Hand mit den Originalanmerkungen der Brüder Grimm* (Stuttgart: Philipp Reclam, 1980), III, 441. Hereafter cited as Rölleke, *KHM* (1857).

3. Archer Taylor (together with Bartlett Jere Whiting, Francis W. Bradley, Richard Jente, and Morris Palmer Tilley), "The Study of Proverbs," *Modern Language Forum*, 24 (1939), 32; also in Wolfgang Mieder (ed.), *Selected Writings on Proverbs by Archer Taylor* (Helsinki: Suomalainen Tiedeakatemia, 1975), p. 66.

4. Johannes Bolte and Georg Polívka, *Anmerkungen zu den Kinder- und Hausmärchen der Brüder Grimm*, 5 vols. (Leipzig: Dieterich, 1913-32; rpt. Hildesheim: Georg Olms, 1963), IV, 25: also p. 39 (hereafter cited as Bolte-Polívka): "Der Redeschmuck besteht nicht in Bildern der poetischen Kunstsprache, sondern in den sinnlichen Ausdrücken des Volkes, die statt der Abstrakta eintreten. . . . Alliterierende Verbindungen (Haus und Hof, Kisten und Kasten, schlecht und recht), Klangmalerien (ritsch ratsch), volkstümliche Vergleiche (vergnügt wie eine Heidlerche, ein Gesicht wie drei Tage Regenwetter), Redensarten (der machte nicht langes Federlesen, ich muß euch über den grünen Klee loben) und Sprichwörter (Aller guten Dinge sind drei, Frisch gewagt ist halb gewonnen, Gleich und gleich gesellt sich gern) verbreiten eine behagliche Stimmung."

5. See Kurt Schmidt, *Die Entwicklung der Grimmschen Kinder- und Hausmärchen seit der Urhandschrift nebst einem kritischen Texte der in die Drucke übergegangenen Stücke* (Halle: Max Niemeyer, 1932; rpt. Walluf-Wiesbaden: Martin Sändig, 1973), pp. 70-72; and Friedrich Panzer (ed.), *Kinder- und Hausmärchen der Brüder Grimm: Vollständige Ausgabe in der Urfassung [1812/1815]* (Wiesbaden: Emil Vollmer, [c. 1948]), p. 43. Hereafter cited as Panzer, *KHM* (1812/1815).

6. Lutz Röhrich, "Sprichwörtliche Redensarten aus Volkserzählungen," in *Volk, Sprache, Dichtung: Festgabe für Kurt Wagner*, ed. Karl Bischoff and Lutz Röhrich (Gießen: Wilhelm Schmitz, 1960), pp. 267-69; rpt. in Wolfgang Mieder (ed.), *Ergebnisse der Sprichwörterforschung* (Berne: Peter Lang, 1978), pp. 131-32.

7. Ibid., p. 275 (in Mieder's reprint p. 135).

8. Jacob Grimm and Wilhelm Grimm, *Kinder- und Hausmärchen*, 3d ed. (Göttingen: Dieterich, 1856), p. 196; now reprinted in Rölleke, *KHM* (1857), III, 196 [208]. The page number in square brackets refers to the pagination of the reprint.

9. Ibid., pp. 254-55 [266-267].

10. Ibid., pp. 37-38 [49-50]. See also Karl Friedrich Wilhelm Wander, *Deutsches Sprichwörterlexikon* (Leipzig: F. A. Brockhaus, 1867; rpt. Darmstadt: Wissenschaftliche Buchgesellschaft, 1964), vol. 1, col. 155, Aschenputtel, no. 1.

11. Rölleke, *KHM* (1857), III, 113 [125], 131 [143], 145-46 [157-158].

12. Ibid., p. 607: "Wie auch immer: Wilhelm Grimm hat mit seinen Umarbeitungen und Erweiterungen unter bevorzugter und oft zugegebener Beachtung volksläufiger Wendungen und Metaphern einen Märchenton gefunden und zu stilistischer Vollendung geführt, der allein schon durch seinen Erfolg gerechtfertigt ist."

13. See Bolte-Polívka, IV, 454: "er paßte dem Volke aufs Maul, um sich seiner Art und Sprechweise zu versichern, und flocht solche Redewendungen, Vergleiche und Sprichwörter in die überlieferte Darstellung ein."

14. See *Briefe der Brüder Grimm an Savigny,* ed. Wilhelm Schoof (Berlin: Erich Schmidt, 1983), p. 188.

15. Wilhelm Grimm, *Kleinere Schriften,* ed. Gustav Hinrichs, 4 vols. (Gütersloh: C. Bertelsmann, 1882), II, 370-71: "sie [Märchen] schildern nämlich mit vollkommener Wahrheit den häuslichen Zustand, Denkungsart, Lebensweise und Sitten eines gerade nicht sehr bekannten Landes. Irländer werden die dargestellten Scenen, einzelne Züge, sprichwörtliche Redensarten, dem Volk zugehörige Scherze und Gleichnisse, unübersetzbare Bulls schneller und mit einem besonderen Vergnügen wiedererkennen, doch auch Fremde pflegen dergleichen zu fühlen und zu schätzen."

16. Bolte-Polívka, IV, 454: "z. B. geschäftig wie eine Maus im Kindbett, ein Erbsenzähler, ein Trübetrost, laß dich heimgeigen, die Petersilie war ihm verhagelt, davon wächst mir kein Speck in die Küche, der hat auch Werg am Rocken hängen; das geht so gut, als wenn einen der Storch laust; de hat en Mul am Kope, de macht mich rechts und links."

17. See several letters attesting to this in *Die Grimms und die Simrocks in Briefen 1830 bis 1864,* ed. Walther Ottendorff-Simrock (Bonn: Ferdinand Dümmler, 1966), pp. 73, 78, 107-8, 117.

18. Reprinted in Rölleke, *KHM* (1857), I, 27: "Auch die sechste Ausgabe hat durch neue Märchen Zuwachs erhalten und ist im einzelnen verbessert oder vervollständigt worden. Fortwährend bin ich bemüht gewesen, Sprüche und eigentümliche Redensarten des Volks, auf die ich immer horche, einzutragen und will ein Beispiel anführen, weil es zugleich einer Erklärung bedarf: der Landmann, wenn er seine Zufriedenheit mit etwas ausdrücken will, sagt 'das muß ich über den grünen Klee loben'; und nimmt das Bild von dem dicht bewachsenen, frisch grünenden Kleefeld, dessen Anblick sein Herz erfreut: schon altdeutsche Dichter rühmen ihn in diesem Sinne (*MS Hag.* 2, 66[b], 94[b])." See also Hermann Schrader, "Etwas über den grünen Klee loben," *Zeitschrift für deutsche Sprache* (Hamburg), 8 (1894-95), 263-64.

19. Heinz Rölleke (ed.), *Brüder Grimm: Kinder- und Hausmärchen, nach der zweiten vermehrten und verbesserten Auflage von 1819, textkritisch revidiert und mit einer Biographie der Grimmschen Märchen versehen* (Köln: Eugen Diederichs, 1982), II, 452 (cited hereafter as Rölleke, *KHM* [1819]): " 'Ja', sprach der Alte zu seinen Söhnen, 'ihr habt eure Zeit wohl benutzt und was rechtschaffenes gelernt.' "

20. Rölleke, *KHM* (1857), II, 204: " 'Ja,' sprach der Alte zu seinen Söhnen, 'ich muß euch über den grünen Klee loben, ihr habt eure Zeit wohl benutzt und habt was Rechtschaffenes gelernt.' "

21. In his article "Vridankes Bescheidenheit" (1835) Wilhelm Grimm speaks of proverbs as "Popularphilosophie." See his *Kleinere Schriften,* II, 450.

22. For the entire text of the fairy tale "Die beiden Wanderer" (KHM 107) see Rölleke, *KHM* (1857), II, 106-17. See also Josef Prestel, *Märchen als Lebensdichtung: Das Werk der Brüder Grimm* (München: Max Hueber, 1938), p. 80. There is also

the extensive tale type study by Reidar Th. Christiansen, *The Tale of the Two Travellers or the Blinded Man* (Helsinki: Suomalainen Tiedeakatemia, 1916).

23. Panzer, *KHM* (1812/1815), p. 155; Rölleke, *KHM* (1819), I, 134–35; and Rölleke, *KHM* (1857), I, 203. 1812: "Der Wirth war neugierig, meinte aller guten Dinge wären drei, und wollte sich in der Nacht den Schatz auch noch holen." 1819: "Der Wirth spitzte die Ohren und dachte: was mag das seyn? Aller guten Dinge sind drei, das sollte ich billig auch noch haben." 1857: "Der Wirt spitzte die Ohren: 'Was in aller Welt mag das sein?' dachte er. 'Der Sack ist wohl mit lauter Edelsteinen angefüllt; den sollte ich billig auch noch haben, denn aller guten Dingen sind drei.' " This example is also cited by Bolte-Polívka, IV, 454–55.

24. Heinz Rölleke (ed.), *Die älteste Märchensammlung der Brüder Grimm: Synopse der handschriftlichen Urfassung von 1810 und der Erstdrucke von 1812* (Cologny-Genève: Fondation Martin Bodmer, 1975), p. 160; Panzer, *KHM* (1812/1815), p. 232; Rölleke, *KHM* (1819), I, 245; and Rölleke, *KHM* (1857), I, 347: 1810: "Nun geht der dritte [Sohn] in Wald u. gibt dem Männchen seinen Kuchen." 1812: "Endlich ging der Dummling hinaus, das Männchen sprach ihn, wie die andern, um ein Stück Kuchen an." 1819: "Da sagte der Dummling auch: 'Vater, ich will hinausgehen und Holz hauen.' Antwortete der Vater: 'Deine Brüder haben sich Schaden gethan, laß du's gar bleiben, du verstehst nichts davon.' Der Dummling aber bat, daß ers erlauben möchte, da sagte er endlich: 'Geh nur hin, durch Schaden wirst du klug werden.' Die Mutter aber gab ihm einen Kuchen, der war mit Wasser in der Asche gebacken und eine Flasche saures Bier. Als er in den Wald kam, begegnete ihm gleichfalls das alte, graue Männchen und grüßte ihn und sprach: 'Gib mir ein Stück von deinem Kuchen und einen Trunk aus deiner Flasche, ich bin so hungrig und durstig.' " 1857: "Da sagte der Dummling: 'Vater, laß mich einmal hinausgehen und Holz hauen.' Antwortete der Vater: 'Deine Brüder haben sich Schaden dabei getan, laß dich davon, du verstehst nichts davon.' Der Dummling aber bat so lange, bis er endlich sagte: 'Geh nur hin, durch Schaden wirst du klug werden.' Die Mutter gab ihm einen Kuchen, der war mit Wasser in der Asche gebacken, und dazu eine Flasche saueres Bier. Als er in den Wald kam, begegnete ihm gleichfalls das alte graue Männchen, grüßte ihn und sprach: 'Gib mir ein Stück von deinem Kuchen und einen Trunk aus deiner Flasche, ich bin so hungrig und durstig.' "

25. Rölleke, *Die älteste Märchensammlung,* p. 162; Panzer, *KHM* (1812/1815), p. 234; Rölleke, *KHM* (1819), I, 246; and Rölleke, *KHM* (1857), I, 349: 1810: "Und er fragte ihn [den Mann] : warum bist du so traurig—ei, ich bin so durstig u. kann nie genug zu trinken kriegen—." 1812: "Der Dummling fragte, was er sich so sehr zu Herzen nähme? 'Ei! ich bin so durstig, und kann nicht genug zu trinken kriegen, ein Faß Wein hab ich zwar ausgeleert, aber was ist ein Tropfen auf einen heißen Stein?' " 1819: "Der Dummling fragte: was er sich so sehr zu Herzen nähme? 'Ei!' antwortete er, 'ich bin so durstig, und kann nicht genug zu trinken kriegen, ein Faß Wein hab ich zwar ausgeleert, aber was ist ein Tropfen auf einem heißen Stein?' " 1857: "Der Dummling fragte, was er sich so sehr zu Herzen nähme. Da antwortete er: 'Ich habe so großen Durst und kann ihn nicht löschen, das kalte Wasser vertrage ich nicht, ein Faß Wein habe ich zwar ausgeleert, aber was ist ein Tropfen auf einem heißen Stein?' "

26. Rölleke, *KHM* (1857), I, 161–64.

27. Ibid., I, 161.

28. Ibid., III, pp. 47–54 [59–66], and p. 454. See also Bolte-Polívka, I, 237–59.

29. Rölleke, *KHM* (1857), I, 49–50 [61–62].

30. Rölleke, *KHM* (1819), II, 408; and Rölleke, *KHM* (1857), II, 147: 1819: "Das Schneiderlein sprach vergnügt: 'Das will ich auch noch vollbringen.'" 1857: "Das Schneiderlein ließ sich nicht abschrecken, war ganz vergnügt und sprach: 'Frisch gewagt ist halb gewonnen.'"

31. For the five texts of the "Hänsel und Gretel" fairy tale see Rölleke, *Die älteste Märchensammlung,* p. 72; Panzer, *KHM* (1812/15), pp. 91–92; Rölleke, *KHM* (1819), I, 64; John M. Ellis, *One Fairy Story Too Many: The Brothers Grimm and Their Tales* (Chicago: University of Chicago Press, 1983), p. 171 (for the text of the fifth edition from 1843); and Rölleke, *KHM* (1857), I, 102: 1810: "Bald darnach hatten sie wieder kein Brod und das Brüderchen hörte [wie de] wieder Abends im Bett, wie die Mutter zu dem Vater sagte, er solle die Kinder hinaus in den großen Wald bringen. Da fing das Schwesterchen wieder an heftig zu weinen, und das Brüderchen stand wieder auf, und wollte Steinchen suchen. Wie es aber an die Thür kam, war sie verschloßen von der Mutter, da fing das Brüderchen an traurig zu werden, und konnte das Schwesterchen nicht trösten." 1812: "Nicht lange darnach, war wieder kein Brod im Hause und Hänsel und Gretel hörten wie Abends die Mutter zum Vater sagte: 'einmal haben die Kinder den Weg zurückgefunden, und da habe ichs gut seyn lassen, aber jetzt ist wieder nichts, als nur noch ein halber Laib Brod im Haus, du mußt sie morgen tiefer in den Wald führen, daß sie nicht wieder heimkommen können, es ist sonst keine Hülfe für uns mehr.' Dem Mann fiels schwer aufs Herz, und er gedachte, es wäre doch besser, wenn du den letzten Bissen mit deinen Kindern theiltest, weil er es aber einmal gethan hatte, so durfte er nicht nein sagen. Hänsel und Gretel hörten das Gespräch der Eltern; Hänsel stand auf und wollte wieder Kieselsteine auflesen, wie er aber an die Thüre kam, da hatte sie die Mutter zugeschlossen. Doch tröstete er die Gretel und sprach: 'schlaf nur, lieb Gretel, der liebe Gott wird uns schon helfen.'" 1843: "Nicht lange darnach war wieder Noth in allen Ecken, und die Kinder hörten wie die Mutter Nachts im Bette zu dem Vater sprach 'alles ist wieder aufgezehrt, wir haben noch einen halben Laib Brot, hernach hat das Lied ein Ende. Die Kinder müssen fort, wir wollen sie tiefer in den Wald hineinführen, damit sie den Weg nicht wieder heraus finden; es ist sonst keine Rettung für uns.' Dem Mann fiels schwer aufs Herz, und er dachte 'es wäre besser, daß du den letzten Bissen mit deinen Kindern theiltest.' Aber die Frau hörte auf nichts, was er sagte, schalt ihn und machte ihm Vorwürfe. Wer A sagt muß auch B sagen, und weil er das erste Mal nachgegeben hatte, so mußte er es auch zum zweiten Mal."

32. Ellis, p. 26. See also Heinz Rölleke's negative review of Ellis's book in *Fabula,* 25 (1984), 330–32.

33. Ellis, p. 85.

34. Rölleke, *KHM* (1857), I, 27: "Auch die sechste Ausgabe hat durch neue Märchen Zuwachs erhalten und ist im einzelnen verbessert worden. Fortwährend bin ich bemüht gewesen, Sprüche und eigentliche Redensarten des Volks, auf die ich immer horche, einzutragen und will ein Beispiel anführen."

35. For the relationship of proverbs and fairy tales see also Otto Crusius, "Märchenreminiscenzen im antiken Sprichwort," *Verhandlungen der deutschen Philologen und Schulmänner,* 40 (1889), 31–47; Heinrich Lessmann, *Der deutsche Volksmund im Lichte der Sage* (Berlin: Herbert Stubenrauch, 1922, 21937); Démétrios Loukatos, "Le proverbe dans le conte," in *IV. International Congress for Folk-Narrative Research in Athens 1964, Lectures and Reports,* ed. Georgios A. Megas (Athens: Laographia, 1965), pp. 229–33; Julian Krzyzanowski, "Sprichwort und Märchen in der polnischen Volkserzählung," in *Volksüberlieferung: Festschrift für Kurt Ranke zur Vollendung des 60. Lebensjahres,* ed. Fritz Harkort, Karel C. Peeters, and Robert Wilhaber (Göttingen: Otto Schwartz, 1968), pp. 151–58; Lutz Röhrich and Wolfgang Mieder, *Sprichwort* (Stuttgart: Metzler, 1977), pp. 83–88; Burckhard Garbe, "Vogel und Schlange: Variation eines Motivs in Redensart, Fabel, Märchen und Mythos," *Zeitschrift für Volkskunde,* 75 (1979), 52–56.

MARIA M. TATAR

Beauties vs. Beasts in the Grimms' Nursery and Household Tales

FAIRY-TALE beauties may all be very much alike, but there are two quite different types of beasts in the Grimms' *Nursery and Household Tales*. First, there are the animal-grooms who make life unpleasant for many a female protagonist: these are the frogs, bears, hedgehogs, and other creatures that press themselves on attractive young girls. But these beasts invariably turn out to be handsome young princes in disguise and generally prove to be perfect gentlemen. The real fairy-tale beasts, even if they are beasts in only the figurative rather than the literal sense of the term, turn out to be murderers masquerading as civilized men: Bluebeard, the Robber Bridegroom (in the tale of that title), and the wizard in "Fowler's Fowl" ("Fitchers Vogel") are the most prominent examples in the *Nursery and Household Tales*.

Bluebeard, the most infamous of this entire lot of beasts, entered the pages of the Grimms' collection, but only in its first edition. For the second, revised edition of 1819, the Grimms eliminated the tale, evidently because it was too close in both substance and verbal realization to its French source. Still, Bluebeard was not done away with entirely. He stood as model for at least one villain in the Grimms' collection, and his wife lent her traits to more than one fairy-tale heroine. For this reason, it will be useful to take a brief detour into the realm of Perrault's Mother Goose, then to trace our way back to a path that leads directly into the world of the Grimms' *Nursery and Household Tales*.

The heroine of Perrault's "Bluebeard" may be a woman of "perfect beauty," but her character is flawed by the nearly fatal sin of curiosity. When her husband tests her by entrusting her with the key to a forbidden chamber, she is so plagued by curiosity that she "rudely" leaves the guests in her house to their own devices, then nearly breaks her neck in her haste to reach the forbidden door. At the door she hesitates as she meditates on the possible consequences of being "disobedient." But the temptation is too great, and she unlocks the door to witness a grisly scene of carnage in the forbidden chamber: "the wives of Bluebeard, whose throats he had cut, one after another."[1] When Bluebeard discovers the evidence of his wife's transgression, he flies into a rage and swears that this woman too will die by his sword. The heroine's brothers arrive in the nick of time to prevent their sister from joining the victims in Bluebeard's chamber.

Perrault harbored no doubts about the meaning and message of this story. "Bluebeard" has two different "moralités" appended to it. The first warns women of the hazards of curiosity, a trait that "costs dearly" and brings with it "regrets." The second reminds us that Bluebeards no longer exist in this day and age: "The time is long gone when there were strict husbands, / And no man will demand the impossible / Even if he is plagued by jealousy and unhappiness."[2] Perrault's description of Bluebeard as a "strict" husband who demands "the impossible" squares with the facts of the text. But his declaration that Bluebeard is "plagued by jealousy and unhappiness" gives us an extratextual piece of evidence concerning the motivation for testing his wives. Bluebeard, Perrault implies, is the victim of sexual jealousy— hence his need to subject each successive wife to a test of absolute obedience. In that test, which becomes as much a test of fidelity as of obedience, Bluebeard's new wife, like all the others before her, fails miserably.

Nearly every reader and rewriter of Bluebeard has fallen in line with the interpretation implicit in Perrault's two morals to the tale. Bruno Bettelheim's view is representative. In Bluebeard he sees a cautionary tale armed with the message "Women, don't give in to your sexual curiosity; men, don't permit yourselves to be carried away by your anger at being sexually betrayed." For Bettelheim, the bloodstained key (in some versions it is an egg) that Bluebeard's wife is obliged to surrender to her husband clinches the argument that she has had "sexual relations" and symbolizes "marital infidelity."[3] For another reader, that key becomes a symbol of "defloration," revealing the heroine's sexual betrayal of her husband during his absence.[4] For a third, it marks the heroine's irreversible loss of her virginity.[5]

What Bettelheim and others do with few hesitations, reservations, and second thoughts is to turn a tale depicting the most brutal kind of serial murders into a story about idle female curiosity and duplicity. These critics follow Perrault's lead and invite us to view the heroine's quite legitimate *cognitive* curiosity (what does her husband have to hide?) as a form of sexual curiosity and sexual betrayal that can only bring in its wake serious "regrets." The genuinely murderous rages of Bluebeard and his folkloric cousins would presumably never have been provoked had it not been for the symbolic infidelity of his wives. As horrifying as those multiple murders may be, they do not succeed in deflecting attention from the heroine's single transgression. That transgression, like the opening of Pandora's box, comes to function as the chief source of evil. In Ludwig Tieck's "Ritter Blaubart," even Bluebeard's wife is appalled by her inability to resist temptation. "O curiosity," she declaims, "damned, scandalous curiosity! There's no greater sin than curiosity!" Her self-reproaches are uttered in full view of the scene of carnage for which her husband bears responsibility. Bluebeard himself confirms his wife's appraisal of her high crimes (by contrast to his misdemeanors): "Cursed curiosity! Because of it sin entered the innocent world, and even now it leads to crime. Ever since Eve was curious, every single one of her worthless daughters has been curious. . . . The woman who is curious cannot be faithful to her husband. The husband who has a curious wife is never for one moment of his life secure. . . . Curiosity has provoked the most horrifying murderous deeds."[6] This is surely a case of the pot calling the kettle black. Whether intentionally or not, Tieck revealed the extent to which literary retellings of Bluebeard blame the victim for the crimes of the villain. Is it any wonder that in the nineteenth century Anatole France attempted to rehabilitate Bluebeard by pointing out that there never really were any corpses in the forbidden chamber: Bluebeard's wife headed for that room with such breakneck speed because a handsome young man was waiting for her on the other side of the door.[7] Here, once again, the heroine's cognitive curiosity in the folktale is taken as a sign of sexual curiosity, while Bluebeard's murderous sexual curiosity (he takes one wife after another) is taken as rage at his wife's sexual curiosity.

As Bluebeard became appropriated by the literary culture of the nineteenth century, it was transformed from a folktale describing the rescue of a maiden from a murderous ogre (AT 312) into a text warning of the evils of female curiosity. Oral folktales (even those of relatively recent vintage) rarely embroider on the theme of curiosity

and disobedience; instead the tales' narrative energy is funneled into
the mounting dramatic tension that arises as the heroine's brothers
race to Bluebeard's castle while the heroine stalls for time, resorting to
various tactics to keep her husband from cutting her throat or decapi-
tating her before the arrival of her brothers. A related tale type (AT
311) focuses on the clever ruses mounted by the youngest of three
sisters to outsmart and defeat an ogre who has slaughtered her sisters.[8]
It was Perrault, in his literary version of an orally transmitted tale, who
took the first steps in the direction of converting a dramatic encounter
between innocent maiden and barbaric murderer into a moral conflict
between corrupt woman and corrupted man.

That female curiosity has been enshrined as the central subject of
this tale is confirmed by a brief glance at the pictorial history of
Bluebeard. One illustrator after another emphasizes one of two "key"
scenes in the tale: the arousal of curiosity is masterfully put on display
in Gustave Doré's illustration for Perrault's "Bluebeard" (see Fig. 1);
the satisfaction of curiosity is depicted in one of ten sketches prepared
by Otto Brausewitz (see Fig. 2). Again and again these two scenes
capture the attention of the tale's illustrators. Walter Crane's drawing
of Bluebeard's wife on her way to the forbidden chamber is also
revealing (see Fig. 3). As the curious heroine slips away from her
guests, she passes by a tapestry that provides a moral gloss on her
action: Eve is shown succumbing to temptation in the Garden of
Eden. The sin of Bluebeard's wife originated with Eve, and all of Eve's
daughters (as the tableau of inquisitive guests opening cupboards,
chests, and drawers tells us) suffer from it. "Succumbing to temptation,"
as one commentator on Bluebeard feels obliged to remind us, "is the
sin of the Fall, the sin of Eve."[9] When women give in to temptation,
they symbolically reenact the Fall, committing a deed tainted with the
evil of sexual curiosity. Like Eve, they may begin their quest in a
search for cognitive knowledge, but it ultimately ends in the desire for
carnal knowledge.

In light of the interpretive vicissitudes of Bluebeard, it is easy
enough to see why the Grimms may have had moral reservations—in
addition to their other objections—for including that story in the
second edition of the *Nursery and Household Tales*. The second edition,
after all, was rewritten with a view toward producing a collection of
tales suitable for children's ears. And Perrault's version of the tale, as
we have seen, lent itself all too easily to interpretations that veered off

Fig. 1. *Gustav Doré 1832–1883. Dessinateur-Peintre-Sculpteur. Album de centenaire* (Paris: SACELP, 1982), p. 254.

Fig. 2. *Märchen, Sagen und Abenteuergeschichten auf alten Bilderbogen neu erzählt von Autoren unserer Zeit,* ed. Jochen Jung (Munich: Heinz Moos, 1974), p. 27.

For a month after the wedding they
    lived and had good cheer,
And then said Bluebeard to his wife,
    "I'll say good-bye, my dear;
"Indeed, it is but for six weeks that I
    shall be away;
"I beg that you'll invite your friends,
    and feast and dance and play;
"And all my property I'll leave con-
    fided to your care;
"Here are the keys of all my chests,
    there's plenty and to spare.

Fig. 3. Walter Crane, *The Bluebeard Picture Book* (London: George Routledge and Sons, 1875). By permission of the Houghton Library, Harvard University.

into areas that most parents preferred to avoid for bedtime reading. For whatever reasons the Grimms decided against including in their collection the tale of Bluebeard that had come into their hands, they were not at all opposed to including variants of that tale type, even in their second edition. Those variants, however, branch out into two radically different directions.

Let us begin with the variant that makes of the tale type a cautionary tale pure and simple—one in which the evils of curiosity are writ even larger than in Perrault's "Bluebeard" and in which the figure substituted for Bluebeard is beyond reproach. "Mary's Child" ("Marienkind") gives us a remarkable recasting of the story of a forbidden chamber. The Grimms' heroine, who has been rescued from starvation and taken up to heaven by the Virgin, cannot resist the temptation to unlock a door to which Mary has given her the key. Behind the door, she sees the blinding splendor of the Holy Trinity and touches it with her finger, which becomes gilded. When Mary discovers the evidence of the girl's transgression, she makes the unrepentant child mute and sends her back down to earth. In one tale variant heard by the Grimms and recorded in their annotations, the Virgin silences the girl by slapping her on the mouth so hard that blood gushes forth. That the Virgin Mary could slip with ease into the same functional slot occupied by Bluebeard is telling and does much to explain why it became easy for rewriters and critics of the tale type to let Bluebeard off the hook. The heroine's disobedience is so unattractive a trait that violence and bloodshed pale by comparison. What is even more remarkable than Mary's adoption of Bluebeard's role is her assumption of the part, in the second half of "Mary's Child," ordinarily played by an ogress. After the heroine's marriage to a king, the Virgin returns on three occasions to demand a confession, each time kidnapping the queen's latest newborn in retaliation for her failure to tell the truth. When the queen confesses at last (just before she is about to be burned at the stake), Mary releases her and restores the three children to her. "Now that you have told the truth," Mary declares, "you are forgiven." The Virgin spells out one lesson of the story; the other lesson has to do with the perils of curiosity, with the girl's inability to avoid taking a peek at the forbidden.

In this story, we have something of a reversal of the ground rules operating in classical children's fairy tales. In the final analysis, it is the heroine's antagonist who wins; the heroine, stubborn as she may be, must admit defeat in the end. "Mary's Child" is only one of several such cautionary tales that side with adults. "Frau Trude," one of the less well known texts in the *Nursery and Household Tales,* is a story that few children could find satisfying. "Once there was a girl who was stubborn and insolent, and disobeyed her parents." In addition, she is unable to curb her curiosity and is driven to see with her own eyes Frau Trude, a "wicked" woman who does "godless things." In the end, the girl is turned into a block of wood that Frau Trude casually throws into the fire to provide heat. Here, the evil witch wins for once. But more than that, the world of adults wins out over the child, taking revenge for childish stubbornness, insolence, and disobedience. There is only one other story in the *Nursery and Household Tales* that surpasses "Frau Trude" in its stark portrayal of the punishment of children. "The Stubborn Child" ("Das eigensinnige Kind") tells of a naughty young-ster who refuses to do what its mother commands. "God was dis-pleased and made it fall sick." The child dies, is buried, but still asserts itself even beyond the grave by thrusting an arm into the air. Only when the mother makes her way to the grave and whips the arm with a switch does the child find peace.

Each of these three stories preaches a straightforward lesson about the virtues of telling the truth, suppressing curiosity, and practicing obedience. It is therefore surprising to hear the Grimms declare, in the preface to the *Nursery and Household Tales,* that their stories were never intended "to instruct, nor were they made up for that reason." These tales seem consciously designed to impart specific lessons framed by adults for children. As cautionary tales, they demonstrate how children with undesirable traits—deceitfulness, curiosity, insolence—come to a bad end.

We have seen how the breathtaking, bloodcurdling story of an ogre's murderous schemes against a young woman could be recast to create a didactic tale celebrating the triumph of adult authority over childish deviousness and deviance. But the conversion took place only with time, as oral folktales moved from *Spinnstuben* and workrooms into the nursery and household, as the audience for the stories shifted from adults to children.[10] The revisions in the Grimms' second edition were motivated in part by harsh contemporary criticism of the first edition, which was deemed adult entertainment rather than children's literature.[11] For the second edition it was logical to replace "Bluebeard," with its forbidden chambers, bloody keys, and maimed corpses, with

"Mary's Child," a story that few adults in the Grimms' day and age would have found offensive. There, the figure who incarnates authority in its most tyrannical form is turned into a saint and therefore becomes impossible to associate with villainy. Instead, evil emanates solely from the tale's obstinately disobedient protagonist, who in the end is punished for her transgression. The quickest way to "teach someone a lesson," as our language puts it, is to punish them. "Mary's Child," with its foregrounding of the transgression/punishment pattern, stands as one of the most striking examples of a fairy tale crafted to teach a lesson both to its protagonist and to its youthful readers.

There is another story in the Grimms' collection that belongs virtually to the same tale type as Bluebeard, yet its conclusion moves in a very different direction, and it is therefore designated as AT 311 rather than 312. "Fowler's Fowl" casts an evil wizard in the role of Bluebeard and features three sisters, two of whom succumb to curiosity, disobey the wizard, discover a bloodbath behind the door forbidden to them, and are executed by their cold-blooded fiancé. The third and youngest sister is "clever and sly." She has the foresight to put into a safe place the egg that her two sisters dropped in their fright at witnessing the scene of carnage. With not a single shred of evidence for her transgression, the wizard loses his power over the heroine, and she is able both to resurrect the mutilated corpses of her sisters and to engineer the downfall of the wizard. The plot of this story follows the classic lines of children's fairy tales: it begins with a display of weakness and victimization at the hands of an all-powerful adversary and ends with a tableau of revenge and retaliation.

In the Grimms' *Nursery and Household Tales,* we have few dragon slayers and giant killers. What we have instead are endless variations on male Cinderellas: Hans Dumm, the youngest of three sons, or a fearless simpleton. Helplessness and abject self-pity are the characteristic poses struck by these figures. Female heroines fare little better: Cinderella, Thousandfurs (Allerleirauh), Snow White, King Thrushbeard's wife, and a variety of princesses must wash dishes, haul firewood, scrub floors, polish boots, and carry out all manner of domestic chores before they are translated into a higher social sphere. But the tables are turned before the tale ends. The hero's accession to wealth and power drains the strength of his adversaries, who become helpless targets of revenge. Punishments overshadow nearly all else in the coda to a large number of the Grimms' tales. The description of Cinderella's wedding is almost wholly devoted to an elaborate account of how doves peck out the eyes of the stepsisters. Snow White's wedding really has only one central event: the death of the stepmother after she is forced to dance in red-hot iron shoes. The king, the queen, and her six brothers may all live happily ever after in "The Six Swans," but not until the queen's wicked mother-in-law has first been burned at the stake. The hero of "The Knapsack, the Hat, and the Horn" triumphs in the end by blowing on his horn until everything around him collapses, crushing to death the duplicitous king and princess of the tale. "Revenge can be as sweet as love," Musäus points out in the version of "Snow White" that he published in his *Volksmärchen der Deutschen.* Revenge comes to function as the main motor of the plot in countless fairy tales.[12]

The protagonists of classic children's fairy tales have never placed a premium on good manners and virtuous behavior. The hero of "The Golden Bird" lies, cheats, and steals his way to success, all the while ignoring the advice of his helper. Rapunzel deceives her enchantress-guardian by arranging secret meetings with a prince. And the princess of "The Frog King" dashes against the wall the importunate amphibian who once came to her aid. Fairy-tale heroes are also rarely prepared to forgive and forget. Wicked stepmothers are forever being stripped and rolled down hills in barrels embedded with nails or turned out into the woods to be devoured by wild animals. That Two-eyes forgives her sisters in the story "One-eye, Two-eyes, and Three-eyes" is a startling exception to the rule of fairy-tale conduct. Virtually any tactic used to work one's way up the ladder of social success is considered legitimate; once on the top rungs, the protagonist has no reservations about toppling those above him. Still, from Perrault on, there has been no end to inscribing moral lessons even on tales that clearly have no moral. When Wilhelm Grimm was preparing the second edition of the *Nursery and Household Tales,* for example, he gave the father of the princess in "The Frog King" an additional line of dialogue: "[The frog] helped you when you were in trouble and you mustn't despise him now." But the father's pronouncements on the importance of keeping promises and remaining loyal move against the grain of the story itself. The Frog King is not released from his enchanted state until the princess displays her contempt for him through an act of physical violence. Passion rather than compassion leads to a happy ending. The protagonists of fairy tales rarely achieve their ends by observing strict ethical codes.

The textual history of "Bluebeard" in the Grimms' *Nursery and Household Tales* illustrates clearly the way in which a single plot can be channeled into two separate and distinct types of stories. The one trusts Perrault's tale and its literary "moralité" on the hazards of curiosity; the other relies on the oral folktales on which Perrault himself probably based his text. What started out as a story pitting a Beauty against a Beast was turned, on the one hand, into a story staging a struggle between a pathological liar and a saint. "Mary's Child" shows us how adult patience wins out over childish disobedience, deception, and stubbornness. Children are guilty of transgressions; adults visit punishments on the transgressors. Power is invested solely in adults, who use their superior strength and intelligence to teach children a lesson. These stories, with their single-minded focus on the transgression/punishment pattern, their unique power relationships, and their explicit morals, belong to a breed apart—one that is best designated by the term cautionary fairy tale.

"Bluebeard," as we have seen, also took another course in the Grimms' collection, one that resulted in the demonization of the figure named in the story's title. "Fowler's Fowl" (along with its variant known as "The Robber Bridegroom") sets up a conflict between a wholly innocent young girl and an evil mass murderer. The contrast between heroine and villain could not be more striking. Against all odds, the helpless heroine triumphs over her powerful adversary. It is easy enough to see just why this particular story would prove attractive to children. A sense of utter vulnerability in the face of a seemingly capricious all-powerful figure replicates perfectly the feelings of the young child toward adults. The movement in this fairy tale, and in others, from victimization to retaliation gives vivid but disguised shape to the dreams of revenge that inevitably drift into the minds of every child beset by a sense of weakness and inconsequence. Fairy tales such as "Fowler's Fowl" put on display the victory of children over adults—power is ultimately put into the hands of the powerless. For the transgression/punishment pattern of cautionary fairy tales, these tales substitute its obverse: victimization/retaliation. They do not have a lesson to preach; if a general truth or moral precept is enunciated in the course of the narrative, it rarely squares with the actual facts of the text. What "Fowler's Fowl," "The Robber Bridegroom," and other such stories give us are classic children's fairy tales—stories in which innocent young Beauties (male or female) always defeat the adult Beasts.

Notes

1. "Bluebeard," in *Perrault's Complete Fairy Tales,* trans. A. E. Johnson et al. (New York: Dodd, Mead, 1961), p. 81.

2. Ibid., p. 88. I have taken the liberty of modifying the translation slightly to make it more literal.

3. Bruno Bettelheim, *The Uses of Enchantment: The Meaning and Importance of Fairy Tales* (New York: Random House, Vintage Books, 1977), pp. 301–2. Bettelheim's interpretation and those of other critics are discussed in my book *The Hard Facts of the Grimms' Fairy Tales* (Princeton, N.J.: Princeton University Press, 1987), pp. 158–61.

4. Alan Dundes, "Projection in Folklore: A Plea for Psychoanalytic Semiotics," in his *Interpreting Folklore* (Bloomington: Indiana University Press, 1980), p. 46.

5. Carl-Heinz Mallet, *Kopf ab! Gewalt im Märchen* (Hamburg: Rasch und Rohring, 1985), p. 201.

6. Ludwig Tieck, "Ritter Blaubart," in *Werke,* ed. Richard Plett (Hamburg: Hoffmann und Campe, 1967), pp. 226, 238.

7. Anatole France, *The Seven Wives of Bluebeard and Other Marvelous Tales,* trans. D. B. Stewart (London: John Lane, 1920), pp. 3–40.

8. For summaries of or references to printed versions of "Bluebeard," see Antti Aarne, *The Types of the Folktale: A Classification and a Bibliography, Translated and Enlarged by Stith Thompson* (Helsinki: Academia Scientiarum Fennica, 1961), pp. 101–4; Paul Delarue, *Le Conte populaire français* (Paris: Erasme, 1957), I, 182–99; and Johannes Bolte and Georg Polívka, *Anmerkungen zu den Kinder- und Hausmärchen der Brüder Grimm,* vol. 1 (Leipzig: Dieterich, 1913), 398–412.

9. J.C. Cooper, *Fairy Tales: Allegories of the Inner Life* (Wellingborough, Northhamptonshire: Aquarian Press, 1983), pp. 72–73. The illustrations are discussed in my book, *The Hard Facts of the Grimms' Fairy Tales,* pp. 161–63.

10. On this point, see Jack Zipes, *Fairy Tales and the Art of Subversion: The Classical Genre and the Process of Civilization* (New York: Wildman Press, 1983), p. 31.

11. See the first chapter of my *Hard Facts of the Grimms' Fairy Tales.*

12. Johann Karl August Musäus, *Volksmärchen der Deutschen* (Munich: Winkler, 1976), p. 115. On revenge in fairy tales, see also Bettelheim, *Uses of Enchantment,* pp. 133–34.

GONTHIER-LOUIS FINK

The Fairy Tales of the Grimms' Sergeant of Dragoons J. F. Krause as Reflecting the Needs and Wishes of the Common People

I F ONE investigates *Grimms' Fairy Tales,* especially the fifty tales in the "small edition" of these *Kinder- und Hausmärchen*[1] that have shaped the image of the fairy tale in Germany, one may ask oneself whether fairy tales and social reality are not mutually exclusive. One could easily conclude that fairy tales have no other mission than to make us forget everyday reality with its cares and problems. And yet, as Lutz Röhrich has demonstrated, even fairy tales cannot escape reality entirely.[2]

If numerous tales in the Grimms' collection leave the impression that reality and the miraculous mutually exclude one another, and that the narrator consciously ignores social realities, one important reason is that most of the Grimms' contributors were of the middle class,[3] and 80 to 90 percent of the tales are from young girls or women. Did not the Wilds, the Hassenpflugs, and the von Haxthausens contribute the largest part, and was it not they who made the collection "Children's and Household Tales"? There were, in addition, also individual contributions from pastors, teachers, and members of other middle-class professions. If we exclude Frau Viehmann, who was to be sure very familiar with the Hessian folk, but who having been born a Pierson and a Huguenot was equally familiar with French fairy tales, then there remain only a few contributors who belonged to the folk, and thus only a few tales that were actually taken from the mouths of the people.

All the greater importance therefore attaches to the person of the sergeant of dragoons Friedrich Krause, who, as Wilhelm Grimm wrote to Achim von Arnim in 1812, traded "a couple of entirely unusual soldiers' tales" for some old clothes.[4] To be sure, we do not know much about Sergeant Krause, only that he was poor and proud, that he was born in 1747 in Breitenbach, was married in Hoof near Kassel in 1779, and died there in 1828.[5] Thus, in 1811 when he told his first tale to the Brothers Grimm, he was sixty-four years old. Since the Grimms saw in fairy tales relics of ancient beliefs and laws, and since folk literature (*Volkspoesie*), as Jacob Grimm wrote to Arnim in 1811, proceeds from the soul of the whole people, while artistic literature (*Kunstpoesie*) is expressive of one person, of the individual, and of subjectivity, they were interested, too, more in the tales' mythical content than in the social relevancies addressed.[6] In the contemporary, or indeed individual, shaping of transmitted narrative they perceived rather a betrayal of tradition. Therefore, too, they did not give the names of their contributors, either in the notes they provided for the first edition or in the commentary in the third volume (1822), although they emphasized in the introduction "that in all living feeling for a piece of literature there lies a process of poetic shaping and further development," indeed that "every region tells stories according to its special nature, every teller narrates differently."[7] The only single narrator that they put forth was "Frau Viehmann," because they believed that she preserved "the old stories firmly in her memory."[8] Therefore, the identity of the individual storytellers has often remained uncertain.

Even Herman Grimm, who paired some of the contributors with the stories that belonged to them,[9] passed over the figure of the old sergeant of dragoons. Only for number 6 of the second volume (1815), "The King of the Golden Mountain," which was later to become KHM 92, did the Brothers Grimm observe in the notes to the first edition: "was told by a soldier."[10] But since they did not give the region from which the storyteller came, it could just as well be a tale by another soldier. Bolte and Polívka, in a note, assign to Krause number 48 of the first edition (1812), "Old Sultan"; the initial version of KHM 54, which appeared as number 37 in the first edition (1812) with the title "About the Napkin, the Knapsack, the Little Cannon Hat, and the Horn"; and also number 16 of the first edition (1812), "Herr Fix und Fertig."[11] Wilhelm Schoof and Albert Schindehütte believed, to be sure, that also the later KHM 16, "The Three Snake Leaves," and possibly KHM 111, "The Skilled Huntsman," could be attributed to Krause,[12] probably because the Grimm Brothers and Bolte-Polívka mention in the commentaries that KHM 16 was retold according to two stories of which "one is from the Lower Hessian village of Habichtswald";[13] and for KHM 111 they wrote, "a third tale from Hof am Habichtswald has the same content."[14] But since for the last two tales we do not know the version that came from the sergeant of dragoons, it seems incumbent on us to limit our discussion chiefly to the three tales known to be from J. F. Krause, and at most to include "The King of Golden Mountain," since it likewise is from a soldier.[15]

Unfortunately, however, we do not know the original versions of these tales, although for the first three we have the still relatively slightly revised text of the first volume of the first edition. For "The King of the Golden Mountain," which appeared with the second volume, Wilhelm was already able to take into consideration the criticisms made by Clemens Brentano, so that the text of this story no longer appears so coarse as that of the other three. Still, we hope, with these tales from the mouth of a soldier, to be able to perceive the wishes and needs of the folk, and, if the opportunity presents itself, the peculiarities of the storyteller as well.

I

"Old Sultan" (no. 48), with its three-part plot, has a simple, single-strand structure. Everything is determined logically from the peasant's plan to kill the old dog because he can no longer fulfill his duties. Since Old Sultan heard this too, he tries, with the help of the friendly wolf, to thwart the plan to test his abilities. Thereupon, the wolf, just as logically, demands a return favor from him. The dog, though, refuses to grant it because it would be detrimental to his master and was not agreed upon in advance. The dog's rejection of the request produces a conflict that is settled with a duel between the two animals. Since the wolf and his second, the hog, misinterpret the peculiar gait of the lame cat that serves as the dog's second, and are afraid of the cat, the catastrophe toward which everything was pointing is avoided at the last moment, and the animals tormented by nature, that is, by old age, carry the day. This unexpected, ironic turn of events, with its burlesque elements surrounding the description of the pairs of animals, provides good balance to the somewhat solemn story of the old dog condemned to death because he is no longer fit for service. In addition, the transposition of the story into the animal world enabled the narrator to present in all plain simplicity the sad situation of the old dog to whom even the bread of charity is denied, and thereby to deflect the tragedy implicit in the story.

The actual point of departure of "Herr Fix und Fertig" (no. 16 in the first edition) is on the one hand the soldier's wish for a new life, in which he could better develop his talents, and on the other hand his boastful claim to know everything and to be able to do anything. Here, too, the course of events follows rather logically from these premises, in that the tale provides the proof of the assertion, so to speak. After a short first test, Fix und Fertig is hired by the king and charged with courting the beautiful princess. The wooing of the bride, which forms the main part of the tale, is retarded by the episode of the threefold obligating of the grateful animals[16] who subsequently help perform the difficult triple task assigned by the bride's father. For the story's conclusion there remain then, in keeping with the frame story, the return with the bride to the king and the rewarding of the extraordinary wooer of the bride.[17] Thus this tale, too, is distinguished by a clear, well-developed structure that is surprising, however, in that aside from the retarding but necessary episode of the grateful animals, everything rushes on smoothly to the end, from the hero's boastful claim to its double fulfillment, without calling into question for a moment that which has been achieved. This straight-line, teleologically oriented tale accords, at the same time, with the name and nature of the hero, Herr Fix und Fertig (Mr. Ready and Waiting).

By comparison, the two other stories prove to be more complex, though they also are clearly structured. In the first part of "The Napkin, the Knapsack, the Little Cannon Hat, and the Horn," the three brothers' poverty is actually already relieved with their journey and their being rewarded with silver, gold, and the napkin. The tale thus could end there, unless—as usually happens—the good fortune so quickly achieved is put in jeopardy once again. There follows though, as was already the case in Hans Sachs's versions,[18] an expansion in the second part that gives the tale a new direction. But whereas in Sachs's versions the trooper is content with the magical donkey, which like the Trojan horse is full of other troopers, the sergeant of dragoons makes the experiment a threefold one. Through a triple exchange and theft, the youngest of the three brothers acquires three magical weapons, the power of which increases from the one to the other.

While the magical napkin is not mentioned any further, so that the connection with the first part remains loose, the third part of the tale is about the effectiveness of the acquired magical weapons, which gain for him the princess's hand and a viceroyship. But then the discontent of the princess, who has been forced to marry, produces a new conflict. In the course of this conflict, she gains the magical weapons from him through trickery. In the end, however, the hero triumphs over this cunning with the magical weapon still in his possession but remains alone, however, since he has destroyed everything.

Characteristic of this tale by the sergeant of dragoons is the commingling of two tales: the story about the trooper who with the help of the donkey regains the magical tablecloth, as in the two versions that Hans Sachs wrote down between 1556 and 1559, and the story of the cunning woman, which first became known through the *Gesta Romanorum* and the chapbook about Fortunatus,[19] as well as an Italian[20] and a French literary tale,[21] of which an echo is found, too, in Musäus.[22] The cunning princess, to be sure, takes the magical objects from one or another of the heroes, but has to return them after a double magical cure that first disfigures her and then heals her again. Through the fusion of the two tales in the sergeant's story, the three magical objects are replaced by three magical weapons. Granted, the new manner of the armed conflict makes the double cure superfluous, but the tale simultaneously acquires an ironic twist through the total weapon that destroys everything. The hero triumphs, to be sure, and now also becomes king, but rules over a devastated no-man's-land, a realm of the dead.

"The King of the Golden Mountain" (II, 6 in the first edition) also fuses several narrative strands. The tale begins with the widely known motif, familiar from "Rumpelstiltskin" (KHM 55) or the tale about the animal bridegroom,[23] about the promise made to a demon or monster to reward him for his help with the first thing one encounters at home. The first part is structured here in the fashion of a devil's pact. The son who is to be delivered up to the demon makes a compromise with it according to which he is to be set adrift on the sea instead of surrendered.

This introduction, which focuses not on the hero but on his father, an impoverished merchant, seems to be rather independent, to be sure, and could easily be replaced by another element. There exists nevertheless a certain connection, at least in atmosphere, between the demonry that dominates the first part and the demonic figures of the second part.

While the Rumpelstiltskin story revolves around the heroine's attempt to ransom herself or to circumvent the stipulations of the contract,[24] so that in the end the little demon is chased off as a cheated devil, in "The King of the Golden Mountain" this motif is used only in the story's first part, which functions to motivate the son's being cast adrift and thereby makes possible the further adventures but does not determine their course or nature. There follows the story of the redemption of a bewitched princess through various tests that must be passed. There are, on the one hand, echoes of the tales of marriage to a spirit (*Martenehe*), as they have become familiar above all through the story of Melusine.[25] Here the princess likewise appears first in the form of an animal; has at her disposal magical things like the water of life and a wishing ring; and in addition, like Melusine, requires of her husband a promise that he then breaks. On the other hand, in the redemptive tests the influence of contemporary horror and ghost stories is evident, as it is also in the "Story of the Youth Who Went Forth to Learn What Fear Was" (KHM 4).

With the breaking of the promise, the third part begins, that is, the renewed search for the lost wife, for which magical objects are necessary that the hero obtains through cunning from the giants who are fighting over an inheritance. But in contrast to the marriage to a spirit (*Martenehe*), in which the knight has to pay dearly for breaking his promise, if not indeed with the permanent loss of the spouse, here a male point of view renders the violation of the command trivial. The violation serves above all to introduce the third part, the search for the missing wife; and in the end the unfaithful queen is punished, not the husband who broke his word.

In all four tales the situation at the beginning is similar. The three brothers in "About the Napkin, the Knapsack, the Little Cannon Hat, and the Horn" (I, 37 in the first edition) were "very poor," so that there was nothing else for them to do but to venture forth to seek their fortunes. The merchant in "The King of the Golden Mountain" (II, 6 in the first edition), too, was after all "a poor man," who had "nothing else left" but a field, since he had forfeited all of his wealth through the loss of two "heavily laden ships." In "Old Sultan" (I, 48), as a result of the transposition into the form of an animal tale, poverty is replaced by infirmity. Old Sultan could no longer "grab hold tightly" of anything. He was like a discharged soldier or an old disabled veteran, who was simply let go without a pension or anything because he had become unfit for service. Only Herr Fix und Fertig, who had "been a soldier for a long time," left the army of his own free will because the war, which alone would have made it possible for a commoner to rise, was now at an end and therefore there "was nothing left to do" for him among the soldiers. He wanted to become "a lackey for a wealthy and powerful gentleman" in the hope that such a post would offer more opportunity for his cunning. Thus it was a matter only of a voluntary change of profession, in which material things played only an indirect role. Yet he, too, wanted to rise, to emerge from the anonymous obscurity of a little soldier in the peacetime army.

II

To be sure, the situation at the beginning usually does not determine the nature of the plot elements. It does, however, determine the goal of the action, for the tale's ending most often compensates in a striking way for the privations attested to at the beginning. Thus the former little soldier Fix und Fertig became "prime minister." And Old Sultan not only had his old rights restored to him; his master granted him, in addition, loving care until his demise. In the other two tales, however, the connection between the beginning and the ending is not so close. These tales, in the last analysis, have two parts, and already the first part—for the one story (I, 37), the finding of the magic napkin, and for the other (II, 6), the contract with the demon—helped overcome the initial poverty, while the second part—in the one case, the soldier's tale, in the other, the tale of redemption—exhibits a finality of its own, even if in the end both the youngest of the three poor brothers and the son of the formerly poor merchant became kings. But these crownings symbolize, above all, victory over the heroes' adversaries. For Fix und Fertig, for the merchant's son, as well as for Old Sultan, the tests are the basic motif that helps bridge the discrepancy between the situations at the beginning and at the end, and that is supposed to guarantee wealth and status to the poor, importance and increase in rank to those whose talents have gone unnoticed, and a peaceful life to those condemned to death. This usually means, though, that the hero's own means are not sufficient for passing the test. The tale is intended to correct reality, and for that there is need of the miraculous, at least temporarily.

Characteristic in this regard are the nature and role of the magical things, as they occur in the soldier's tale "About the Napkin . . . " (I, 37). The oldest brother was content with silver, the first best thing that he found on his wanderings. The second was content with gold, while the youngest, who wanted "to try his luck still further," found a magical napkin that served up all the dishes that he wished for. That not gold, as usual in folktales, but the magical napkin—simultaneously a symbol of the upper classes—assumes the highest rank is surely typical for the poor people's dreams, for their anxiety about procuring their daily bread. With these gifts, however, service was not being rewarded that had been done for a supernatural being; nor were the gifts given to the heroes under any sort of condition. They were really for free, like gifts from heaven, while in Hans Sachs's versions the peasant and the trooper received the gifts from St. Peter as a reward for their hospitality or their generosity; and in Musäus's tales, Roland's three pages had to earn their gifts—a magic penny, a little dishcloth, and a thumb that makes one invisible—with hard work, in that they had to help a terribly old ugly hag undergo a rejuvenating cure by affording her their services as lovers. The sergeant's tale, in rewarding the poor free of charge, reveals a world that radically changes reality, even if it does not turn that world into its opposite. If, though, the youngest of the brothers subsequently exchanges his napkin first for a military knapsack, out of which soldiers emerge, as soon as one slaps it; then for a hat that can fire like a whole battery of cannons; and finally for a little horn that is able to put everything to flight; and then moreover steals back his napkin from charcoal burners with the help of his soldier's knapsack, the world of folktale in the end again becomes a mirror of a cruel reality. The weapons made the elevation possible and simultaneously destroyed the seeming idyll, just as if the soldier's world and the world of fairy tale were in the last analysis incompatible.

In both of the other stories, magic plays a different role. In "Herr Fix und Fertig" it is limited to the fulfilling of three difficult tasks—the gathering of the sown poppy seeds, the fishing out of the ring that had

been lost in the water, and the slaying of the dangerous unicorn—tasks
that the hero accomplishes with the help of the grateful animals.

In "The King of the Golden Mountain," the impoverished merchant makes a pact with a little black man who is reminiscent of the
demonic figures in "Rumpelstiltskin" and in the Faust legend; thus,
the contract, like a pact with the Devil, must be certified with a
signature and seal. In contrast to Rumpelstiltskin, the little man is not
depicted at all comically. In the mind of the merchant, he is a demon.
Therefore, the son has himself blessed by a priest and draws a magical
circle in order to deal with the demon from inside this secure island.
In contrast to the cheated devils in some tales in the Grimms' collection,
the little man is not deprived of the return payment. In true merchant
fashion, a compromise is agreed upon. In the second part of the tale,
the hero has to survive a test that is repeated for three nights and made
more difficult each time. At the end of those tests he is even beheaded,
but at the stroke of midnight the test is over and the bewitched castle
and the princess, who had been changed into a snake, are redeemed,
and she then revives him with the water of life. It is not said, however,
who cast the spell on the castle and the princess or who gave her the
water of life and the magical ring, with the help of which one can wish
oneself wherever one wants. Nevertheless, a connection between the
redemption of the princess and the pact with the little black man is
indicated, since she has waited for her liberator for twelve years and
this was the date that the little man had stipulated for the surrender of
the merchant's son, as though he had appointed him for that role and
through the son's exposure on the seas had allowed him to fulfill the
task. Thus, however, the demon appears as an ambiguous figure, half
devil and half magical helper. In the third part, the hero steals a sword
from the giants that beheads everything, an overcoat that makes the
wearer invisible, and a pair of boots that perform the same service as
the magical ring. Thanks to these magical things, he can wish himself
back with his unfaithful wife, dupe her without being seen, and finally
take revenge at court for her disdain of him. As in "About the
Napkin . . . ," the interest lies, above all, in the weapons that enable the
hero to survive the struggle with the unfaithful wife and her retinue.

The animal tale contents itself, by contrast, with the fact that the
dog overhears his master's plan the way Hansel overhears that of his
parents (KHM 15), and speaks about it with his friend the wolf, who like
a sorcerer knows ahead of time what the peasant woman will do the next

morning. This magic results simply from the transposition of the action into the animal realm and the concomitant anthropomorphization.

In this tale, the narrator does not give free rein to fantasy. If the magic in the animal tale results from transposition, in fairy tales it is indispensable, above all, to shape the magical realm as contrary to the real world. Only in "The King of the Golden Mountain" does the magic come from demonic figures, the little black man or the giants. In these soldier tales, though, the fairy-tale realm is divided. It is not only a contrary world, where the poor man is presented with riches and the disregarded man is rewarded. It compensates for the hero's sad fate in the real world. But this magical realm is at the same time full of malice and to that extent also mirrors the cruel reality that the heroes had tried to escape. Insofar as the magical things procure material goods, they create a happy counterworld, but to the extent that they give the hero the means to gain revenge, they destroy this counterworld again. Significantly, revenge plays an important role in two tales in our group.

In these tales, the moral does not refer to any transcendent authority. Rather, it centers strictly on the hero, as though everything he does is right and everything that is inflicted on him is wrong. While Fix and Fertig can count firmly on the animals' gratitude, Old Sultan is able to receive his keep for his old age only by deceiving his master. For that reason, he agrees with the wolf that the wolf should steal the peasant's child, but drop it again so that Old Sultan could return it unharmed and thereby appear to have rescued it. This ruse seems to be the necessary answer to the mercilessness of the peasant, as though one cannot exist in the world without deceit. But even this has its limits. When the wolf wants to steal a sheep from the peasant as the reward for his help, the dog not only opposes that, he betrays the wolf to his master, and the wolf therefore denounces him as a bad fellow. Thus, corresponding to the spirit of the times, the dilemma of loyalty to one's master or to one's friend is decided in favor of middle-class morality.

In "About the Napkin . . ." and in "The King of the Golden Mountain," the heroes deceive the three charcoal burners and the three giants, respectively, who trusted them.[26] But when the youngest brother has the napkin taken away from the charcoal burners again after an honest bargain, and thereby cheats his peers of the magical weapon, it is because the weapon was of no use anyway to the peaceful forest dwellers. Otherwise, the story would have gone differently, and he would have had to give his napkin to the first charcoal burner. Therefore, they actually did not lose anything, except at most the temporary illusion of being able to eat for free, thanks to the magical napkin. Compared to the loutish giants, too, the fairy-tale hero emerges as the craftier fellow, as he did compared to the charcoal burners. A crafty fellow who makes use of his natural advantage, his cunning, normally represents a departure from the popular moral code; yet in justification of the hero there echoes the unspoken conviction that he did well to rob the dangerous giants of the means of harming people. In the third part, with regard to the little black man and the wife who mostly is more cunning than the stupid husband, popular morality, however, is changed from a Christian, or phallocratic, perspective into its opposite, in that now stupidity is equated with honesty and cunning with dishonesty. Therefore, the merchant's son reproaches the little black man with having "deceived and seduced" his father, for the latter did not know what he was promising, while the little demon surely foresaw whom the merchant would encounter first. For the same reason, the youngest brother takes revenge on his wife, who deceived him twice, in the cruelest way. (Indeed, in both tales in which magical weapons play a role, the reaction appears disproportionate and at the end a cruel lust to destroy dominates.) In the first conflict with his brothers, he has his soldiers "fill their humpbacks with blows," and in the marital argument he brings war to the whole country and ends indeed by burning everything down.

Except for "The King of the Golden Mountain," where psychology plays a larger role, both to elucidate the merchant's spiritual anxiety after signing the contract with the demon and to differentiate between the characters of the father and the son, the psychology is, above all, functionally tied to the respective episode. Thus, if the hero is sometimes craftier than the upright charcoal burners, he is, at the same time, occasionally stupider than the cunning princess. A similar illogic also results when Fix und Fertig, to be sure, does not want to disturb the birds at prayer, yet without hesitation has one of his horses run through so that the ravens will "not suffer hunger" on his account. This mixture of sensitivity and insensitivity further strengthens the impression that he helps the animals out of pure calculation, since he himself notes that the birds will "serve him sometime," as the fish then confirms. In the face of this utilitarian mentality, the moral lesson that sympathy for poor animals is mostly rewarded loses its meaning.

Since the narrator in the first edition mostly contents himself with reporting the events without adopting a position, the narrative stance remains amoral. But since no authority—not even fate, which controls the action—corrects or punishes the attitude of the hero, his view ultimately prevails. What is permitted is what suits him.

III

The world depicted in these tales is bipolar, in that the world of the poor people and their poverty are contrasted with the wealth, magnificence, and power of kings. Precisely with regard to the basic necessity, eating, the poverty of the people becomes clear. The charcoal burners are hospitable, to be sure, but can only offer their visitor "potatoes without fat." The wealth of kings is usually indicated above all by gold, but in this case, however, it is shown by the magnificence of the clothes and the pomp, so that the difference is obvious. They ride "a half-open carriage harnessed with six." They have "personal coachmen, guards, runners, lackeys, a cook," and everything that is proper for a monarchy. But not only clothes make the man. Character and attitude are also determined by class. The social distinctions show themselves most clearly in the female characters. While the princesses are beautiful if also malicious, in the case of the female commoners there is no talk of beauty. In the poor people's families, the traditional patriarchal distribution of sexual roles still prevails. Thus, the peasant shows himself to be harsh with the old watchdog, while his wife has more of a heart and begs for old-age care for the veteran guard, though in vain, for the decision belongs to the husband and he turns a deaf ear to his wife's pleas. Only after the dog appears to have rescued his child does the peasant show a sentimental, emotional trait, in accord with the spirit of the times and of the Grimms' tales.

Even in the world of the poor people, things are not always comradely. While the hero deceives the charcoal burners, his brothers, who have meanwhile come into money, scorn him because he is wearing "an old tattered coat," with the result that he has them beaten black and blue. Only the village community is still intact, insofar as the villagers rush to the brothers' aid. In other words, the social hierarchy is neutralized by a hierarchy of rich and poor. Whereas the poor people are prepared to share with a guest the little that they have, the rich show themselves to be mostly cold and heartless.

If the story does not concern a usually old, discharged soldier, the hero's profession is generally not very clearly specified. He is simply a son or a brother, but always the child of poor people. Nevertheless, like the fairy-tale hero he does not only wish to become wealthy. He also desires to achieve recognition. The soldier Fix und Fertig did not just want to become the lackey of an important man; he also wished at the same time to raise himself above his peers. He wanted to become "*Herr* Fix und Fertig," so everyone would have to "obey his orders." He wanted to go woo the princess for his master only in "princely clothes" and with princely pomp, so that the innkeeper took him to be a "foreign king," although (as the narrator notes) he was "but only a Sir Servant." Fix und Fertig seemed to be wooing on his own behalf, for he did not mention his master. Yet when, with the help of his cunning and foresight, he succeeded in winning the bride, he did not lay claim to her hand himself. She remained reserved for his master; and she fell to his master's lot doubtless as a result of his royal status, although he did not lift a finger and had contented himself with decking out his wooer in princely fashion. As a reward, Fix und Fertig received the position of prime minister, just as though even in a fairy tale he would not forget his subordinate status, and could not forget that princesses are not for the likes of him, that he was born a servant and remained one, even if he was the country's first servant—after the prince.

The owner of the magical weapons, by contrast, experienced an incomparable rise. Without his having especially gone to any trouble himself, with the signing of the peace he even received the princess as his wife, so to speak in recognition of his military prowess; in addition, he was made viceroy. But here, too, the gulf between rulers and poor people, to whom the hero belongs, is called to mind, for the princess was vexed that she had had to take "such an old fellow as a husband," and she wanted nothing more than to get rid of him again. In contrast to the later editions, where "the princess" lamented "that her husband was a commoner,"[27] in the first edition her vexation is not motivated by class distinctions, but by the difference in age. Yet if in the first edition of 1812 she scorns her husband as an "old fellow," then the pejorative expression acquires a social connotation, since up until that point there had been no talk about the hero's age.

In "The King of the Golden Mountain," social distinction does not have nearly as great a role, as though the merchant's son does not have the same perspective as the poor brothers. Thus, here the queen's unfaithfulness is no longer motivated by the difference in class between the marriage partners, but by the trespass against the command.

The difference in the depiction of the social dimension in "The King of the Golden Mountain" could be attributed not only to the tradition of the tying together of motifs, but also to the personality of the narrator; for in contrast to this tale, in the tales that can definitely be attributed to Sergeant Krause, the socially limited horizon of the poor storyteller is clearly evident. Thus, it is significant that the possessor of the magical napkin knew, to be sure, what he scorned, but was not able to indicate any more closely what he was able to set before the charcoal burner in place of "potatoes without lard." In listing the dishes, the storyteller remained extremely laconic, and noted only that the hero found "a table furnished with many sorts of dishes" and that he offered the charcoal burners "everything one could wish for"; but what this menu consisted of went unreported.

Our narrator's discretion in such matters is all the more telling since he likes to expand on what he knows well, namely military things. While Hans Sachs only reported that troopers climbed out of the donkey, the sergeant is able to recount vividly that everytime someone slapped the soldier's knapsack "a corporal and six fully armed soldiers" came out of it. A hidden identification between the hero and the narrator may possibly have contributed to the princess's describing her husband as an "old trooper" ("einen alten Kerl"). As an old soldier, the narrator did not know anything better to wish for than a "pipe and tobacco";[28] therefore Fix und Fertig, too, believed that the king's "desire" was the very same, as though people's wishes and needs remained identical irrespective of class. Equally characteristic, it seems, is the fact that the hero and the narrator never completely forgot that they were born as servants and in the end had to remain in a subservient position. Was it a coincidence that the hero who had risen to viceroy saw his position in doubt, and only Herr Fix und Fertig, who was content with the second-highest position and renounced all other personal wishes, retained his rise in status unchallenged once he had achieved it? His comrade remained as king at the end, to be sure, but ruled, as we saw, over a realm of the dead. And precisely this ironic ending, which is not otherwise familiar from folktale tradition, is entirely our storyteller's property; it reflects the old sergeant's skepticism, which he never quite overcame. He transported himself, to be sure, into the world of fairy tale, but at the same time he never forgot entirely that everything was after all only a beautiful dream, and that afterwards he found himself again in an unchanged gray reality, in his very own miserable condition.

IV

In spite of all the related features shared by the four tales, there is a certain noteworthy difference between "The King of the Golden Mountain" on the one hand and the other three stories, in that social problems find much more pronounced expression in the latter.[29] Of course, this difference can be owing to the Brothers Grimm, since as is well known they revised the style of the tales in the second volume of the first edition much more than they did for the first volume, in order to counter the charge of immorality raised by Clemens Brentano. Nonetheless, the difference can be traced above all to the fact that "The King of the Golden Mountain" was from another soldier. As August von Haxthausen reported, not only old discharged soldiers told stories; active soldiers, too, whiled away the time facing the enemy in the trenches by narrating tales.[30]

In Krause's tales, it is a matter of varying familiar themes and combinations of motifs that in part were already set. Nonetheless, it appears improbable that the old sergeant of dragoons had any knowledge about such things. Even Musäus's *Volksmärchen der Deutschen* (Folktales of the Germans) was at that time hardly known among the folk. And even if J. F. Krause could read and write,[31] in his poverty he seems hardly likely to have had access to books. Therefore, he appears, with his repertoire, to bear testimony to the contemporary oral tradition among the people, more in any case than the Grimms' middle-class contributors, who were also familiar with the literature of the times.

What we have of Krause's repertoire appears rather uniform and reflects both the misery and wishes of the old soldier and his discontent with the world and with society (not least of all, his joy in depicting destruction bespeaks his misogyny). This contrasts with his consciousness of his worth, his ability, and his cunning, though his consciousness of his subservient position also remains evident. Finally, he is characterized by a certain joy at telling stories, which can be seen from the complex, compound structure of his tales, as well as a sense of irony about the discrepancy between the fairy-tale world and reality.

Although, or precisely because, these tales testified to the sergeant's independent personality, the Brothers Grimm, after their initial enthusiasm, about which Wilhelm's letter to Arnim speaks, appear not to have thought much of these stories. Why otherwise would they, in the second edition, have replaced "Herr Fix und Fertig" with "The Three Snake Leaves," combined other stories by the sergeant with those of other sources, and expanded "About the Napkin . . . " considerably? To be sure, "The Knapsack, the Little Hat, and the Little Horn" (KHM 54) is distinguished, compared to number 37 of the first edition, by a greater vividness and clearer motivation. But since the hero stopped blowing at the last moment, after the king and his daughter had been slain, and "since no one further opposed him" when he made himself "king of the whole land," Krause's skeptical irony has given way to a happy ending, so that the tale was made to conform to the spirit of *Grimms' Fairy Tales.*

Notes

Translated from the German by James M. McGlathery.

1. Jacob Grimm and Wilhelm Grimm, *Kinder- und Hausmärchen: Kleine Ausgabe* (Berlin: Reimer, 1825). Ten editions of these selected tales appeared during the Grimms' lifetime.

2. Lutz Röhrich, *Märchen und Wirklichkeit* (Wiesbaden: Franz Steiner, 1956), and Waltraut Woeller, "Der soziale Gehalt und die soziale Funktion der deutschen Volksmärchen" (Diss., Berlin-Humboldt, 1955).

3. Heinz Rölleke, *Wo das Wünschen noch geholfen hat: Gesammelte Aufsätze zu den Kinder- und Hausmärchen der Brüder Grimm* (Bonn: Bouvier, 1985), pp. 39ff., 55ff., and *passim*, as well as Gabriele Seitz, *Die Brüder Grimm: Leben—Werk—Zeit* (Munich: Winkler, 1984), pp. 58ff., and Walter Nissen, *Die Brüder Grimm und ihre Märchen* (Göttingen: Vandenhoeck & Ruprecht, 1984), pp. 51ff.

4. Reinhold Steig, *Achim von Arnim und Jacob und Wilhelm Grimm* (Stuttgart: Cotta, 1904), p. 215; Wilhelm's letter to Arnim of 26 September 1812. (This is vol. 3 of Steig's *Achim von Arnim und die ihm nahe standen.*)

5. Wilhelm Schoof, *Zur Entstehungsgeschichte der Grimmschen Märchen* (Hamburg: Ernst Hauswedell, 1959), p. 88; Schoof also presents the texts of two letters from Krause to the Grimm brothers. See also Albert Schindehütte (ed.), *Krauses Grimm'sche Märchen* (Kassel: Johannes Stauda, 1985), pp. 100–102.

6. Steig, *Achim von Arnim*, III, 109ff.

7. Preface to the second edition of 1819, quoted from the text of the seventh edition of 1857, in Jacob Grimm and Wilhelm Grimm, *Kinder- und Hausmärchen*

(Munich: Winkler, 1949), p. 36: "daß in allem lebendigen Gefühl für eine Dichtung ein poetisches Bilden und Fortbilden liegt"; and "daß jede Gegend nach ihrer Eigentümlichkeit, jeder Mund anders erzählt."

8. Ibid., p. 33.

9. Ibid., pp. 20ff., in Herman Grimm's "Die Brüder Grimm: Erinnerungen."

10. Jacob Grimm and Wilhelm Grimm, *Die Kinder- und Hausmärchen: Vollständige Ausgabe in der Urfassung,* ed. Friedrich Panzer (Wiesbaden: Vollmer, [1955]), p. 526. The present interpretation is based on the text of this edition, and uses its numbering of the tales, while the KHM numbers refer to the later editions.

11. Johannes Bolte and Georg Polívka, *Anmerkungen zu den Kinder- und Hausmärchen der Brüder Grimm,* 5 vols. (Leipzig: Dieterich, 1913–32), II, 19, n.1.

12. Schoof, *Zur Entstehungsgeschichte,* p. 90, and Schindehütte, p. 5; and more cautiously, Heinz Rölleke, in Schindehütte, p. 17.

13. Jacob Grimm and Wilhelm Grimm, *Kinder- und Hausmärchen* (Leipzig: Reclam, n.d.), III, 31, and Bolte-Polívka, I, 126.

14. Jacob Grimm and Wilhelm Grimm, *Kinder- und Hausmärchen,* III, 207; and Bolte-Polívka, II, 503.

15. In addition, there are still other soldier's stories in *Grimms' Fairy Tales:* "Des Teufels rußiger Bruder" (KHM 100); "Das blaue Licht" (KHM 116); "Die zertanzten Schuhe" (KHM 133); and in the second volume of the first edition (1815), "Die lange Nase" (No. 36). See also Röhrich, *Märchen und Wirklichkeit,* pp. 181, 169.

16. Cf. Bolte-Polívka, II, 19.

17. Cf. "Ferenand getrü und Ferenand ungetrü" (KHM 126).

18. "Warumb die lanczknecht der trümel zulawffen," which is adapted as an etiological tale, and "Der lanzknecht mit dem Esel," in Hans Sachs, *Sämtliche Fabeln und Schwänke,* ed. Edmund Goetze, 6 vols. (Halle: Niemeyer, 1893–1913), II, 180ff., and VI, 357 resp.

19. Cf. Bolte-Polívka, I, 482ff.

20. The "Historia di tre giovani e di tre fate"; see Bolte-Polívka, I, 483.

21. Jean Paul Bignon, "Histoire du Prince Tangut et de la Princesse au pied de nez," in *Les Avantures d'Abdalla, fils d'Hanif* (Paris: Pierre Witte, 1712); there were numerous editions in the eighteenth century, also in the *Cabinet des Fées,* ed. Charles Joseph de Mayer, 41 vols. (Amsterdam and Paris: Hotel Serpente, 1785–89), XII, 460ff. Cf. "Die lange Nase," no. 36 in the second volume of the first edition (1815) of the Grimms' *Kinder- und Hausmärchen.*

22. "Rolands Knappen," in Johann Karl August Musäus, *Volksmärchen der Deutschen,* I (Gotha: Carl Wilhelm Ettinger, 1782).

23. E.g., "Das singende springende Löweneckerchen" (KHM 88).

24. Cf. Gonthier-Louis Fink, "Les Avatars de Rumpelstilzchen: La Vie d'un Conte Populaire," in Ernst Kracht (ed.), *Deutsch-französisches Gespräch im Lichte der Märchen* (Münster: Aschendorff, 1964), pp. 46ff., and Lutz Röhrich, *Sage und Märchen: Erzählforschung heute* (Freiburg im Breisgau: Herder, 1976), p. 272.

25. The *Historia und Geschichte von Melusina;* see Claude Lecouteux, *Melusine et le chevalier au cygne* (Paris: Payot, 1982).

26. This deceit is softened, however, in the later editions. Cf. "Der König vom goldenen Berg" (KHM 92), in Jacob Grimm and Wilhelm Grimm, *Kinder- und Hausmärchen* (Munich: Winkler, 1949), p. 405, where the injustice results not from evil intent but from carelessness, since without thinking, the hero wishes himself back with his wife, and his wish is fulfilled immediately. Cf. also "Der gelernte Jäger" (KHM 111).

27. Ibid., KHM 54, p. 256; cf. "Des Teufels rußiger Bruder" (KHM 100).

28. Cf. "Das blaue Licht" (KHM 116).

29. Cf. "Die drei Schlangenblätter" (KHM 16).

30. Letter of Jacob Grimm to Wilhelm Grimm of 18 January 1814, in Herman Grimm and Gustav Hinrichs, *Briefwechsel zwischen Jacob und Wilhelm Grimm aus der Jugendzeit,* 2d rev. ed. (Weimar: H. Böhlaus Nachfolger, 1963), p. 238: "Auf einer Vorpostenwacht in der Nacht hat er sich ein Märchen von seinem Kameraden erzählen lassen, der am anderen Tag hinter ihm totgeschossen wurde." Which tale is the one in question is not known, however. Possibly, it was "Die zertanzten Schuhe" (KHM 133).

31. See, on the one hand, Krause's letters to the Grimm brothers, in Schindehütte (pp. 118, 125), as well as Rölleke's description of the sergeant's intellectual horizons (in Schindehütte, p. 16).

AUGUST NITSCHKE

The Importance of Fairy Tales in German Families before the Grimms

FAIRY TALES have been told to children ever since the later Middle Ages. Before that, the situation was different. Bishop Burchard of Worms, in the eleventh century, for instance, was convinced that women were taking the persons in fairy tales seriously. They would—he thinks—really bring toys to the dwarfs, and for the sisters who would only appear in fairy tales they would prepare food and drinks.[1] Even the mother of Hermann of Weinsberg spoke with her son about the dwarfs that they had seen one day, so they believed.[2] In the fifteenth and sixteenth centuries fairy tales were told to children, but grown men took fairy tales so seriously that they would interpret them symbolically. Geiler of Kaisersberg, for instance, and Martin Luther were able to interpret the Cinderella story in such a way. They foretold a good future for those persons working in the kitchen as humbly and shyly as Cinderella did.[3] Others such as Cardinal Giovanni Dominici opposed fairy tales because he thought they could foster vanity such as toys might—like the wooden horses or the pretty trumpets or the artificial birds or the golden drums—or because they might frighten children.[4]

Modern psychologists have argued the pros and cons of fairy tales. Disciples of Sigmund Freud have been of the opinion that fairy tales could help children understand their own experiences from early childhood.[5] Disciples of Jung have argued that fairy tales might provide the possibility of becoming acquainted with the process of separation from the parents.[6] Bettelheim believed fairy tales to be valuable because they could teach children to observe an obvious boundary between good and bad and thus to become sensitive toward the order

164

of the world.[7] None of those psychologists has so far asked which experiences the children themselves actually had in the time before the Grimms collected their stories. It is this topic to which I would like to direct attention here.

I understand "fairy tales" to signify stories

—related orally,

—describing persons such as dwarfs or giants whom one normally does not meet,

—depicting animals speaking with humans—such as the wolf talking to Little Red Riding Hood,

—telling about witchcraft, the effects of which one normally does not take into consideration.

It has frequently been shown that fairy tales in this sense were related in spinning-rooms (i.e., their tradition was oral) and that spinning-rooms existed in the countryside up to the twentieth century.[8] It has also been known that some of these fairy tales from the spinning-rooms were written down long ago—and underwent changes in the course of this process—and that written stories, too, were retold in the spinning-rooms, provided their contents and form took the shape of fairy tales.[9] I shall, then, not distinguish terminologically between stories originally of oral tradition[10] and stories added in part at least from books at a later point in time. I shall call all such stories "fairy tales" to which this term was applied during the time before the Grimms, under the condition that they assumed the character just described.

Felix Platter, in the sixteenth century, reports in his autobiography that he liked listening to stories, especially—and this is nothing peculiar—to fables and fairy tales. "And then the old women," so he says, "used to chat a lot about ghosts," and he took their stories seriously and even became frightened. He subsequently refused to stay by himself, especially at night when he cried and screamed. He did so because he had heard about one Üllengry who used to bite off people's heads. And so he had refused to stay by himself at night unless he was permitted to lie in his father's bed. Felix Platter also reports that as a child he was afraid of the Black Spittelku because he also thought that she wanted to bite people. When his sister Margretlein was ill with the plague, he and his other sister, Ursel, had gone to stay with a neighborhood printer he was especially fond of. In the printer's house Felix and Ursel woke up in the morning when all the others had gone to church. Through a crack in the window they saw the sun shining and something moving, and they became terror-stricken, believing that Üllengry had come. They cried so fearfully that the neighbors called their hosts back from church, and they did not want to stay there any longer at all and moved back home.[11]

Thus, fairy tales make children frightened. Nothing is said about good qualities being rewarded and nothing is said about the world order in which one becomes confident. It is pure fright that seizes the children. The humanist Vegio, likewise, reported his own fear of the persons in the fairy tales.[12]

There is other evidence for this from the end of the eighteenth century. Karl Philipp Moritz tells us in his autobiographical novel *Anton Reiser:*

> But beginning in his second or third year he used to remember the infernal tortures that he was afflicted with from the fairy tales of his mother and his cousin, both when he was awake and when asleep. In his dreams he would see many friends suddenly staring at him with faces turned into ugly grimaces, and he would mount a high and dark staircase and a frightening figure would prevent him from returning. . . . At the time when his mother and he lived in a village every old woman would frighten him because he had heard so much about witches and sorceresses. . . . Also, he had a similar fear of Christmas. During Advent he was afraid of the coming of Ruprecht. . . . There was not a single day in the course of which no strange noise such as the ringing of bells or a scraping in front of the door or a dull voice could not be heard, . . . and there was not a single night during which he did not wake up stricken with terror and with sweat on his forehead. . . . This went on until his eighth year.[13]

Another report: Wilhelm Harnisch, who was born in 1787, informs us that "My father himself was an excellent storyteller, and in the evenings he would frequently tell us long stories of witches having fattened children in order to devour them, and then I would feel terrible trying to fall asleep in the evening when witches performed their dances around me." One might conceive of Hansel and Gretel as the fairy tale just mentioned.[14]

It was not the fairy tales themselves that helped against such fright, but the Christian faith of the father. Harnisch himself, at least, goes on to say that he should have been thankful to his father for having told these fairy tales: "In our sinful life on earth there is no trust in God without fright, and therefore I am not discontented with my blessed father, for he planted so much discomfort in my soul, through the biblical stories and also through the fairy-tale world into which he led me. But especially I have to be grateful to him for having shown me the path leading out of the discomfort of this earthly world into the quietness of heavenly peace, when frequently in the evening and probably also during other times of the day I could hear him and see him kneeling and praying from the bottom of his heart."[15] One concludes, therefore, that it is not the fairy tale but faith that helps young men to find their way out of the world—a world to which the fairy tales themselves indeed belong.

The situation had changed thoroughly by the end of the eighteenth century. It may have been shortly before 1780 that young Ernst Moritz Arndt listened to fairy tales told by his mother. The children were taught writing and reckoning by their father. It was their mother's task to care for other exercises and, according to Ernst Moritz's opinion, "she stimulated our young and unsteady spirits through stories and fairy tales that she was able to retell in a wonderfully sweet way."[16] What he really meant becomes evident from the report of Jung-Stilling, born in 1740. He also had listened to many stories and mixed up everything. He was told, or had read to him, legends, oriental fairy tales, German popular literature, and gothic novels. He made use of them for the creation of a new fantastic landscape. At that time he lived together with his father. He was only allowed to play in a small fenced-in part of the woods where he could be seen by the father, and was not allowed to meet even a single neighborhood child.[17]

This wooded area he turned into a sequence of ideal landscapes: "There was an Egyptian desert in which he transformed a bush into a cave. In the cave he would hide and imagine he was St. Anthony, and it may have been that he said prayers from the bottom of his heart. In another area he imagined the fountain of Melusine. There was Turkey, where the sultan and his daughter the beautiful Marcebilla lived. On a rock he imagined the castle of Montalban in which Reinhold used to live. . . . He used to conduct daily pilgrimages to these places. Nobody can conceive of the joy that the boy had then. His mind was over-productive; he stammered rhymes and had poetical illusions."[18] Fairy tales as well as other stories here make one imagine places and, as we know from other juvenile reports, assign roles to oneself.

This was a world in which the parents consciously protected their children from the environment, however. More characteristic are those reports in which the children were exposed to threatening, embarrassing, or frightening situations. We have such a report from Friedrich von Klöden born in 1786. His parents had become separated due to a longer absence of his father, who had become a drunkard. When he came home drunk, Frau von Klöden scolded him severely, and he reacted correspondingly, and thus depressing scenes occurred "in the course of which we children experienced dreadful situations." In Berlin, the child had had anything but beautiful experiences. In his neighborhood, girls seven and nine years of age had been beaten by their mother whenever they failed to knit what they had been assigned for the day. There was a cooper living in the same courtyard whose wife used to beat her son and chase him around the courtyard shouting at him and scolding him. Friedrich's family then moved to a Polish town, where their situation became really poor, with their Polish neighbors being convinced that the mother did not take enough care of her husband—an opinion that the husband liked to hear.[19]

In such an environment von Klöden's mother was able to create a happy counterworld on occasion at Christmas. He relates, "In order to be able to buy toys she would continue to work well into the night during the final three or four weeks before Christmas, would sing herself Christmas carols, and would tell to us, as long as we stayed awake, Christmas memories from her childhood as well as stories of events she had experienced, and fairy tales and other stories that she had read and of which she had a tremendous memory. We had frequently heard all that, but always rejoiced when we had a chance to hear it again. Mother was a good storyteller, and we even corrected details that she had told in a way different from that of years before, and we would also provide those details that by chance she had omitted."[20]

Here the fairy tales gain a new and completely different significance for the children. They create an atmosphere free of tension and full of confidence in close temporal connection with Christmas, a festival aimed at providing nothing but happiness. In this case it is not the contents of the fairy tales nor the endings that are of importance to the children. The fairy tales lead to a close personal connection between the children and the person telling them. The happiness stemming from the fairy tales consists in their power to create, in the depressing course of the persons' lives, a certain period of time set aside from all pressures, which was provided by the mother.

It was also by the end of the eighteenth century that through fairy tales children started to create their counterworld opposed to the world of adults. In 1769 Caroline Pichler was born. She belonged to the upper stratum of society. In her family, also, the mother occupied a central position. The mother conducted historical research: "The male sex was not evaluated particularly highly in all these studies, and my mother was very inclined to construct a system according to which women had originally and by nature been destined to rule."[21] A self-reliant girl like Pichler did not like to subordinate herself to the adults: "It was easy for me to learn things, to apprehend fast, and I had an excellent memory—all gifts from nature for which I did not deserve any credit.... For me such easiness often did do harm. I did not like to study."[22] This child used her reading of fairy tales to construct a world counter to that of the adults, even when she was attending classes in school: "I found it intolerable to sit on a chair, to pay attention and to be occupied with one and the same object all the time. So I used my gift of apprehension and my good memory, took my toys or my fairy-tale book to school, half listened to what the teacher explained and half played or read, contenting the teacher by repeating what he had just said."[23]

In this case, a child used the fairy tales to construct her own world as opposed to that of the adults.[24] The young lady—like the young Rousseau a few decades before her[25]—experienced that at the age of eight she was able to separate her situation from what she conceived of as her lost childhood. In her diary she noted: "The days are gone that made me happy."[26] For such precocious children, the reading of fairy tales offered a possibility for protest and allowed them to oppose the adults or to recall a time during which they had felt happy because of having been children and having loved fairy tales.

Thus, it appears that children between the sixteenth and early eighteenth centuries reacted to the weird elements in fairy tales and tended to become frightened by them. By contrast, beginning with the second half of the eighteenth century, the storytellers became important. They transported the children to a better world that stood in marked contrast to depressing everyday reality. Mothers might be able to create such a world, yet at the same time children experienced fairy tales as something belonging to themselves and read fairy tales to prevent themselves from being drawn into the sphere of the adults.

In this situation fairy tales have offered the impression to children that different states of community exist in the world: a relaxed one, free of tension and occasioned by hearing fairy tales, that is frequently lost with childhood, and a depressed and tense one characteristic of the remaining world.[27]

All these experiences were not created through the fairy tales but existed independently of them.[28] By no means were these experiences created by the Grimms' collection, for they published their fairy tales only later. Thus, in their collection the Grimms present an experience being had by children of their time, an experience shared in an extremely intensive way by the Grimm children—not only by Wilhelm and Jacob but also and especially by Ludwig. For them the family and being together with their mother was a world in itself; they were shy in the presence of other persons, and even in old age yearned to live once more like children.[29]

Subsequently, though, the Grimms' tales indeed served to deepen these experiences. Georg Ebers reports that his mother used to "play" fairy tales with him. In this example, the moral of the fairy tales is of no concern at all, not the ending either, and not at all whether or not the ending was good. On the contrary, mother and son greatly liked evil endings and even created them occasionally. What was important was the close relationship that arose between mother and child when fairy tales were told:

> It was most exciting when we played Little Red Riding Hood. I used to be the little girl walking into the woods and she was the wolf. Always when the bad animal had covered itself with the hood of the grandmother I not only used to pose the prescribed questions: "Grandmother, how come you have such large eyes? Grandmother, how rugged your coat is!" and so on, but also created new questions in order to postpone the ending, and these might be: "Grandmother, how come you have such big and sharp teeth?" followed by the answer "So that I can bite you well," the wolf then attacking me in order to eat me. Instead of the bites, however, I received kisses and instead of its teeth the monster that was a tender mother merely used its lips and hands, now teasingly pushing me away and then pulling me back.[30]

In this way the fairy tale creates a relationship with the mother and the world that she created: "These friendly images that used to populate my imagination return to my mind countless times whenever the world around me has darkened, and among them there also appeared the image of the beloved woman from whom I had heard the first fairy tales."[31]

Over the course of the nineteenth century, however, the situation changed. Children again looked for the frightening in the fairy tales, and Shockheaded Peter (Struwwelpeter) came along to give them a fright. Once again they invented figures, as did Isolde Kurz, who imagined that a Häkelmann, long, skinny, with a long green tailcoat and red stockings, was trying to pull children afraid of him out from under tables and beds "by means of a long hook.... My screams of anguish were terrible."[32] Sometimes, however, fairy tales were thought of as not frightening enough anymore: "Therefore we indifferently skimmed through fairy-tale books, but keenly and shudderingly we heard of the recently deceased mayor of M. dragging back to its former place a boundary-stone that he had illegally displaced"—such is the report by Friedrich Ratzel.[33]

Indeed, it is regrettable that our sources are talking about fairy tales, magic tales, and numinous legends without making any distinction between them. But one point is obvious. We have no evidence of any reaction to fairy tale being different from that to a legend or a fanciful tale. So the different attitudes of the children cannot reflect the diversity of the genres. One may mistrust the change of effects the tales appear to have had through the centuries; but we have a control group for our results. We have not only the autobiographical sources but also—though not well known—data about the symbolic interpretation of fairy tales given by parents, priests, and other fairy-tale tellers. Analyzing these symbolic interpretations, one finds a comparable change in attitudes over the centuries.[34] Thus, our inferences are not as uncertain as at first glance it may seem.[35]

Before I sum up let me say again that the results I shall propose are tailored for historians. They will surely not impress psychologists, who as a rule know in advance how fairy tales are supposed to affect children. Historians are not quite as sure. The only thing they can do is to rely on the statements of the children. I am associated with a special group of historians. As an historian of modes of behavior I study formal processes of actions—not the aims and causes of actions.[36] My interest is to find out how the processes of actions of the various persons in the fairy tales affect each other so that I may be able to describe preferred modes of dynamics.[37] My other question is how an event outside the sphere of the hero's human actions, for example the change of seasons, may affect his actions, and whether or not the hero will adjust himself to such an event. With the help of this method it is possible to redate some fairy tales.[38] Finally—this has just been said—I want to know the effects of the processes of the telling of fairy tales upon the audience. The focus of my interest is thus upon interactions. Judging from the evidence cited above, one may conclude that fairy tales do not offer a better world that one may long for; they do not render experiences with father and mother in early childhood conscious or unconscious. They do not depict the process of becoming an adult, and they do not show that the world has a moral order in which one may place one's trust. We do not have a single report testifying about such matters. On the contrary, children select different figures out of the context of the fairy tales at different times. For many centuries these were figures causing fright. If one deprives children of fairy tales or if fairy tales are denounced as childish then children will look for other stories fulfilling the same function, e.g., for legends or reports from the neighborhood.

Beyond that, fairy tales gained specific importance for families within a specific epoch, in the course of the eighteenth century and just a few decades before the Grimms started to publish their collections. This was a period in which the world was viewed in a new way. People then differentiated between a relaxed state of community familiar to them and another state that was depressing, restless, and full of tension.[39] The relationship between fairy-tale tellers and children assisted the children in gaining a feeling of that familiar state of community. Having the feeling and the knowledge of these two different worlds, children and adults wanted to build a better, tensionless world, to work hard for this goal, to reform the constitution, to develop the economy, and to create new industries.

From this point of view it now becomes evident how many children the Grimm brothers helped with their collection of household tales. They put together those fairy tales children and adolescents were longing for, not because these children were especially keen on the content, but because what the children wanted was to have someone telling the fairy tales to them or acting them out with them. If a fairy tale like Little Red Riding Hood was interpreted pedagogically and if it had a positive ending respectful of order, mothers were smart enough to change the contents of these fairy tales in such a way that only the terror or weirdness remained—a type of terror, however, that could provide occasion for tender affection. In this way, the mothers allowed their children to come to an understanding of the world in which familiar and discomforting aspects were clearly separated, thus reaffirming that these two states of community existed. Under these conditions, through the telling of fairy tales a mother living together with a drunken husband gained courage and handed that courage on to their children.

In our time storytellers can create a very amusing atmosphere, but not the close connection between mother and child that we have found in the late eighteenth century. We live in a completely changed world. In our world psychologists and historians have to be grateful to the Grimms for the attention they paid to the contents of fairy tales. During the time of the Grimms, however, families could be grateful to them for the possibility of creating a relationship free of tension through the telling of fairy tales.

Notes

1. Hermann J. Schmitz, *Die Bussbücher und das kanonische Bussverfahren* (Düsseldorf: L. Schwann, 1898), p. 432, 443.

2. Hermann von Weinsberg, *Das Buch Weinsberg: Kölner Denkwürdigkeiten aus dem 16. Jahrhundert,* ed. Konstantin Höhlbaum, vol. 1 (Leipzig; A. Dürr, 1886), p. 49.

3. Johannes Bolte and Georg Polívka, *Anmerkungen zu den Kinder- und Hausmärchen der Brüder Grimm,* vol. 1, 2d ed. (Hildesheim: Georg Olms, 1963), pp. 185f.

4. Giovanni Dominici, *Regola del governo di cura familiare,* ed. Donato Salvi (Florence: A. Garinei, 1860), p. 151.

5. Sigmund Freud, "Märchenstoffe in Träumen," in Wilhelm Laiblin (ed.), *Märchenforschung und Tiefenpsychologie* (Darmstadt: Wissenschaftliche Buchgesellschaft, 1969), pp. 20, 52ff.

6. Marie Luise von Franz, "Bei der Schwarzen Frau: Deutungsversuch eines Märchens," in Laiblin (ed.), *Märchenforschung,* p. 332; Hedwig von Beit, *Symbolik des Märchens,* vol. 2: *Gegensatz und Erneuerung im Märchen,* (Berne: Francke, 1956); Carl Gustav Jung, "Die praktische Verwendbarkeit der Traumanalyse," in Jutta von Graevenitz (ed.), *Bedeutung und Deutung des Traums in der Psychotherapie* (Darmstadt: Wissenschaftliche Buchgesellschaft, 1980), p. 115.

7. Bruno Bettelheim, *The Uses of Enchantment* (New York: Alfred A. Knopf, 1976), p. 309.

8. Andreas Gestrich, *Traditionelle Jugendkultur und Industrialisierung: Sozialgeschichte der Jugend in einer ländlichen Arbeitergemeinde Württembergs* (Göttingen: Vandenhoeck & Ruprecht, 1986), pp. 92ff.

9. Heinz Rölleke, *Die Märchen der Brüder Grimm* (Munich: Artemis, 1985), p. 16.

10. August Nitschke, *Soziale Ordnungen im Spiegel der Märchen,* vol. 1, *Das*

frühe Europa (Stuttgart-Bad Cannstatt: Frommann-Holzboog, 1976), pp. 22f.

11. Felix Platter, *Tagebuch (Lebensbeschreibung 1536–1567)*, ed. Valentin Lötsche (Basel and Stuttgart: Schwabe, 1976), p. 59: "Ich hab seer gern zu geloßt, wan man etwas historien erzelt unnd sunderlich wie die iugendt pflegt, fablen und merlin erzellet. Do dan di alten weiber domolen vil von geisten redten, dem ich ernstlich zugeloßt hab, aber gar schreckhaft und forchtsam darvon worden, also daß ich nienan allein sein dörfen, besunder znacht nit allein ligen, auch etwan in der nacht mich geförchtet, daß ich geschruwen, do mir allerley wiß ich etwan gehört von Üllengry, so den leuthen den kopf abbeiße, unnd andre narry fir kamen, dorumb auch einest in der nacht nienen bleiben wolt, ich lege dan in meines vatters bett, mit iomeren, die schwartze spittelku (wie ich sy dan gegen zeoben alher gesach in die scheur hinuß fir unser huß dreiben) wolte mich freßen." P. 62: "Ich bleib aber gar ungern, und alß wir die nacht in der oberen kammer schliefen unnd sy alle am suntag zerkilchen ganen waren, alß wir erwachten sachen wir durch die spelt die sunnen durchscheinen und etwaß do rin wie geschicht zwitzern, erschracken wir seer, vermeinendt, eß wer der ülenkry, so die kinder sagen, biße die köpf ab, schruwen und weinten also, daß die nachburen, dorunder der Glieger genant vorüber sas, unserem hußvolck uß der kirchen riefen mußten. Nach dem eßen wolt ich nit lenger bleiben, nam mein hobel unnd segen in die handt, zog wider heim."

12. Maphaeus Vegius, *De educatione liberorum,* ed. Maria W. Fanning (Washington, D.C.: Catholic University of America, 1933), book 1, chap. 1, pp. 31ff.

13. Karl Philipp Moritz, *Anton Reiser: Ein psychologischer Roman* (Munich: Winkler, 1971), p. 23: "Aber von seinem zweiten und dritten Jahre an erinnerte er sich auch der höllischen Qualen, die ihm die Märchen seiner Mutter und seiner Base im Wachen und im Schlafen machten: wenn er bald im Traume lauter Bekannte um sich her sahe, die ihn plötzlich mit scheußlich verwandelten Gesichtern anbleckten, bald eine hohe düstre Stiege hinaufstieg, und eine grauenvolle Gestalt ihm die Rückkehr verwehrte, oder gar der Teufel bald wie ein fleckiges Huhn, bald wie ein schwarzes Tuch an der Wand erschien.

Als seine Mutter noch mit ihm auf dem Dorfe wohnte, jagte ihm jede alte Frau Furcht und Entsetzen ein, so viel hörte er beständig von Hexen und Zaubereien; und wenn der Wind oft mit sonderbarem Getön durch die Hütte pfiff, so nannte seine Mutter dies im allegorischen Sinn den handlosen Mann, ohne weiter etwas dabei zu denken.

Allein sie würde es nicht getan haben, hätte sie gewußt, wie manche grauenvolle Stunde und wie manche schlaflose Nacht dieser handlose Mann ihrem Sohne noch lange nachher gemacht hat.

Insbesondere waren immer die letzten vier Wochen vor Weihnachten für Anton ein Fegefeuer, wogegen er gerne den mit Wachslichtern besteckten und mit übersilberten Äpfeln und Nüssen behängten Tannenbaum entbehrt hätte.

Da ging kein Tag hin, wo sich nicht ein sonderbares Getöse wie von Glocken, oder ein Scharren vor der Türe, oder eine dumpfe Stimme hätte hören lassen, die den sogenannten Ruprecht oder Vorgänger des heiligen Christs anzeigt, den Anton denn im ganzen Ernst für einen Geist oder ein übermenschliches Wesen hielt, und so ging auch diese ganze Zeit über keine Nacht hin, wo er nicht mit Schrecken und Angstschweiß vor der Stirne aus dem Schlaf erwachte. Dies währte bis in sein achtes Jahr."

14. Wilhelm Harnisch, *Mein Lebensmorgen: Nachgelassene Schrift: Zur Geschichte der Jahre 1787–1822,* ed. H. E. Schmieder (Berlin: Hertz, 1965), p. 20: "Ja mein Vater war selbst ein trefflicher Erzähler und öfter erzählte er lange Geschichten an den Abenden von Hexen, die Kinder fett gemacht, um sie zu verspeisen, und es war mir dann sehr schauerlich zu Muthe, wenn ich des Abends einschlafen wollte und die Hexen mich umtanzten."

15. Ibid., p. 21: "Ohne Furcht aber ist in unserm irdischen Sündenleben kein Gottesbewußtsein, und ich bin darüber nicht unzufrieden mit meinem seligen Vater, daß er mir in den biblischen Stoffen, die ich durch ihn erhielt, und in der Mährchenwelt, in die er mich führte, manche Beunruhigungen in mein Gemüth gelegt hat. Ich muß ihn aber besonders dafür danken, daß er mir auch den Weg zeigte, auf dem man aus dieser Unruhe der getrübten Welt in die Ruhe des himmlischen Friedens gelangen kann, indem ich ihn öfters des Abends und wol auch zu andern Zeiten auf den Knieen liegend aus dem Herzen beten hörte und sah."

16. Ernst Moritz Arndt, *Erinnerungen aus dem äußeren Leben,* ed. Robert Geerds (Leipzig: Reclam, 1892), p. 19: "die Mutter hielt die Leseübungen und machte unsere jungen flatternden Geister durch Erzählungen und Märchen lebendig, die sie mit großer Anmut vorzutragen verstand."

17. Johann Heinrich Jung-Stilling, *Lebensgeschichte,* ed. Gustav Adolf Benrath (Darmstadt: Wissenschaftliche Buchgesellschaft, 1976), p. 46.

18. Ibid., p. 47: "Da war eine egyptische Wüste, in welcher er einen Strauch zur Höhle umbildete, in welcher er sich verbarg und den heiligen Antonium vorstellte, betete auch wohl in diesem Enthusiasmus recht herzlich. In einer anderen Gegend war der Brunnen der Melusine: dort war die Türkei, wo der Sultan und seine Tochter, die schöne Marcebilla, wohnten. Da war auf einem Felsen das Schloß Montalban, in welchem Reinold wohnte usw. Nach diesen Örtern wallfahrte er täglich, kein Mensch kann sich die Wonne einbilden, die der Knabe daselbst genoß. Sein Geist floß über, er stammelte Reimen und hatte dichterische Einfälle."

19. Karl Friedrich von Klöden, *Jugenderinnerungen* (Leipzig: Insel, 1911), p. 56.

20. Ibid., p. 93: "Um die Ausgaben zu Spielzeug für ihre Brüder, später für ihre Kinder zu bestreiten, arbeitete sie die letzten drei bis vier Wochen bis tief in die Nacht hinein, sang sich Weihnachtslieder und erzählte uns Kindern, solange wir wach blieben, teils Weihnachtserlebnisse aus ihrer Kinderzeit, teils Geschichten, die sie erlebt, teils Märchen und andere Erzählungen, die sie gelesen hatte und für die sie ein bewunderungswürdiges Gedächtnis besaß. Wir hatten alles das schon oft gehört, aber es machte uns immer neues Vergnügen, es wiederzuhören, denn die Mutter erzählte gut, ja wir berichtigten sogar einzelnes, wenn es mit dem früher Gehörten nicht wörtlich übereinstimmte, oder wir ergänzten auch, wenn etwas weggelassen wurde."

21. Caroline Pichler, *Denkwürdigkeiten aus meinem Leben,* vol. 1 (Munich: G. Müller, 1914), p. 48.

22. Ibid., pp. 34f.

23. Ibid.: "Auf einem Stuhle sitzen, acht geben und mit einerlei Gegenstand mich beschäftigen, das alles waren mir unerträgliche Dinge. So benützte ich jene Fassungskraft und mein gutes Gedächtnis, nahm mein Spielzeug oder ein Märchenbuch mit zur Lektion, hörte, während ich spielte oder las, mit halbem Ohr auf das, was der Lehrer erklärte und fertigte ihn... damit ab, daß ich ihm genau wiederholte, was er soeben gesprochen [hatte]."

24. Regarding children's construction of their own world, see August Nitschke, *Kunst und Verhalten: Analoge Konfigurationen* (Stuttgart-Bad Cannstatt: Frommann-Holzboog, 1975), pp. 146ff. For the opposition of children to adults in European history since the beginning of the fifth century, see August Nitschke, *Junge Rebellen: Mittelalter. Neuzeit. Gegenwart: Kinder verändern die Welt* (Munich: Kösel, 1985), pp. 15ff., 63ff., 79ff.

25. Nitschke, *Junge Rebellen*, pp. 44ff.

26. Pichler, p. 44.

27. Nitschke, *Junge Rebellen*, pp. 44ff.

28. August Nitschke, *Revolutionen in Naturwissenschaft und Gesellschaft* (Stuttgart-Bad Cannstatt: Frommann-Holzboog, 1979), pp. 120ff.

29. Ludwig Emil Grimm, *Erinnerungen aus meinem Leben*, ed. Adolf Stoll (Leipzig: Hesse & Becker, 1911), pp. 74 and 90f.

30. Georg Moritz Ebers, *Die Geschichte meines Lebens: Vom Kind bis zum Manne* (Stuttgart: Deutsche Verlags-Anstalt, 1893), p. 18: "Am schönsten war es, wenn wir Rotkäppchen spielten. Ich stellte immer das kleine Mädchen dar, das in den Wald geht, sie aber den Wolf. Wenn sich das böse Tier dann mit der Haube der Großmutter unkenntlich gemacht hatte, richtete ich nicht nur die vorgeschriebenen Fragen: 'Großmutter, was hast Du für große Augen?' 'Großmutter, wie rauh ist Dein Fell?' und so weiter an sie, sondern erfand auch neue, um den großen Schlußeffekt hinauszuschieben, und der bestand darin, daß nach der Frage: 'Großmutter, was hast Du für große, scharfe Zähne?' und nach der Antwort: 'Damit ich Dich gut beißen kann,' der Wolf sich auf mich stürzte, um mich zu fressen. Statt der Bisse gab es dann aber nur Küsse, und statt der Zähne brauchte das Untier, das eine zärtliche Mutter war, nur Lippen und Hände, um mich bald neckisch fortzustoßen, bald an sich zu ziehen." Cf. Paul Göhre, *Denkwürdigkeiten und Erinnerungen eines Arbeiters* (Leipzig: Eugen Diederichs, 1903), pp. 30f.; Wilhelm Hamm, *Jugenderinnerungen* (Darmstadt: Schlapp in Comm., 1926), pp. 73f.

31. Ibid., p. 19: "Unzähligmale kehrten diese freundlichen Gemälde, die damals meine Einbildungskraft bevölkerten, mir wieder in die Vorstellung zurück, wenn sich die Welt um mich her verfinstert hatte, und in ihrem Gefolge erschien dann auch das Bild der geliebten Frau, von der mir die ersten Märchen erzählt worden waren."

32. Isolde Kurz, *Aus meinem Jugendland* (Stuttgart and Berlin: Deutsche Verlags-Anstalt, 1918), p. 16: "Die Mißgestalten des Struwwelpeters arbeiteten zum Nachteil meines Seelenfriedens in meiner Phantasie, die genötigt war, im Traum noch mehr solcher Ungeheuer zu erzeugen. Eins der schrecklichsten war der Häkelmann, eine Gestalt, die mich jahrelang verfolgte. Er war lang und mager mit grasgrünem Frack und roten Beinkleidern und fuhr blitzschnell durch alle Zimmer, indem er mit einem langen Haken die Kinder, die sich vor ihm verkrochen, unter den

Tischen und Betten hervorzuhäkeln suchte. Wann er erschien, brachte er das ganze Haus um den Schlaf, so furchtbar war mein Angstgeschrei."

33. Friedrich Ratzel, *Glücksinseln und Träume* (Leipzig: F. W. Grunow, 1905), p. 18: "Darum lasen wir gleichgiltig in den Märchenbüchern, hörten aber mit Grauen von dem kürzlich verstorbnen Bürgermeister von M., der Nachts ächzend einen Grenzstein, den er zu Unrecht versetzt hatte, wieder an seine Stelle schleppte."

34. August Nitschke, "Symbolforschung und Märchenforschung," in Manfred Lurker (ed.), *Beiträge zu Symbol, Symbolbegriff und Symbolforschung* (Baden-Baden: Valentin Koerner, 1982), pp. 127ff.

35. In analyzing the autobiographical sources, it was possible to demonstrate that we have some in which the author controls his memory, but there is also a possibility of "inner control"; for the relationship between a child younger than six years old and his environment must be different from the relationship to the environment on the part of a child older than six years. You can determine the quality of a source by observing the author's method of telling stories about the first years of his or her life. See Nitschke, *Junge Rebellen,* pp. 105ff.

36. August Nitschke, *Historische Verhaltensforschung: Analysen gesellschaftlicher Verhaltensweisen: Ein Arbeitsbuch* (Stuttgart: Ulmer, 1981), p. 75.

37. Nitschke, *Soziale Ordnungen,* vol. 2, *Stabile Verhaltensweisen der Völker in unserer Zeit* (Stuttgart-Bad Cannstatt: Frommann-Holzboog, 1977), pp. 15ff.

38. Nitschke, *Soziale Ordnungen,* vol. 1, pp. 21ff; Nitschke, "Symbolforschung und Märchenforschung," pp. 132ff.

39. Nitschke, *Revolutionen in Naturwissenschaft und Gesellschaft,* pp. 120ff.

WALTER SCHERF

Jacob and Wilhelm Grimm: A Few Small Corrections to a Commonly Held Image

F ROM TIME to time, the civilized world—or at least certain parts of it—is seized by an urge to explore fairy tales. We find ourselves now in the midst of such a period. The famous collection by Jacob and Wilhelm Grimm is, next to the Bible, indeed the most widely distributed book in the world. But this did not happen yesterday, nor only since the recent billowing wave of products of fantasy. Compared to these, *Grimms' Fairy Tales* seems much too modest and unassuming. And yet, it still has a greater impact.

We do not need to join in stoutly enumerating those things that show, as everyone recognizes already, how much in demand those transmitted fairy tales are nowadays. At the same time, it may be useful to call attention to less well noticed aspects of the Grimm phenomenon; and in view of the scholarly zeal that has developed in recent years, to do so is not very difficult. Scholars have studied Wilhelm Grimm's diary of dreams, and, in a strictly medical way, his particular heart ailment. They have traced the French influences on the collection of tales, which for so long was considered to be entirely Hessian; at first, this was done carefully and circumspectly, then later with speculative abandon. Meanwhile, scholars are occupied, too, with critically exploring the brothers' relationship to their other siblings. And it will not much longer be left to local organizations to analyze the folktale treasure, for example, that was contributed by Dorothea Viehmann, the tailor's wife from Zwehrn near Kassel. We are now informed, even, about the origins of the first illustrations of *Grimms' Fairy Tales,* done by Jacob and Wilhelm's brother, the painter Ludwig Emil Grimm; and we may admire the patience and perseverance with which their painter brother's lovingly realistic observations made according to nature had to be reconciled with Wilhelm Grimm's artistic ideas of a mystical and romantic sort that probably were influenced by the works of the contemporary painter Philipp Otto Runge, whom he greatly admired.

The essence of the new discoveries, it seems to me, is something different. What made the tales so important to the Grimm brothers, so that they lived with them throughout their lives and for five decades placed their great and amazing learning in now closer, now broader relationship to these stories, was the experience of an un-anticipated chorus of narrative memories that burst forth from their and their friends' childhoods. In the almost siblinglike circles of girlfriends gathered about their sister Lotte, Jacob and Wilhelm's favorite occupation with traditional forms of folk poetry opened a treasure of mutually supporting tales that Jacob, then twenty-three, and Wilhelm, a year younger, began to write down together—Jacob at first hesitatingly, Wilhelm with increasing vividness and ever more under the spell of this new world filled with inner human truth that opened itself to him.

To be sure, first Jacob, who as a seventeen-year-old student at the University of Marburg was already called "the old one," and soon thereafter Wilhelm, called "the little one," had come upon their first great task through meeting the young Friedrich Carl von Savigny, who was lecturing on Roman law, and through him his friends Clemens Brentano and Achim von Arnim. Full of unparalleled zeal, they had put themselves to work for Arnim and Brentano, those two already famous fire sprites of the Romantic movement, contributing to the latter's great work, *Des Knaben Wunderhorn: Alte deutsche Lieder* (The Boy's Miraculous Horn: Old German Songs) by busily excerpting from German Renaissance and Baroque authors like Fischart and Moscherosch, Rollenhagen and Grimmelshausen. They had even put their problem child, their brother Ferdinand, to work on this great undertaking of combing through literature (a habit Jacob and Wilhelm themselves retained all their lives), because Ferdinand wrote a fine hand. But the Grimms' recognition of the dramatic, magnetic power of the seemingly so plain folktales and of the unexpected extent of their inner connection with life did not occur until a little while later. The first writing down of stories told in the circle of their sister's eight- to twenty-year-old girlfriends did not begin until the year 1808.

Excerpting texts of presumed folk poetry from venerable old books is a completely different world from participating in the rediscovery and mutual telling of tales among young people. Jacob and Wilhelm, indeed, had grown up with fairy tales. We know, for example, that in their childhood the stories "Mrs. Fox's Wedding" (KHM 38), "How the Children Played Butcher" (KHM *Anhang* 3), and the tale about "The Little Gnome" (KHM 91) were told to them, for example.

The occasion for this mutual storytelling did not arise accidentally, one must remember. When the Grimms' father, whom they passionately loved, died in early 1796, and his sister, who up to that time had likewise been a dependable support for the family, died later that same year, their mother was left alone with five young sons and the little daughter Lotte. In addition, the household budget had to be reduced almost overnight and the family moved out of the stately official residence, under constant pressure from the father's successor in office. Now that is all well known, and one can read about it anywhere. It evidently has remained hidden from countless biographers and writers of articles, however, that the sudden change made Jacob, the oldest of the boys, his father's successor as head of the household. Jacob, who was then only eleven years old, felt he owed this to his mother and to himself. And his brother Wilhelm, who had always been close to him and followed his lead, recognized at the very same time where his place was: next to the eldest brother, and with him, to replace the father as the great motivator for the younger siblings, and also to compensate their mother, who was falling into ever-greater financial difficulties, for her love and selfless sacrifice as fast as they could. What Jacob and Wilhelm Grimm gained from this heavy blow that cut them off from a happy childhood was their incredible diligence—about which Heinrich Heine once said that it bordered on obsession—and their devotion to their life together and with their brotherly and sisterly circle. The little literary circle, to which Lotte belonged, had a different degree of importance than one might at first assume. The members, including Jacob and Wilhelm, integrated themselves into it both intellectually and emotionally. It is also no accident that, in a similar manner, Wilhelm found his way into the Bökendorf circle of his school chums August and Werner von Haxthausen and through his enthusiasm for folktales and folk songs made of it a comparably sibling circle of mutual storytelling, collecting, and communicating of tales.

Yet it was not only this curious double occurrence that shaped the

Grimms. Presumably Jacob Grimm's experiences as a young diplomat in Vienna, at the congress following the collapse of the Napoleonic empire, in the circle of friends who championed the newly self-aware peoples of southeastern Europe, their language, and traditions (we need only think of the Slovenic librarian Kopitav) helped. The European peoples also became family in his eyes: siblings whose joys and sufferings one should share and whose surviving cultural treasures one should enjoy, and in whom one should find comfort and support. Those who have perceived this early acquired, basic attitude of the brothers Jacob and Wilhelm Grimm will not be so foolish as to declare that these two founders of Germanic studies and, especially, folktale research, were, along with certain contemporary scribblers, partially the cause of a ludicrous patriotism (or *Deutschtümelei*) and ruthless nationalism. On the contrary, they viewed the Napoleonic striving for power as a horrible mistake. But the southeastern Europeans' fire of enthusiasm, such as that of their friend Vuk Stefanović Karadžić for the revival of his native Serbian language and traditions, was not only something they shared; they made it their model—in a brotherly way.

The rediscovery of the importance for children of our folktale tradition is not the sole property of our times and those of the Grimm siblings; even earlier it had noteworthy consequences. I shall not speak of the teller of the famous tales about Rübezahl, Johann Karl August Musäus, who is presently having an important anniversary. In pre-Goethean Weimar, that curious mixture of a village and a home of the muses, Musäus was wont to fetch children from the street, and carters and old women spinners, into his living room and have them tell stories. He made of these stories at the end of the eighteenth century almost a different—to be sure, very amusing—literary genre. No, I mean the court society of Versailles, including its bourgeois participants in Paris, at the time of Louis XIV, or more specifically in the last decade of the seventeenth century. It was the same puzzling phenomenon. Grown men and women of precisely this luxury-loving epoch that saw the greatest development of political power told fairy tales to one another. They exchanged letters about their childhood memories about fairy tales, told them to their children, or had their children tell the stories to them, and wrote them down for one another, so that they could indeed have the stories passed around. To be sure, this undertaking was a naive one only at its inception. Their fine ironic humor was restrained at first, as a humorous appreciation of human mistakes and frailty, at least in Charles Perrault's case. He attempted to be a substitute for his children's dead mother, and encouraged his favorite son, Pierre Darmancourt, to take down carefully the stories that he told to the children. This became a nicely bound present for the daughter of the court's second lady.[1] This gift was intended, of course, to serve Perrault's son, who was fifteen or sixteen years old at the time, as the first rung on the ladder to success in the court society of those days—a project that had a tragic ending, to be sure. But is it not worth noting that one could at all hope to reach that first rung with Red Riding Hood and Bluebeard, Sleeping Beauty and Cinderella, Puss in Boots and Tom Thumb? Certainly, it is worth combing through the letters of Liselotte of the Palatinate with this question in mind.[2] There one easily finds more than one reference to childhood impressions and fairy tales. Most amusing is the allusion to the coarse children's tale about the doll that excretes gold and is tossed upon the very manure pile on which soon thereafter a prince wishes to relieve himself. The little doll grabs hold of the princely hind parts, and in this remarkable, miraculous way brings about the happy marriage of the thoroughly good owner of the doll and the Crown of Life. With this tale, which was somewhat unusual for Versailles and is to be attributed no doubt rather to her native Palatinate, the duchess of Orléans is ridiculing for her friend, the countess (*Rauhgräfin*) Louise, the censorship of their letters by the old minister of state Colbert, son of the great Colbert. She wishes for both herself and her friend that their stationery could bite, like the little doll in the fairy tale (a story that one or the other reader may know, indeed, in the almost house-trained version by Ludwig Bechstein, the court librarian of the Meiningers, entitled "Das Dukaten-Angele").

The passion at the Versailles court for rediscovering old folktales gave way, as one knows, to a luxurious fairy fad in magnificient oriental dress, for which Jean-Antoine Galland's first European translation of the *Arabian Nights* must be held partly to blame. But the terrible results of the originally quite naive rediscovery of folktales is not our subject (although one is tempted to cast a side glance at the interesting case of Sophie von Kamphoevener[3]).

We could go yet another step backwards in time and take a look at the conditions surrounding the origins of Giambattista Basile's magnificent literary work. His *Pentamerone* of 1634–36, written in the Neapolitan idiom, is not only a collection of five times ten fairy tales.

Rather, a frame story binds together each group of ten stories told on one of the five evenings, as well as the whole group of fifty stories. And Boccaccio's narrators tell his one hundred tales in a social group that has fled the town to escape the plague. Is this only a fictive detail? Certainly, but still it was hardly just plucked from the air. Telling stories to one another must have suggested itself to people living in those earlier times, and especially in intellectual circles. Certain clues indicate that in the scholarly Academy, to which Basile belonged, along with his editor and successor in tale-gathering, Pompeo Sarnelli, the floor was open not only for scholarly debate but for telling one another tales and anecdotes, which were amusingly stylized and spiced with vivid baroque wit. The Neapolitan cannonades of abuse, which certain of Basile's characters are wont to fire off, are in themselves an incomparable delight, initially no doubt for Basile's listeners and then, posthumously, for his readers.

But enough of such excursions to visit the Grimms' predecessors. We want to occupy ourselves, after all, with the collection by Jacob and Wilhelm Grimm that has remained so significant for children and adults alike. If we count the tales that were subsequently dropped and those added later, there are at least five basic groups, viewed according to the stories' provenience.

The first group is comprised of those tales that were taken from older printed or manuscript sources and modified to fit the model of charming and unpretentiously told stories. As an example of this type, one could point to the not especially successful attempt to divest the amiable Weimar satirist Musäus of his witty, critically topical allusions and bizarre ironic jests (as the Grimms attempted to do with his "Bücher der Chronika der drei Schwestern," the result of which they published as "Die drei Schwestern," no. 82 in this first volume of 1812).

The second group consists essentially of the stories from Lotte's circle of friends. These texts put their stamp on the first volume of 1812. They reflect the experience of passage to adulthood. On closer investigation, it was no accident that Lotte Grimm became involved not only with the daughters of the neighboring Wild family (the pharmacist Wild was from Berne, his wife from a family from Basle), but also with the daughters of the pastor of the fourth French congregation in Kassel, Charles François Ramus, and of the Hassenpflug family that was thoroughly at home in French culture. The two eldest Hassenpflug daughters were very well read, well educated, and

intelligent. They can be considered to have been the actual intellec-
tuals among the girls. Curiously, Wilhelm called this intellectual
argumentativeness their "overweening nature" and complained that
even the youngest of the sisters, Amalie, was already infected with it.[4]

The Grimms' sister Lotte later was wed to Ludwig Hassenpflug,
the girls' brother, while Wilhelm Grimm married Dortchen Wild
after a long engagement. Jacob Grimm, though, found his home for
life in Wilhelm's household. Actually, no one should be surprised
that the Grimms were so intimately connected with Huguenots.
In Hanau and Steinau, the Grimm family was concerned to remain
faithful to the Calvinist confession. The Grimms' grandfather, like
the great-grandfather and one of their father's elder brothers, was
a Reformed pastor. One was not supposed to become too intimately
acquainted with Lutherans—so Jacob Grimm retrospectively wrote in
his autobiography—not to mention Catholics, who occasionally surfaced like colorful figures from another world.[5] In short, an important
part of the first volume of 1812, including a number of readers'
favorites down to the present day, derives from French storytelling
traditions. Presumably, texts published in books played the decisive
role in this.[6] In the present context, it is unimportant whether the
tales came from France, Switzerland, or the Netherlands, or whether
they were printed in Germany in French with and without vocabularies,
as was customary at that time, or were translated into German (as in
the *Blaue Bibliothek der Nationen,* edited by Friedrich Justin Bertuch in
Weimar). What counts is that the young people set about to recall
their childhood memories and, for a time, were once again deeply
moved by those experiences.

We have already mentioned the most important of the French tales
by Perrault. To those, some must be added from the collections by
Jean de La Fontaine, the Countess d'Aulnoy, and others, for example,
"Persinette" by Mlle de la Force that became the Grimms' "Rapunzel"
(KHM 12) and remains today one of the best-loved stories.[7] But when
we speak of the second group of stories in the Grimms' collection, we
must not forget to mention an experience that determined Wilhelm
Grimm's stylistic aims throughout his life. This was, of course, his
reading of the Low German versions of two stories for which we are
indebted to the mystically romantic painter Philipp Otto Runge, from
Wolgast in West Pomerania. These two texts that seem at first so
modest are in reality two great masterpieces of Low German literature:

"The Juniper Tree" (KHM 47) and "The Fisherman and His Wife" (KHM 19). Against these seemingly naive stylizations, and from his first reading of them, Wilhelm Grimm measured all subsequent texts that came his way; and he determinedly revised and adapted these texts to fit those two model tales. Readers who simply let the leitmotivic verses in the two stories work their magic can gauge what Philipp Otto Runge achieved, and what sort of effect he necessarily had on someone like Wilhelm Grimm, who was always attentive to gentle poetic murmurings. One's appreciation of Runge's achievement is greater still when one compares his verses with the innumerable texts and song strophes that have survived in many other European languages.[8]

The third group of fairy-tale texts are those that were received by Wilhelm Grimm primarily in the so-called Bökendorf circle, which represented a duplication of the little circle in Kassel. It was there, too, that the notable encounter between Wilhelm Grimm and the important nineteenth-century German author Annette von Droste-Hülshoff took place. "She was dressed entirely in flaming purple," he wrote, recording a dream in a letter of 1814, "and pulled out individual strands of her hair and cast them through the air at me; they turned themselves into arrows and could easily have blinded me if the whole thing had been serious."[9]

These tales, written down mostly in the Westphalian dialects of Paderborn and Münster, have long since been thoroughly studied and written about. It is a shame that our enjoyment of surviving dialects has to this point been dampened by our rather unbalanced educational aims and productivity goals, if such enjoyment has not indeed been driven out entirely. Only a very few of the stories from the Bökendorf circle have come to be included in the volumes of selected tales that completely dominate the market. The fate of the tale of the worn-out dancing shoes (KHM 133), contributed in High German by Annette's sister Jenny, was decidedly better.

The second volume of 1815, however, received its decisive character not from the Bökendorf circle but from the stories told by Frau Dorothea Viehmann—an influence that continues still today. With her contributions we have reached the fourth group of texts in the Grimms' treasure chest of fairy tales. People should not allow themselves to be misled by tourist advertising in Niederzwehrn near Kassel to think that the old Hessian *Fachwerk* house (newly listed as 11 Fairy Tale Way, or "Märchenweg Nr. 11") is the cozy place where a wise old primevally Hessian peasant woman, surrounded by an audience of children, told native stories to the learned librarians who had traveled out from Kassel in their frock coats. Those who do have lost their way behind the stained-glass windows of a German romanticism that is the latest of the late. The painting that was done by a certain Louis Katzenstein in 1892 and that, strange as it may sound, one may still see passed off as a contemporary pictorial document in the Rowohlt monograph on the Grimms,[10] is from start to finish an invention of a sentimental cult of things German. Frau Viehmann also was not a peasant woman, but a tailor's wife. Once each week, she carried the products of their small farm to the homes of her regular customers in Kassel. And since she was from a Huguenot family (her great-grandfather was the first mayor of the Huguenot settlement Schöneberg that was founded near Hofgeismar, though he was presumably not a Frenchman, but a Dutch merchant from the Lothringian city of Metz) the French pastor Ramus was among her customers. It was the two Ramus daughters who provided the tie to the Grimms. Thus it happened that Frau Viehmann also knocked at the door of Jacob and Wilhelm Grimm, stopped by for a cup of coffee, and told stories that were eagerly written down by the two brothers, sometimes for hours at a time. We can read of Wilhelm's joy over this unexpectedly discovered source in a letter he wrote to his brother Ferdinand, a loner who was staying in Munich at the time.[11] Katharina Dorothea Viehmann, a kindhearted, very alert, and gifted person, soon ran into misfortune, however, when she took in the sick, downtrodden family of her daughter. She died in need at the end of 1815, at the beginning of which a first, large part of her tales had been published.

Not much that was French, it seems to me, found its way into Frau Viehmann's treasury of tales, despite all the recent speculation. Considerably more probable is the assumption that, as the daughter of the innkeeper on the Knallhütte, along the much traveled highway from Frankfurt am Main to north Germany by way of Kassel, Dorothea listened attentively to the stories told by the carters and soldiers, the visitors to the fair at Frankfurt am Main, and whatever other people gathered in the popular and well-run establishment. And we know that she preserved everything in her memory until one day she began to tell stories herself—when, we do not know, but perhaps for her own children, or perhaps only later, for the children of her customers in Kassel. One may point to the story "Hans My Hedgehog" (KHM

108) as a particularly impressive example of her narrative art, from among the more than twenty tales that she contributed.

The fifth and last group of the Grimms' tales, however, came to them through various transmissions from friends, schoolmates, and acquaintances, both new and old. Much of this material was employed only to add to stories that were already in the collection, or to communicate it in their commentary on the individual tales. As an excellent example from these texts, one may single out the story of "The House in the Forest" (KHM 169) that Karl Goedeke communicated to them from Delligsen on the Deister, and that Wilhelm Grimm included in the fourth edition of 1840. The Grimms knew Goedeke from his student days in Göttingen. He remained a loyal co-worker; for in this enterprise the Grimms were not merely collectors, after all. In the narrower sense, indeed, they no longer heard or wrote down any tales themselves after the second edition of 1819. Instead, they became unprecedentedly far-reaching instigators well versed in many languages, traditions, and mythologies who circumspectly and loyally maintained a correspondence across all political boundaries. Among the European collections of fairy tales that have become classics, there is none that did not come into being directly or indirectly through the activities of Jacob and Wilhelm Grimm—from the Norwegians Peter Christen Asbjørnsen and Jørgen Engebretsen Moe to the Moscow archivist Aleksandr Nikolaevič Afanas'ev. As far as German collections and individual publications were concerned, with each of their seven editions the Grimms were on the lookout for particularly well told stories and examples of story types that were not yet represented in their collections. Thus, as late as 1857, in the last edition during their lifetime, they were able to include the story of "The Sea-Hare" (KHM 191) from Josef Haltrich's collection of tales from Transylvania. And in 1843, "The Hare and the Hedgehog" (KHM 187) found its way into the fifth edition from its printing in the Hannover *Volksblatt*, where it had appeared under the title "The Race between the Hare and the Hedgehog on the Buxtehuder Heath" ("Het Wettloopen tüschen den Haasen un den Swinegel up der Buxtehuder Heid").

The romantic legend about the two vigorous hikers who, up and down and all across the country, listened to the nation's last fairy-tale tellers in their smoky cottages is patently false. How that type of work looks can be seen most strikingly in the collections by Wilhelm Wisser (east Holstein) and Evald Tang Kristensen (north Jutland); and we may hope that someday the Balkan travel diaries of Felix Karlinger will be published.

In two circles of young people in Kassel and Bökendorf, the Brothers Grimm caused childhood memories to be awakened, and experienced the magic of those memories. And they had an elderly female story-teller come by herself to tell stories time and again, and to them alone. The much-praised storyteller Marie from the Wild pharmacy, though, is obviously a myth. There was, to be sure, a housekeeper by that name working for the Wilds, but presumably she did not contribute a single tale. The stories that were attributed to her were in reality told by Marie Hassenpflug, who in 1808 was just in her twentieth year.[12]

Beyond the five groups of tales discussed above, everything else consists of literary excerpts, written contributions, and borrowings, except for the few tales by a discharged sergeant of dragoons. This material testifies, as the Grimms' astounding, extremely rich correspon-dence shows, to an unprecedented involvement with the surviving treasures of the folk literature of all nations.

We owe it to these two German literary scholars and folk-poetry treasure seekers, as one said it so nicely in those days, to remove the superfluous retouching done on their work. That we know so much more about them today, and with such greater reliability, we owe, above all, to the former Kassel librarian Ludwig Denecke and to Heinz Rölleke at the University of Wuppertal.[13]

But one question remains unanswered. What is so extraordinarily important about telling fairy tales to one another, and reading them, that today a whole industry owes its existence to this? The answer could be spelled out with a long lecture on literary sociology and psychoanalysis, but one can present the heart of the matter in a few sentences. All human beings must loosen the ties from early child-hood that bind them to their parents in order to find out who they are themselves. One must internalize what the people nearest and dearest to one have to offer and adapt it to one's own aims and goals. Loosening ties and steering one's own course is thus the key theme of childhood; overcoming immature regressive ties, building of an inde-pendent partnership, and unselfish dedication to another person with whom one wants to lead one's life together would be the key theme of the second part of our drama. Fairy tales, however—the actual ones that are sometimes called magical tales (*Zaubermärchen*)—are nothing else but a constant challenge to project onto them, as though onto an open stage, the constellation of figures from our childhood and adolescent conflicts, our loosening of ties, and our efforts at steering our own course and finding a partner, and to play through these processes, without being conscious of what is actually happening. What distinguishes fairy tales from many other so-called media offerings is that they do not merely send up signals saying, "Here is where your conflict lies!" No, fairy tales do considerably more. They draw us through self-identification in their dramatic spell, strap us in, and lead us through a highly dramatic chain of action and processing of our own inner reality. A return to what has not yet been worked through? Yes, yet not a letting go of oneself but a creative regression.

Finally, to remove one last bit of retouching from the customary image of the two brothers who were so intimately and sincerely devoted to one another: Wilhelm Grimm, who not merely by accident tended to the fairy-tale collection virtually by himself beginning with the second edition, never had it easy with his older brother's acerbity and indeed inconsiderateness, as Ludwig Denecke put it. Wilhelm deferred to Jacob. He lovingly smoothed things over. He gave Jacob a home. But in a dream that he wrote down in 1813, Wilhelm saw with great clarity his own relationship to his brother and his mother, and his severing of childhood ties. He was always inclined to meditate on the puzzling processes of our inner being, for which dreams and fairy tales give equal occasion. In the dream, he saw himself returning to Steinau, saw the lonely, neat and tidy household, and noticed that everything seemed covered as though with a layer of fine dust. He saw his mother and brother sitting across from one another at a small table, her with her sewing and Jacob reading. "It was," Wilhelm wrote, "as though, with my dust-covered boots and brightly colored traveling clothes, I did not belong in there with them."[14]

Notes

This essay appeared in German in slightly different form in *Die Märchenzeitung* (Lebach), May, 1986, pp. 5–10. The translation into English is by James M. McGlathery.

1. Elisabeth-Charlotte, Duchess of Orléans (Liselotte of the Palatinate, born 27 May 1652 in Heidelberg, died 8 December 1722 at Saint-Cloud). Her daughter

was Elisabeth Charlotte, Mademoiselle de Chartes (1676–1744), who was married in 1698 to Duke Karl Leopold of Lorraine.

2. Walter Scherf, "Das Dukaten-Angele," in Scherf, *Lexikon der Zaubermärchen* (Stuttgart: Kröner, 1986), pp. 83–86; cf. the edition of these letters by Wilhelm Ludwig Holland, *Briefe der Herzogin Elisabeth Charlotte von Orléans* (Tübingen: Literarischer Verein in Stuttgart, 1879), p. 293; cf. also the earlier edition by Wolfgang Menzel, *Briefe der Prinzessin Elisabeth Charlotte von Orléans an die Raugräfin Louise* (Stuttgart, 1843), Letter of 3 October 1720, p. 473.

3. The novelist and elocutionist Elsa-Sophia von Kamphoevener (b. 14 June 1878 in Hameln; d. 27 July 1963 in Traunstein, Oberbayern) maintained that her very successful collections of fairy tales came from the oral tradition of Turkish nomads. Folkloristic criticism has decidedly rejected this claim, and has shown in detail the actual origin of her two-volume work *An den Nachtfeuern des Karawan-Serails.* See the review by A. Tietze and W. Anderson in *Fabula,* 1 (1958), 294–95, and 2 (1959), 292–94.

4. Heinz Rölleke, "Familie Hassenpflug," in his *Die älteste Märchensammlung der Brüder Grimm* (Cologny-Genève: Fondation Martin Bodmer, 1975), pp. 391–92. Regarding Amalie Hassenpflug, see Jacob Grimm's letter to his brother Wilhelm of 3 September 1809.

5. Jacob Grimm, "Selbstbiographie" (1831), in Jacob Grimm and Wilhelm Grimm, *Schriften und Reden,* ed. Ludwig Denecke (Stuttgart: Reclam, 1985), pp. 15–34, esp. pp. 15–16.

6. Gonthier-Louis Fink, *Naissance et apogée du conte merveilleux en Allemagne* (Paris: Les belles lettres, 1966).

7. Max Lüthi, "Die Herkunft des Grimmschen Rapunzelmärchens," *Fabula,* 3 (1960), 95–118; cf. Walter Scherf, "Rapunzel," in Scherf, *Lexikon der Zaubermärchen,* pp. 305–9, including the bibliographical references there.

8. Michael Belgrader, *Das Märchen von dem Machandelbaum* (Frankfurt a.M.: Peter Lang, 1980).

9. Heinz Rölleke, "Wilhelm Grimms Traumtagebuch," in Ludwig Denecke (ed.), *Brüder Grimm Gedenken,* vol. 3 (Marburg: Elwert, 1981), pp. 15–37; see p. 27 for the passage from the letter of 12 January 1814 to Ludowine von Haxthausen.

10. Hermann Gerstner, *Brüder Grimm in Selbstzeugnissen und Bilddokumenten,* 2d ed. (Reinbek bei Hamburg: Rowohlt, 1983), p. 46.

11. Letter of 17 July 1813 in Robert Friderici, "Wer entdeckte die Märchenfrau?" *Hessische Blätter für Volkskunde,* 60 (1969), 166–67.

12. Heinz Rölleke, Afterword to his *Brüder Grimm: Kinder- und Hausmärchen,* 3 vols. (Stuttgart: Reclam, 1980), vol. 3, pp. 590–617, esp. p. 600, from Ludwig Hassenpflug's still unpublished autobiography. Cf. Rölleke, *Die älteste Märchensammlung.*

13. From among their many scholarly publications, only a few representative ones can be cited here. See, for example, Ludwig Denecke, *Jacob Grimm und sein Bruder Wilhelm* (Stuttgart: Metzler, 1971), and his "Die Brüder Grimm heute: Zum Stand der Grimmforschung," in Charlotte Oberfeld and Andreas C. Bimmer (eds.), *Hessen: Märchenland der Brüder Grimm* (Kassel: Röth, 1984), pp. 116–32, 170–72; Heinz Rölleke, *Die Märchen der Brüder Grimm* (Munich: Artemis, 1985);

his *"Nebeninschriften": Brüder Grimm–Arnim und Brentano–Droste-Hülshoff* (Bonn: Bouvier, 1980), and his *Wo das Wünschen noch geholfen hat* (Bonn: Bouvier, 1985).

14. Rölleke, "Wilhelm Grimms Traumtagebuch," pp. 35–36, based on the record of a dream from 1813 published in Hans Daffis, *Inventar der Grimm-Schränke in der Preußischen Staatsbibliothek* (Leipzig: K. W. Hiersemann, 1923), pp. 116–17.

RUTH B. BOTTIGHEIMER

From Gold to Guilt:
The Forces Which Reshaped
Grimms' Tales

JACOB AND Wilhelm Grimm have been chiefly known to the general
public for the collection of fairy tales that bears their name. Therein
lies the problem. Are they *Grimms'* (or *Grimm's*) *Tales* quite literally?
Or is it more accurate to conclude that they belong to and emanate
from what the German title specifies, *Kinder- und Hausmärchen*, the
audience for the tale telling—children—and the locus of the narrative
act—the nursery? Many other collections, particularly in the late eighteenth century, had also assumed this stance. For example, *Ammen-
märchen* (nurses' or old wives' tales) specified the narrative voice; and
Märleinbuch für meine lieben Nachbarsleute (Book of Little Stories for
My Dear Neighbors) or *Kindermärchen* (Children's Tales) emphasized
the fictive or real intended audience.[1] As far as the Grimms' title is
concerned, it is remarkable for the fact that it does not include the
touchstone word *Deutsch*, which sets it strikingly apart from the
Grimms' own styling of so many of their other publications.[2] Their
non- or suprageographical title also distinguishes their collection
from other (though not all) collections of fairy tales and folktales
published at the end of the eighteenth and well into the nineteenth
century, so many of which bore regional or national specifications,
like Franconian tales or East Frisian tales.[3] But once it appeared in
conjunction with their names, the Grimms' own designation of their
collection seemed to exert an independent influence, for there appeared
a goodly sprinkling of collections which simply adopted the Grimms'
title, *Kinder- und Hausmärchen*.[4] The title of the collection represents
a small but nonetheless fertile field in which to cultivate questions
about what one may infer concerning the relationship between the

192

collection and its intended readership, its origin, or its relationship to regional or national identity.

Whose voice we hear in the tales, a far more significant inquiry, has repeatedly surfaced as a central question in Grimm scholarship. Both nineteenth- and twentieth-century critics of *Grimms' Tales* have tried to characterize and identify the social milieu from which the tales as a whole emerged. Central to Marxist revisionist work of the 1970s and 1980s,[5] this concern has become more focused with critics' increasing awareness that a process of thoroughgoing editorial change took place in *Grimms' Tales* between 1810 and 1857. In only one instance did Wilhelm Grimm publicly celebrate a particular narrative voice; it was the voice of Dorothea Viehmann, whose portrait has introduced the second volume of *Grimms' Tales* for more than 150 years. Recent inquiries into the Grimms' sources have resulted in assigning a great many of the tales to specific and identifiable informants,[6] assignments which often differ from those traditionally assumed and which were themselves based on attributions offered by Wilhelm Grimm's son Herman. But in the overwhelming number of tales, changes in vocabulary and style transformed the tales—to a lesser or greater extent—in succeeding editions of the collection. We may legitimately ask—and indeed we must ask—whose voice is responsible for these alterations?

In this essay I will touch on three points which have been hotly debated in the past few years, as well as on a fourth which represents a new direction in Grimm scholarship: (1) the process by which *Grimms' Tales* took shape; (2) the social-historical implications of the publishing history of *Grimms' Tales;* (3) the revisionist implications, especially with reference to Marxist criticism in the last decade; and (4) the critical position of *Grimms' Tales* at a turning point in German literary, political, and social history.

For several decades, there has been a lively discussion about the direction, the causes, and the effects of editorial change in *Grimms' Tales.* I hope that this essay will initiate a dialogue about whose voice we hear in the collection, a dialogue which will extend the discussion to include many aspects of nineteenth-century German history not previously adduced as relevant in considerations of *Grimms' Tales.*[7] Traditional wisdom has suggested that what is audible (or legible) is the voice of the folk, celebrated as a fount of wisdom, especially in those jingoistic and xenophobic years in the nineteenth century when the German nation was being hammered together from a motley group of former bishoprics, principalities, dukedoms, and margravates. In those years, German schoolchildren and their parents were told that the one undivided German folk spoke through these tales, and subsequent critics enthusiastically embraced this theme and exuberantly developed it. Wilhelm Grimm's son, Herman, created the myth of the thoroughly Hessian nursemaid informant "Old Marie," widow of a village blacksmith, whether intentionally or unwittingly we'll never know, but certainly in the spirit of the times.[8] During the Third Reich commentators had a heyday with the tales: what they recognized in Cinderella, for example, was the racial purity which distinguished her from her "racially alien" (*rassenfremd*) sisters.[9] Postwar German critics with little else to cling to in their immediate past continued to propagate the idea that *Grimms' Tales* captured the voice of the folk; but now the folk was understood in a worldwide sense, making of the collection a psychological sketchbook of transcendent validity.[10]

In the same period during which fairy tales were being defined psychologically as narratives above and beyond time and place, an opposing trend developed in both Germany and America, where revisionist critics trenchantly criticized and radically revised literary traditions. While American feminists were pointing out that *Grimms' Tales* together with the Disneys' versions of them were inherently antifeminist and occasionally misogynistic,[11] Heinz Rölleke in Germany was uncovering persuasive evidence that the tales owed a great deal to nineteenth-century bourgeois sources. By clear reasoning, hours in archives, and a lot of detective work that included scrutinizing the Grimms' social calendar, he concluded that "Old Marie" was not an impoverished Hessian blacksmith's widow, but the oldest sister in the wealthy Hassenpflug family. By piecing together datebook entries and the dates noted by the Grimms in the margins of their personal copies of the *Kinder- und Hausmärchen* Rölleke deduced that Marie Hassenpflug had provided them with many of the tales in their collection when Wilhelm and Jacob came to her parents' house for coffee and conversation. The bourgeois parlor is a great psychological and social distance from the rural cotter's dooryard, and the distance requires that a very different set of questions be put to the text. In the last ten years Grimm scholars have largely accepted the thesis of the bourgeois inception of the collection and many have also gone on to assume that subsequent reformulation was equally bourgeois-based, but popular belief in an unbroken chain of oral folk tradition has proved difficult to amend.[12]

The association of the bourgeoisie with *Grimms' Tales* was perfect grist for Marxist interpreters and critics who put feminist concerns together with their own and concluded that nineteenth-century bourgeois informants had shackled their female fairy-tale readers with a set of restrictive and punitive paradigms for female behavior. This direction was taken further by a recent publication which claimed that the Grimms, themselves thoroughly bourgeois, knew exactly what they were doing in changing the tales from one edition to the next, embedding ever more unpleasant outcomes for women, making the tales ever more bourgeois.[13] But are these assumptions correct about the intimate connection between nineteenth-century bourgeois values and the tales as they now stand? And are these assumptions even tenable?

My own work has produced results which agree with parts of each of the positions outlined above. However, when this information is put together in a model which takes into consideration historical change in the Germanies as well as changes in bourgeois attitudes in the course of the nineteenth century, the results suggest very different conclusions. The nationalistic nineteenth- and twentieth-century critics and commentators whose work has been so thoroughly discredited in the past years and decades seem to have been right after all, though for the wrong reasons. The voice in *Grimms' Tales* may be that of the folk, as well as that of the bourgeoisie. But we need to look closely at what it means to say that one hears the voice of the folk in the tales, and we also need to look closely at how the Grimms went about collecting the tales in the early years of the nineteenth century and at how Wilhelm continued the process of collecting together with collating and editing the tales in the collection from 1815 to 1857.

Throughout the collecting process that produced *Grimms' Tales*, literary sources loom large. However, these literary sources emerge from two very different social, national, and literary traditions at the beginning of and later in the collecting and editing process. It seems beyond reasonable doubt that the Grimms' first informants were young women of their bourgeois circle in Kassel, who were modestly brought up and well educated. For entertainment, they met for coffee, went on picnics, did needlework, and read or told *Märchen* to each other. The tales they told derived, principally, from the French courtly or bourgeois tradition and many were available in German translations for those who did not read French. The Hassenpflugs, a wealthy banking family attached to the court in Hesse-Kassel, even spoke French at home. These young women belonged to a refined urban tradition, and the tales they read and told reflected that tradition. As in Perrault's "Cinderella," girls in these tales could take the initiative: they could talk and even suggest that they have a chance to try on the tiny slipper.

From 1815 onward, the Grimms' literary sources were no longer the courtly French Perrault but the robust, gutsy, rough-hewn tradition of early modern German literature that provided narratives for their retelling: Hans Sachs (KHM 77, 119, 147, 148, 180), Johann Pauli (KHM 11, 145), Eucharius Eyering (KHM 164), Jakob Frey (KHM 32A, 35A), Jörg Wickram (KHM 35, 170), Martin Montanus (KHM 20), and Hans Wilhelm Kirchhoff (KHM 35, 119, 168, 174, 177).[14] These writers addressed a bourgeois book-buying readership that also included those of limited—or no—education.[15] Their style and their genre was that of the brief chapbook narrative which made its point quickly within crude comic situations. The *Schwank* rather than the *conte de fée* was the norm for Wilhelm Grimm's later sources, and, though produced for sixteenth- and seventeenth-century bourgeois consumers, the *Schwank* reflected the coarse world of the peasant and the artisan, not the cultivated Biedermeier parlor of the Kassel bourgeoisie. Looking backwards into the sixteenth and seventeenth centuries, it is all too easy to graft contemporary assumptions onto past reading habits. At first glance small leatherbound books ostensibly intended to pass the time on a coach trip and clearly affordable only by the more affluent would be thought to offer a worldview different from that in chapbooks and broadsheets addressed to the semiliterate. Cost rather than content principally differentiated the one from the other, so that the distinctions "folk," "artisan," and "bourgeois" fade into one another as far as the narratives themselves are concerned.

Why—if Grimm was primarily interested in making his collection bourgeois, as the Marxists assume—did he turn to sources like these to fill it out? How did he get from the polite drawing room to the rude cottage and the bawdy marketplace? Everyone knows, or at least talks about, the fact that the publication of the first volume of *Grimms' Tales* resulted in an outpouring of contributions from all over Germany. That may overstate the case, but even a glance at Wilhelm Grimm's annotations to the *Tales* indicates that many of these tales were widespread throughout Germany, not to mention the entire European continent.[16] The patterns in the tales he added later corresponded more to the misogyny of the sixteenth- or seventeenth-century *Schwank* with its stereotyped nagging wife and brutal husband than to the refined manners of the Kassel drawing rooms which Jacob and Wilhelm frequented.[17] It would seem that Wilhelm Grimm's editorial direction after 1812, the year the first volume of the first edition appeared, was set more by a desire to approach and incorporate the German-speaking "folk" than to embrace bourgeois values, at least as they had been understood in eighteenth- and nineteenth-century Germany up to the years of the Napoleonic invasions and occupation of 1806–13.[18]

At this point, I would like to reinterpret the changes made to the text of the *Kinder- und Hausmärchen* by Wilhelm Grimm, for it was he who was principally responsible for editorial change in the collection. A review of some familiar tales and the changes introduced into them in the early years of the collection's editorial history will put my inquiry into perspective. "Rumpelstiltskin" (KHM 55) provides an excellent starting point. In its earliest extant Grimm version (1810),[19] the heroine's problem centers on the fact that everything she spins turns to gold, which she finds troublesome. Two short years later, the story flows very differently. Now her father boasts (falsely) that his daughter can spin straw to gold; the king hears of this, takes the girl to his palace and says that she must spin roomfuls of straw to gold—or die. A very different tale indeed! In "Cinderella" (KHM 21: "Aschenputtel"), the shifts are more subtle and are evident within the language of the text rather than in alterations to the plot. The first extant Grimm version (1812) is a German-language carbon copy of Perrault's sparkling tale in which Cinderella joins in the general chat and herself suggests in the final scene that she be allowed to try on the shoe. Only a few years later (1819), she speaks hardly at all, while the wicked stepmother gives vent to the most horrid pronouncements in a set of shifts which equate female verbosity with wickedness.[20] In "Hansel and Gretel" the father is steadily exonerated for his moral absence in edition after edition. In "Our Lady's Child" (KHM 3) little Marienkind's sufferings increase in intensity as Wilhelm piles on adjectives to convey precisely how debased, exposed, and miserable she is in the forest, while at the same time he removes the fairy-tale golden trappings she had enjoyed in the earliest versions; and in "The Three Spinners" (KHM 14) a steady process of isolating the heroine leaves her alone, prey to happenstance, to fulfill the impossible task that has been set for her.[21]

The isolation which comes to surround most fairy-tale heroines in the course of the editorial history of *Grimms' Tales* was not the norm for bourgeois families in early nineteenth-century Germany, nor was it the case among the Grimms' circle in Kassel. Their datebooks bespeak and the drawings, paintings, and autobiography of their brother, Ludwig Emil, reveal a highly sociable life both for themselves and for the women in their families.[22]

If, then, isolation and silence for heroines creeps inexorably into *Grimms' Tales* and if their association with gold disappears from the tales, it is not from bourgeois experience, but is, instead, part and parcel of the restrictive values that emerge from the "folk" versions of the tales. These folktales differ from the bourgeois form in which Wilhelm had first heard them from his Kassel acquaintances. It is the folk, not the bourgeoisie, which preserved harsh patterns of conduct for girls and women. The immediate literary precursors for such tales are sixteenth-century broadsheets and chapbooks. It is the dictates of hard peasant and artisan life that produce domestic tyranny, female silence, and isolation in *Grimms' Tales.* Among contemporary informants, it is the voice, above all, of the common soldier Krause which tells misogynistic tales, and not that of Wilhelm Grimm or of his friends, the Wilds or the Hassenpflugs.

What's peculiar—and unique—about *Grimms' Tales,* however, is that eventually they came to be understood as a pattern of folk life in Germany, and in the later nineteenth century, everyone, even the upper classes and the bourgeoisie, wanted to identify with the folk to a very large extent for nationalistic reasons. Furniture and household goods produced for the middle and upper economic classes—sofas, chairs, tables, lampshades, and screens, as well as dishes—incorporated decorative motifs which their buyers thought of as "folk": everything from tillers of the soil to scenes from the Siegfried cycle, for example. At the same time, painters and poets of many stripes took to the village in the late nineteenth century to find folk truth, a particularly striking example of which is the Worpswede colony, where Rilke, Heinrich Vogeler, and Paula Modersohn-Becker were active members.

The rough values which inhere in *Grimms' Tales* didn't gain the upper hand within the nineteenth-century German bourgeoisie without a scuffle, however. As much as the bourgeoisie as a group supported the nationalistic tendencies of the expanding Prussian empire (in whose service the Grimms themselves were from 1840 onwards), privately they at first seemed to reject the coarseness of *Grimms' Tales,* for at mid-century *Grimms' Tales* were still being outsold by Bechstein's editions of fairy tales.

Many of Bechstein's versions of familiar tales are similar to the Grimms' in every respect except closure. The Grimms' tales frequently end violently: witches are burnt at the stake, boiled in oil together with snakes and vipers, rolled down a hill in a perforated barrel into a river, or dragged through town inside a barrel studded with nails. Instead of those horror-inspiring endings, Bechstein's tales conclude far more gently—for example, the witch's magical ring falls off and she simply disappears. This suited the refined sensibilities of the mid-century German bourgeoisie far better than the gory endings of many of *Grimms' Tales*. But only a generation later, *Grimms' Tales* had been taken up by the German bourgeoisie in full cry. What had happened to change their taste?

The intervening years—the decade from 1861 to 1871—had produced a unique conjunction of events and requirements. National fervor went from high to high in Prussia as it first annexed Schleswig-Holstein and followed this coup with a seven weeks' war against Austria (1866), which resulted in enormous gains both in territory and population (25,000 square miles and five million inhabitants). Finally, Prussia provoked the Franco-Prussian War, which it won handily, adding Alsace and Lorraine to its possessions. The course Bismarck had charted resulted in the proclamation of the German Empire in 1871 under Prussian Hohenzollern leadership.

Jacob and Wilhelm Grimm had been in the service of the king of Prussia from 1840 and remained there until their deaths. Whatever the route by which it came to be decided in the council chambers in Berlin, *Grimms' Tales* became an integral part of the expanding Prussian empire when it was introduced into the Prussian elementary school curriculum (1850) twenty years before the Franco-Prussian War. It thus became part of the unquestioned national heritage and national canon.

We have to ask why *Grimms' Tales* lent themselves to this sort of exploitation. The answer has to do with the language into which Wilhelm Grimm had recast the tales.[23] It was a language stripped of time- and place-specified vocabulary. At a very early point in the editorial history of the *Tales* the Grimms had defined the *Märchen* as a genre whose narrative stood beyond time and place, and Wilhelm went on to produce just that, a collection of tales which contained no clues as to time and place, though of course the tales are located within a time frame identifiable as "traditional," even though above—or beyond—a precise historical moment. It was this apparent transcendence that imbued the collection with its alleged universality.

In one sense, *Grimms' Tales* clearly expresses universal values, but not within a familiar bourgeois context. The harsh ethic which inheres in these tales, especially as far as the role and position of female characters is concerned, is similar to the folk ethic and folk values that emerge from the narratives of most agrarian cultures characterized by limited resources and even more limited education.[24] What is peculiar and even unique about *Grimms' Tales* is that this carefully collated and crafted body of folk literature became a standard for the bourgeoisie. Its earlier lively tales of golden girls had given way to a tradition in which guilt inhered in the female persona. The shift from gold to guilt represents a mighty displacement in worldview, and it coincides with the shifts in German national life during the period in which the Grimms began their collection and proceeded to refine it.

Literarily the Grimms' collection can be taken as the fulcrum between clumsy classic attempts to deal with the genre *Märchen* and the full-fledged fantasy of later Romantics. For example, Goethe's genial intellect, which encompassed the classic world in *Iphigenia* and *Faust II,* as well as the broad sweep of European historical events and their tragic effect on individual lives in *Egmont,* failed pathetically in its attempts to enter the world of the fantastic in "Das Märchen" and "Zauberflöte Part II." At the other end of the spectrum lies the work of E. T. A. Hoffmann, who tailored seamless fantasies one after the other, tales of magic and transformation. The Grimm collection lies somewhere in between, with magic serving wish fulfillment but rarely existing for its own sake as it does in Hoffmann. The Grimms desperately craved the approval of their classic predecessor, Goethe, but he withheld it; instead, their collection earned the approbation of subsequent generations, becoming a source for literary and artistic reworkings up to the present day.

Historically the Grimms' lives were in step with the steady development from *Kleinstaaterei* to *Reich.* Their father had served the Count of Hanau; they themselves entered the service of a landgrave who became a prince elector; they were employed by a relatively minor king in Hannover when they taught at Göttingen; and they ended up at the court of the Prussian monarch in Berlin. Their path took them from a small agrarian principality to an industrializing European power.

Their collecting and editing activity also coincided with significant sociocultural shifts in German-speaking central Europe. In the first place, the bourgeoisie shifted away from a conscious identification with French culture as a result of the nationalistic Francophobia which followed Napoleon's occupation of the central German states between 1806 and 1813. This xenophobic response had thoroughgoing consequences in terms of the books people read and the social models they turned to. As far as children were concerned, schooling shifted in the same period generally from church-supported and -staffed schools to a centrally administered secular system in the early to mid-nineteenth century. At the same time Protestantism was becoming monolithically Lutheran with the disappearance of minor but influential Protestant sects, a process which resulted in the fading of one significant tradition of socially liberal Protestant thought, a process which had profound consequences for curricula in the state schools.[25] The Grimms themselves were an example of the extinguishing of this tradition, since their own great-grandfather and grandfather had been pastors of the Reformed Church, whereas they themselves moved steadily away from this tradition, as did Germany as a whole.

And finally, their collection took shape just as possibilities for women seemed to be narrowing drastically. Women writers as well as salons led by women had existed in relatively large numbers in the eighteenth and early nineteenth centuries, but there seemed to be a sudden loss of opportunity in these areas for women in the decades of the mid-nineteenth century.[26]

The precise pathways which resulted in revaluations of fairy-tale heroines from producers of gold to bearers of guilt wind in and out of the social, cultural, and historical processes which have been introduced here. In some of these shifts, the Grimms were passive, silent participants, unseeing spectators of contemporary developments; in others, their work may have played a part in forming a new ethic which burst the confines of their peasant and artisan origins (at least in terms of plot) to become valid for German society in general. In each of these areas—literary, historical, political, religious, and social—the Grimms were moving with the tide of the times, and their collection, *Grimms' Tales,* reflects that fact. Looking into their work, we find both cause and effect, an exhibit, as it were, of a dynamic cultural process.

Notes

1. Attributed to Christian August Vulpius (1791–92); by Johann Gottlob Muench (1799) and by Albert Ludwig Grimm (1809), respectively.

2. For example, *Deutsche Grammatik, Geschichte der deutschen Sprache, Deutsche Sagen, Die deutsche Heldensage, Altdeutsche Wälder, Deutsche Mythologie, Deutsches Wörterbuch,* and *Deutsche Rechtsaltertümer.*

3. Johann Karl August Musäus, *Volksmärchen der Deutschen* (1782–86); Benedikte Naubert, *Neue Volksmärchen der Deutschen* (1789–93); Ludwig Bechstein, *Thüringische Märchen* (1845).

4. For example, the Austrian collection of Ignaz and Josef Zingerle, published in Innsbruck in 1852. There had been one or two collections with the same name before the Grimms published in 1812, but they were rarely if ever reprinted and cannot be accounted as influential as the Grimm collection.

5. See Jack Zipes, *Fairy Tales and the Art of Subversion: The Classical Genre for Children and the Process of Civilization* (New York: Wildman, 1983).

6. Heinz Rölleke (ed.), *Kinder- und Hausmärchen.* 3 vols. (Stuttgart: Reclam, 1980), III, 559–74: "Beiträger und Vermittler der Märchen."

7. See the discussion of "Präzisierung des Historischen" (pp. 274–75), "Soziale Problematik in und um die Volkserzählung" (p. 279), and "Der sozialhistorische Gehalt von Volkserzählungen" (pp. 281–82) in Rudolf Schenda, "Tendenzen der aktuellen volkskundlichen Erzählforschung im deutschsprachigen Raum" in Isac Chiva and Utz Jeggle (eds.), *Deutsche Volkskunde—Französische Ethnologie: Zwei Standortsbestimmungen* (Frankfurt and New York: Campus Verlag; Paris: Éditions de la Maison des Sciences de l'Homme, 1987); also Schenda, "Volkserzählungen," *Studia Fennica,* 20 (1976), 185–91.

8. Heinz Rölleke, "The 'Utterly Hessian' Tales by 'Old Marie': The End of a Myth," in Ruth B. Bottigheimer (ed.), *Fairy Tales and Society: Illusion, Allusion and Paradigm* (Philadelphia: University of Pennsylvania Press, 1986), pp. 287–300.

9. *Rassenpolitische Unterrichtspraxis,* quoted in Ulrike Bastian, *Die Kinder- und Hausmärchen der Brüder Grimm in der literaturpädagogischen Diskussion des 19. und 20. Jahrhunderts* (Frankfurt a.M.: Haag & Herelsen, 1981), pp. 161ff.

10. Hedwig von Beit, *Symbolik des Märchens* (Berne: Francke, 1956–57); Bruno Bettelheim, *The Uses of Enchantment* (New York: Vintage, 1977); Marie-Louise von Franz, *An Introduction to the Interpretation of Fairy Tales* (New York: Spring, 1970).

11. Kay Stone, "Things Walt Disney Never Told Us," *Women and Folklore* (special issue of *American Folklore*), 88 (1975), 42–50.

12. See, for example, an article on illustrations for *Grimms' Tales,* "From the Bookish Brothers Grimm, a Flood of Fantasy," *Smithsonian* (May, 1985), 108–19, for which I served as editorial consultant. Despite my numerous corrections on the galleys, the magazine's editors could not bring themselves to give up the old myths; and so they reinstated "Old Marie" and Wilhelm sitting under the village linden tree.

13. John M. Ellis, *One Fairy Story Too Many* (Chicago: University of Chicago Press, 1983).

14. Rölleke (ed.), *Kinder- und Hausmärchen,* III, 559-74.

15. The generally elevated language of the medieval texts, H. Rupp writes in "Schwank und Schwankdichtung in der deutschen Literatur des Mittelalters," *Deutschunterricht,* 14, no. 2 (1962), 29-48, suggests courtly and patrician audiences for the thirteenth- and fourteenth-century *Schwank,* but his argument does not take into account the occasions on which medieval manuscripts represented a bridge between the literate and oral traditions when they were read aloud. For a balanced discussion of the nature of Baroque readership see Elfriede Moser-Rath, "Die Publikumsfrage" in her *"Lustige Gesellschaft": Schwank und Witz des 17. und 18. Jahrhunderts in kultur- und sozialgeschichtlichem Kontext* (Stuttgart: Metzler, 1984), pp. 262-72. From clear directions for reading the books aloud given in some of them, one may conclude that the sixteenth- and seventeenth-century *Schwank* collections, like their medieval manuscript predecessors, both bridged and linked the literate and the illiterate, mistress and servant, master and seasonal laborer.

16. See the Grimms' own notes to KHM 50: "Dornröschen" or KHM 89: "Die Gänsemagd" as particularly good examples, in the 1812-15 edition in, Jacob Grimm and Wilhelm Grimm, *Kinder- und Hausmärchen,* ed. Heinz Rölleke, 2 vols. (Göttingen: Vandenhoeck & Ruprecht, 1986); in their own notes to the 1857 edition, in Jacob Grimm and Wilhelm Grimm, *Brüder Grimm: Kinder- und Hausmärchen,* ed. Heinz Rölleke, 3 vols. (Stuttgart: Reclam, 1980); and in the expanded notes of Johannes Bolte and Georg Polívka, *Anmerkungen zu den Kinder- und Hausmärchen der Brüder Grimm,* 5 vols. (1913-32; rpt. Hildesheim: Georg Olms, 1963).

17. See Moser-Rath, esp. the section "Erotica und Eheszenen," pp. 80-130.

18. A different approach is taken by Cay Dollerup, Iven Reventlow, and Carsten Rosenberg Hansen in "A Case Study of Editorial Filters in Folktales: A Discussion of the Allerleirauh Tales in Grimm," *Fabula,* 27, nos. 1-2 (1986), 12-30. They conclude that Wilhelm Grimm did everything possible to expunge non-middle-class values, and that his success in doing so was responsible for the collection's positive reception among the burgeoning middle class in nineteenth-century Germany.

19. Jacob Grimm and Wilhelm Grimm, *Die älteste Märchensammlung der Brüder Grimm,* ed. Heinz Rölleke (Cologny-Genève: Fondation Martin Bodmer, 1975), p. 238.

20. Ruth B. Bottigheimer, *Grimms' Bad Girls and Bold Boys: The Moral and Social Vision of the Tales* (New Haven: Yale University Press, 1987), esp. "'Cinderella': Editorial Change and Content Development," pp. 57-70.

21. Bottigheimer, *Grimms' Bad Girls and Bold Boys,* esp. "Prohibitions, Transgressions, and Punishments," pp. 81-94; "Spinning and Discontent," pp. 112-22; and "Towers, Forests, and Trees," pp. 101-11.

22. Ingrid Koszinowski and Vera Leuschner (eds.), *Ludwig Emil Grimm 1790-1863: Maler, Zeichner, Radierer* (Kassel: Weber & Weidemeyer, 1985); also Ludwig Emil Grimm, *Erinnerungen aus meinem Leben* (1913; Berne: Herbert Lang, 1971).

23. Max Lüthi, *The European Folktale,* trans. John D. Niles (Philadelphia: Institute for Human Issues, 1982), esp. chaps. 2–6.

24. Shirley Ardener (ed.), *Women and Space: Ground Rules and Social Maps* (London: Croom Helm, 1981).

25. I am referring here to Protestantism from the pulpit, not to academic liberal Protestant theological inquiries, which began to be heard in the 1820s, especially from Tübingen.

26. Priscilla Robertson, *An Experience of Women: Pattern and Change in Nineteenth-Century Europe* (Philadelphia: Temple University Press, 1982). See also the individual essays in Ruth-Ellen B. Joeres and Mary Jo Maynes (eds.), *German Women in the Eighteenth and Nineteenth Centuries* (Bloomington: Indiana University Press, 1986).

JACK ZIPES

Dreams of a Better Bourgeois Life: The Psychosocial Origins of the Grimms' Tales

For, my dear Wilhelm, let us never ever separate, and even supposing that one of us wanted to go to some other place, the other would at once have to give up everything. We have now become so accustomed to our communal life (*Gemeinschaft*) that even this present separation could be enough to drive me to death.

Jacob Grimm to Wilhelm Grimm
Paris, July 12, 1805[1]

Otherwise, dear Jacob, what you write about staying together is all very beautiful, and it moved me. That has always been my wish, for I feel that no one cares for me as much as you do, and I certainly love you just as much.

Wilhelm Grimm to Jacob Grimm
August 10, 1805[2]

ALTHOUGH the tales of the Brothers Grimm have been examined from various psychoanalytical viewpoints up to and through Bruno Bettelheim,[3] there have been surprisingly few attempts to investigate the psychosocial origins of the Grimms' tales. Such neglect may be due to the fact that, until recently, most critics who have written about psychology and the Grimms' tales assumed that the tales were genuine folktales. In other words, even though their psychoanalytical approaches varied, these critics believed that the tales were products of a *Volksgeist* or the common people and thus represented phantastic projections of either the collective unconscious as described by Jung or the universal psyche as outlined by Freud. Indeed, the tales were fair game for their analysis because they firmly believed the stories were hundreds of years old (if not thousands) and contained general symbolical patterns to which they could assign psychological meaning, quite often in most convincing, authoritative terms.

Now that we know, however, that the Grimms substantially rewrote

205

the tales they collected and that they endeavored to re-create a cultural tradition of folk poesy in literate form, it is time we shift the
analytical eye to examine the possible psychological motives behind
the Grimms' collecting of tales and their revisions within a socio-
historical context. It is important here to bear in mind that the
Grimms identified themselves closely with these tales and thus felt
represented by them. Such identification raises numerous questions.
Why were the brothers drawn to old German literature and folktales
in the first place? Why did they rewrite the tales so carefully and to
what purpose? What determined their selection process? What kinds
of family prototypes did they favor in their tales and to what extent
did their types correspond to their bourgeois notions of how people
should act in an ethical way? What type of wish fulfillment (*Wunsch-
Erfüllung*) did the tales convey for the brothers, who had a deep love
for one another and for home (*Heimat*) and fatherland (*Vaterland*)?

To provide a starting point for answers to these questions, I want to
focus on some key incidents in the years preceding the publication of
the first volume of the *Kinder- und Hausmärchen* (Children's and
Household Tales) in 1812. My concern will be with how these incidents had affected the Grimms psychologically and how they reacted
to them in formulating principles for their literary historical and
folklore research. Furthermore, I shall suggest some guidelines for
examining the tales from a psychosocial perspective by studying the
manner in which the Grimms reconstituted various texts of the Ölenberg
manuscript of 1810 in preparing them for publication in 1812. Even
though the tales that the Grimms collected may, in fact, be traced
back hundreds of years, they infused them with their own psychological needs, utopian dreams, sexual preferences, and sociopolitical views.

Loss, fear of separation from loved ones, work, industry, and diligence
as compensation for a decline in social status, dreams of peace, quiet,
and stability to lead the good clean life as opposed to the evil chaotic
life of the unjust: let us remember all this as we review the psychosocial
origins of the Grimms' tales.

In 1796 their father, Philipp Wilhelm Grimm, a respected and
pious magistrate, died in Steinau. Not only was this loss traumatic for
the Brothers Grimm, but for the entire family, which was compelled
to abandon the large, comfortable house that went with their father's
position. In addition, the family experienced a sharp drop in social

status and was often treated unjustly by so-called superiors. In imagining the extent to which Jacob and Wilhelm, the two oldest sons in the family, were affected by their father's death, it is useful to recall Alexander Mitscherlich's statement in *Society without the Father:* "The situation of the child in relation to the father . . . provides the foundation for all respect for authority in him. The collapse of paternal authority automatically sets in train a search for a new father on whom to rely. Trying to substitute for him any other element in the family constellation, for instance, a sibling order, awakens deep anxiety. The reaction to which is irrational hatred of those who dare suggest such a thing. The weakness or fallibility of the father has to be made good and wiped out by putting in his place a new one of still undiminished strength."[4]

In the Grimms' case, Jacob was just eleven years old when their father died, and as the leading male figure, he was expected to help provide for the family's future as soon as possible. By no means was he expected to replace the father, but it was incumbent on him to bring order to the family, to reorder the family relations and keep everything stable. For instance, right after his father's death, he wrote the following letter to his aunt Henriette Zimmer, his mother's sister and the first lady-in-waiting at the prince's court in Kassel: "I commend myself to your love and care with my four brothers and sister, and I am convinced that this is not a vain request. I know how deeply concerned you are about our great loss so that I should like to call on you and tell you personally about all the matters that are close to my heart. How much there is to tell you about my dear suffering mother! I am sure you will console me and give me good advice."[5]

The loss of the father could have meant great deprivation for the Grimm family and disintegration if a "good fairy" like Henriette Zimmer and other relatives and friends had not offered financial assistance and emotional support. Even here, help meant that the brothers were obliged to leave their family in Steinau, which they often described in idyllic terms as a paradise.[6] The departure occurred in 1798, which was incidentally the year in which their grandfather, Johann Hermann Zimmer, died—another man on whom they had relied for support. The brothers were enrolled at the Lyzeum in Kassel, and the bond between Jacob and Wilhelm, which had always been strong, deepened during the next four years. Not only were they emotionally tied together as brothers, but they also shared the same bed and took all their lessons together. The absolute trust each placed in the other was one way they compensated for loss of father, family, and home. Together Jacob, the more authoritative, introspective one, and Wilhelm, the more flexible, outgoing one, sought to reconstitute a semblance of family away from home. In addition, the brothers compensated through work: they had six hours of formal schooling six days a week at the Lyzeum and another four or five hours of private lessons daily. Though this schedule was imposed upon them to a great degree, the brothers also wanted to prove themselves and become the best pupils at the school. In some instances they suffered slights because of their "low" social status, and this treatment caused them to work even harder to win the respect and admiration of their peers and teachers. Moreover, they wanted to live up to their dead father's expectations and pursue their studies at a university to become lawyers. The four years of rigorous schooling in Kassel did not have a negative effect on Jacob's health and constitution. Instead the training strengthened his resolve to succeed and to help his mother bring up the four other children in an orderly fashion. For Wilhelm, whose physical stamina was weaker than Jacob's, the pace brought about an attack of scarlet fever and asthma, from which he suffered the rest of his life, and he had to postpone his studies at the university for one year.

Despite the talents of the brothers and their accomplishments at the Lyzeum, they both needed special dispensations to study law at the University of Marburg because they lacked the proper social qualifications. Again the Grimms turned such unfair policy into a just cause to motivate themselves; that is, they were motivated to show how unjust the class favoritism was by excelling at the university and in their scholarly work. Loss and injustice were to be overcome by industry, diligence, and dedication to goodness and justice. Dreams of a better bourgeois life were put into action.

The years at Marburg—1802–5 for Jacob; 1803–6 for Wilhelm— were hard ones: they lived like ascetics and had little money and clothes to participate fully in the student social life. At the same time both became increasingly aware of their deep desire to study old German literature, which was not bound to be profitable. This choice, one that meant abandoning their dead father's legal profession, was somewhat ironic since it was Friedrich Karl von Savigny, the young professor of law, who influenced them to take an interest in old German literature, customs, and traditions through the study of law. It was Savigny's historical approach to jurisprudence, his belief in the organic connection of all cultural creations of the *Volk* to the historical development of this *Volk,* which drew the attention of the Grimms. Furthermore, Savigny stressed that the present could only be fully grasped and appreciated by understanding the past. Therefore, he insisted that one must study the legal system synchronically and diachronically to establish the connection between the customs, beliefs, values, and laws of a people. For Savigny—and also for the Grimms— culture was originally the common property of all members of a *Volk.* This culture became divided over the years into different realms such as law, literature, religion, and so on, and their cohesion could only be restored through historical study. Savigny saw his mission, as researcher and professor of law, to be to reconstitute the development of the legal system so that the German people might retain certain truths about their culture and use them as building blocks for a better future. The Brothers Grimm felt that language rather than law was the ultimate bond that united the German people. They were thus more drawn to the study of old German literature, though they were in agreement with Savigny's methods and with his desire to create a better future for the German people.

The interest in literature was stimulated to a great extent by the German romantics, in particular Ludwig Tieck, Clemens Brentano, and Achim von Arnim, who introduced them to the folk literature of the European-German Middle Ages. However, the Grimms felt that Tieck, Brentano, and Arnim tampered too much with the old German literature, and therefore began collecting chapbooks (*Volksbücher*) and documents about German customs and beliefs to preserve the "pure" essence of folk culture. They threw themselves into the study of both old German literature and law in their typically intense manner so that, by the time Jacob left Marburg in 1805 to go and work with Savigny as a research assistant in Paris, they were well on their way to becoming formidable scholars of old German literature—all this at the tender ages of nineteen and twenty.

What fascinated the Grimms and compelled them to concentrate on old German literature was a belief that the most natural and pure forms of culture—those which held the community together—were linguistic and were to be located in the past. Moreover, modern literature, even though it might be remarkably rich, was artificial and thus could not express the genuine essence of *Volk* culture which bound a people together. In their letters between 1807 and 1812 and in such early essays as Jacob's "Von Übereinstimmung der alten Sagen" (1807) and "Gedanken wie sich die Sagen zur Poesie und Geschichte verhalten" (1808) and Wilhelm's "Über die Entstehung der deutschen Poesie und ihr Verhältnis zu der nordischen" (1809), they began to formulate similar views about the origins of literature based on tales and legends, or what was once oral literature. The purpose of their collecting folk songs, tales, proverbs, legends, and documents was to write a history of old German poetic literature and to demonstrate how artistic literature evolved out of traditional folk material and how this new *Kunstpoesie* gradually forced *Naturpoesie* (tales, legends, etc.) to recede during the Renaissance and take refuge among the folk in an oral tradition. According to the Grimms, there was a danger in this development that the natural folk forms would be forgotten and neglected, and thus the Grimms saw their task as literary historians to be the preservation of the *pure* sources of modern German literature and to reveal the debt or connection of literate culture to the oral tradition. In two important letters to Achim von Arnim, Jacob stated his position on this matter most clearly—a position that was shared wholeheartedly by Wilhelm:

> Poesy is that which only emanates from the soul and turns into words, thus it springs continually from a natural drive and innate ability to capture this drive—folk poesy stems from the soul of the entire community (*das Ganze*). What I call art poesy (*Kunstpoesie*) stems from the individual. That is why the new poetry names its poets; the old knows none to name. It was not made by one or two or three, but it is the sum of the entire community. We cannot explain how all came together and was brought forth. But it is not any more mysterious than the manner in which the water gathers in a river in order to flow together. It is inconceivable to me that there could have been a Homer or author of the *Nibelungen*. . . . The old poesy is completely like the old language, simple and only rich in itself. In the old language there are nothing but simple words, but they are in themselves so capable of such great reflection and flexibility that the language performs wonders. The new language has lost innocence and has become richer outwardly, but this is through synthesis and coincidence, and therefore it sometimes needs greater preparation in order to express a simple sentence. . . . In addition the old poesy has a form of eternal validity that evolves from itself; the artful form passes over the secret of this and ultimately does not need it any longer. . . . Therefore, I see in art poesy or whatever you want

to call it what I designate as preparation, even though the word is good and does not refer to anything dead or mechanical. In the nature poesy there is something that emanates from itself.

May 20, 1811[7]

All my work, this is what I feel, is based on learning and showing how a great narrative poesy (*epische Poesie*) has lived and held sway all over the earth, how the people have gradually forgotten and neglected it, perhaps not entirely, but how the people are nourished by it. In this way a history of poesy is for me based on something unfathomable, something that cannot be entirely learned, and something that provides real pleasure.

October 29, 1812[8]

Between 1802 and 1812, the Grimms knew they had to establish careers for themselves as quickly as possible to look after the rest of the family. Out of a sense of loss of their father they became absorbed by a quest to reconstitute the old German tradition in its oral and written forms so that it would not fade from the memory of the German people. Put more positively, the Grimms saw old German literature as the repository of valid truths concerning German culture. In particular, they believed that a philological understanding of old German literature would enable Germans to grasp the connections between the customs, laws, and beliefs of the German people and their origins. In addition, by comparing the motifs and themes in the German tales and legends with those from other countries, they hoped to learn more about the distinctive qualities of German culture. Such a desire to reconstitute the old German tradition in its pure form, I want to emphasize again, was based on a desire to resurrect the authority of their father and his heritage, to regain a lost, untarnished home or realm. Simultaneously this pure, innocent realm was implicitly upheld as better than the artificial realm of the ruling class. The quest to uncover the truths of the old German tradition was unconsciously a desire to prove the worth of the Grimms' personal bourgeois ethics. Their values were based to a great extent on the reformed Calvinist religion, the faith in which they were raised. It was due to their religious beliefs and upbringing that they stressed diligence, industry, honesty, order, and cleanliness as the ingredients necessary for success. Indeed, the Grimms were success-oriented, and their value system based on the Protestant ethos favored a utilitarian function within the formation of the German bourgeois public sphere, as Jürgen Habermas has described it.[9] Therefore, the Grimms' ethics assumed the form of self-validation that was also a validation of patriarchy in the family and public realm. To this extent, the elaboration of their ethics in their tales has left us with problems in socialization through literature that still have to be resolved.

As I have already tried to show, the merging of the personal and the political in the Grimms' work on folk and fairy tales can be attributed to various circumstances that affected their lives between 1802 and 1812. And there is more to be considered here.

When Jacob began his studies at Marburg in 1802, he felt under pressure to make a quick career choice and begin helping his mother, who was barely managing to look after the other four children and whose health was rapidly deteriorating. After his trip to Paris with Savigny in 1805, he realized that he would never have the money to carry on extensive research in that particular field of law, as only a rich man could afford to do. Moreover, he wanted to stay close to his family in Hessia, and a law profession would have demanded that he travel a great deal and live elsewhere. To help the family, which was now installed in Kassel, Jacob abandoned his formal studies and took a job in 1806 with the war ministry (Kriegskollegium) while two of his younger brothers, Ferdinand and Ludwig, attended the Lyzeum. Wilhelm joined him in the spring of that year after he had passed the law examinations, but he could not find employment because of the Napoleonic wars and the military situation. Both brothers were now completely dedicated to the study of old German literature, but since Jacob was the only breadwinner for the entire family, they were plagued by financial difficulties that hampered their work and hurt their health. Not only was there very little to eat and wear, but the French made matters even worse by defeating Prussia in the fall of 1806. Kassel was occupied by French forces, and early in 1807 Jacob resigned his position at the Kriegskollegium. Thus, for a while no one was earning money to support the family. Wilhelm, who was suffering from asthmatic attacks, had to postpone a cure treatment, and the family sought outside help for support. Then, in May of 1808, the Grimms' mother died. Her loss was felt deeply by everyone in the family. In his letter to their aunt Henriette Zimmer, who had taken refuge with the royal family of Kassel in Gotha, Jacob wrote: "We are now in the most inconsolable and saddest condition and still do not know how to help ourselves. . . . God will give you the strength to bear these ill tidings more easily. I cannot write anything more."[10]

Fortunately for the family, and despite his aversion toward French rule, Jacob was able to obtain the position of librarian for King Jérome's personal library in Kassel, and he could help the family regain some financial stability. However, Wilhelm's health became so poor that, in 1809, he had to travel to Halle for several months to be treated for his asthma and a weak heart. At the same time, Ludwig left home to study art at the academy in Munich, creating additional financial burdens. The separation between Jacob and Wilhelm was just as painful as all their earlier separations and perhaps even more so, because it came soon after their mother's death and led to certain misunderstandings. Wilhelm felt guilty that he had left Jacob alone to look after the welfare of the family, and Jacob, though unwilling to admit it, resented being left alone to cope with all the family problems—lack of food and clothing, the difficulties caused by Ferdinand and Carl, who were unsuccessful in their endeavors to establish careers for themselves. In 1810, Wilhelm, still unemployed, rejoined Jacob in Kassel, and together they began preparing their first book publications. Nevertheless, the pecuniary situation of the Grimms did not allow for a conducive atmosphere for their work, or, put another way, they had to work under the most adverse conditions as young scholars while preparing major publications on folklore. Wilhelm's letter of May 11, 1812, is most revealing with regard to the way the Grimms had been living during the past several years:

> We recently received a letter from Ludwig. He is healthy and industrious. Of course, he is costing us a lot of money, and that is the reason why we cannot make do with our yearly income. We curtail our needs as much as propriety allows, but we cannot go much further. If we had another source from which we could draw our income, we could live well off it, but it does not work here. We five people eat only three portions and only once a day. I usually save something for breakfast because I cannot bear waiting until five o'clock. Jacob usually eats only breakfast when each of us drinks but a single cup of coffee and eats nothing more than milk bread. We have done away with tea because sugar is much too expensive. But we cannot go around wearing improper clothing.[11]

In addition to this letter, there are other important ones that portray the Grimms' dreams, hopes, and needs during this difficult period. On June 25, 1809, Jacob wrote to Wilhelm:

My wish for me and for us is a small city of 2,000 to 3,000 people where we could stay. I would like to know how things will continue for me because so much repulses me now that I cannot concentrate. I know that, even though I am for my part completely calm when I work. If God would only grant us just enough so we could lead an outwardly moderate life, independent from earning money.... In any case there must be peace in Germany first. Oh, if only God could provide peace. For my part, I do not believe that people in Germany have ever prayed for anything with such accord and in such a noble way. I could give up everything for this and let everything drop, and often I think how is it possible not to keep thinking about it and how sinful it is that one is passionately involved with other things. If only the misfortune would stop just once.[12]

Wilhelm replied to Jacob on July 1, 1809:

Why not go directly to a village in the country like Allendorf where it is so beautiful, quiet, and peaceful, or nearer to a large city? For I don't see why we should give up all the advantages of a large city out of opposition, and in this way we could keep the advantages of both. Even more, I'd love to ask God for a farm estate where it would be even more quiet. Sometimes a friend would visit. In addition, there would be the glorious pleasure of a garden.[13]

Later that year, on September 10, 1809, Jacob wrote to Wilhelm again indicating how much he felt the loss of their mother and a real home: "Oh, if only our mother were still alive. Since her death our house has become uncomfortable because there is nothing that binds us together, and there is no longer any order at mealtime. Often I feel as though I would like to go to an inn, perhaps because I must concern myself with so many petty details or listen to them. And I feel for certain that if one lives moderately and quietly as we do, then order and cleanliness are the things that matter most."[14]

There is an interesting connection that could be made here between the Grimms' almost desperate search for a stable home, order, and cleanliness and their social concern for the welfare of Germany disturbed by war and the French occupation. The personal becomes very much political in their work, and their act of collecting folktales and reconstituting them according to their needs and ethical notions of the pure German language and literature was essentially an act of compensation for the loss of father and homeland. Here I also want to suggest that the Grimms' controversial lines in their preface to the

1812 edition of the *Kinder- und Hausmärchen* must be understood as part of their sincere if not obsessive endeavor to restore respectability to themselves and the German people and to regain their lost heritage. Let us reconsider what they stated in that preface:

> We have tried to write down these tales as purely as possible. In many cases the story is interrupted by rhymes and verses which sometimes even clearly alliterate, but they are never sung while being told, and precisely these are the oldest and the best. No circumstance has been added through our poetic efforts or embellished or changed, for we would have shied from augmenting tales that were so rich in themselves with their own analogy and reference. They cannot be invented. There is no collection of this kind yet in Germany. One has almost always used the tales only as material in order to make longer narratives out of them. They have been arbitrarily expanded and changed to get the most value out of them. Whatever the case may be, that which belongs to children has always been torn out of their hands, and nothing has been given to them in return.[15]

Important here is not the misleading assertion that the Grimms did not change, embellish, or augment anything but rather the emphasis on preserving the tales "as purely as possible" and restoring a heritage to children that was "torn out of their hands." The Grimms obviously used their original handwritten notations of the tales as drafts for the more complete versions they developed for the 1812 publication. The changes they made were intended to respect the purity of the oral tales as they had heard them. To be sure, they embellished their tales, both oral and literary, but in no way did they take great liberties in the manner of Musäus, Goethe, Wieland, Tieck, and Brentano, who developed the genre of the artistic fairy tale in Germany. Moreover, given the inconsistencies and roughness of the tales in the Ölenberg manuscript of 1810, the Grimms' evidently planned to reconstitute the originals from the beginning in a manner they believed would best represent the pure folk style. As Heinz Röllcke has argued,[16] it appears that the two dialect tales by Phillip Otto Runge, *The Fisherman and His Wife* and *The Juniper Tree,* served as their models. Certainly, there is some truth to this, but I would argue that the Grimms were influenced by a variety of gifted storytellers, and it seems to me that they were striving to synthesize many different stylistic elements to create their own model of the ideal folk narrator as they prepared the first edition for the press. At the same time, though, they used their aesthetic and ideological preferences in selecting and reworking the motifs in tales that had a bearing on their own lives.

To illustrate this last point I want to discuss two tales that focus on the brother-sister relationship and the reconstitution of family and home. Here it is possible to argue that the Grimms, whose temperaments were quite different (Jacob, the reticient recluse, the strong, indefatigable writer; Wilhelm, the outgoing, cheerful brother, but tender in health) unconsciously saw their own relationship in the brother-sister relationship (among others) and reconstituted the tales along personal lines. Certainly, the notion of home and household in the tales is very much shaped by the Grimms' need for order (*Ordnung*) and cleanliness (*Reinlichkeit*).

As I have pointed out elsewhere,[17] the portrayal of the family in the Grimms' tales reflects the dissolution of the original family, whereby the protagonist or protagonists must go on a quest to establish a new realm. The loss of family must be compensated by the recreation of a new type of family that incorporates a sense of the Grimms' own bourgeois ethics. Two good examples of the reconstitution of home can be found in "Twelve Brothers" and "Brother and Sister."

In the Ölenberg manuscript, "Twelve Brothers" has the title "Twelve Brothers and the Little Sister." The original handwritten version was recorded by Jacob, while Wilhelm prepared the text for the 1812 publication. The pattern of the oral tale is basically retained. The twelve brothers, who are threatened by their royal father, are saved by their mother's warning. Their sister, who was the cause of all their difficulties, seeks to redeem them. Once she finds and joins them, she takes care of their house but must demonstrate her loyalty to them once more after she inadvertently transforms them into ravens. Though she marries a king and is threatened by a jealous mother-in-law, she keeps silent for twelve years and is saved by her brothers before she can be burned at the stake. Wilhelm's reworking of the tale emphasizes two factors: the dedication of the sister and brothers to one another, and the establishment of a common, orderly household in the forest, where they lived peacefully together.

Aside from reinforcing their notions of industry, cleanliness, and order, Wilhelm was obviously drawn to the tale—as Jacob was too— because of its theme: *several* or more brothers and *one* sister overcome adversity after separation from their parents. The parents are never mentioned again, that is, their loss is permanent, and it is clear that the brothers and the sister, whose reputation is restored at the end, will have a new home and live together in contentment. This theme was so appealing to the Grimms that Jacob later translated a similar tale, "The Seven Doves," from Basile's *Pentamerone.*

Jacob also translated a version of "Brother and Sister" from the *Pentamerone,* though the Grimms' 1812 version of "Brother and Sister" did not rely on Basile's work: it was based on oral tales gathered by both brothers and prepared for publication by Wilhelm. The plot of the oral tales concerns a brother and sister who wander in the forest. The brother is changed into a doe because he drinks water from an enchanted spring. His sister takes care of him and remains faithful to him even after she marries a king. However, the king's mother endeavors to ruin her reputation and to have her put to death. In the end, the sister's innocence wins the day.

The changes made by Wilhelm in the 1812 publication are much greater in this tale than the ones he made in "The Twelve Brothers," but the synthesis of the variants recorded by him and Jacob does not distort the essence of the tale type. The new components do, however, give us an idea of what the Grimms themselves felt were important for an ideal family life:

1. The brother and sister are forced to go into the forest because their mother has died and their stepmother beats them. Loss brings about injustice that must be overcome.

2. The brother and sister set up a quiet, comfortable household in the forest. This is not a totally ideal state yet, but a transitional one.

3. Their stepmother discovers that the sister has married a king and has given birth to a child. She goes to the castle with her own ugly daughter and kills the sister. The evil forces come from the outside.

4. The sister shows her devotion to her brother and child by returning to the castle and asking after them. Such loyalty is emphasized throughout the Grimms' tales.

5. Once the sister returns to life, the stepmother is punished, and the brother and sister are reunited in a new realm in which justice prevails. The ideal state is a reconstitution of personal and political relations.

There are numerous sibling tales[18] that were collected by the Grimms, who reworked and revised them to convey their notions of family, ethical behavior, and homeland. The ideals which are stressed in their reconstitution of home were based on a sense of loss and what they felt should be retained if their own family and Germany were to be united. In the process of reconstitution they shaped their dreams of a better life, dreams they reformulated in their remarkable collection and integrated into the entire corpus that we are still interpreting with a belief in its therapeutic utopian power. Yet, as much as the Grimms were intent on reconstituting the tales with powerful utopian motifs and themes to validate their bourgeois notions of a better world, we must ask whether these dreams are valid today, for there are many oral and literary tales in our present society that surpass the utopian vision of the Grimms. Nonetheless, despite the shortcomings in the Grimms' tales, such as the sexist stereotyping and fetishism with regard to order and industry, it is still worthwhile to reconsider why the Grimms dreamt and worked as they did, in order that we may better understand the nature and thrust of our contemporary tales.

Notes

1. Herman Grimm, Gustav Hinrichs, and Wilhelm Schoof (eds.), *Briefwechsel zwischen Jacob und Wilhelm Grimm aus der Jugendzeit,* 2d rev. ed. (Weimar: Hermann Böhlaus Nachfolger, 1963), p. 67. This and all subsequent translations into English are my own, unless otherwise indicated.

2. Ibid., p. 75.

3. Bruno Bettelheim, *The Uses of Enchantment: The Meaning and Importance of Fairy Tales* (New York: Knopf, 1976).

4. Alexander Mitscherlich, *Society without the Father* (New York: Schocken, 1970), pp. 300–301.

5. Irma Hildebrandt, *Es waren ihrer Fünf: Die Brüder Grimm und ihre Familie* (Cologne: Eugen Diederichs, 1984), pp. 34–35.

6. Ibid., pp. 11–30.

7. Gabriele Seitz, *Die Brüder Grimm: Leben—Werk—Zeit* (Munich: Winkler, 1984), p. 48.

8. Gunhild Ginschel, *Der junge Jacob Grimm 1805–1819* (Berlin: Akademie-Verlag, 1967), p. 40.

9. Jürgen Habermas, *Strukturwandel der Öffentlichkeit* (Berlin: Luchterhand, 1962).

10. Seitz, p. 19.

11. Ibid., p. 31.

12. Herman Grimm et al. (eds.), *Briefwechsel,* p. 115.

13. Ibid., p. 119.

14. Ibid., p. 156.

15. Jacob Grimm and Wilhelm Grimm, *Kinder- und Hausmärchen der Brüder*

Grimm: Vollständige Ausgabe in der Urfassung, ed. Friedrich Panzer (Wiesbaden: Emil Vollmer, [1955]), p. 61.

16. See Heinz Rölleke, *Die Märchen der Brüder Grimm* (Munich: Artemis, 1985), pp. 52–60.

17. See the chapter "The Fight Over Fairy-Tale Discourse: Family, Friction, and Socialization" in Jack Zipes, *Fairy Tales and the Art of Subversion* (New York: Wildman, 1983), pp. 134–69.

18. Altogether there are eight tales focusing on the brother-sister relationship; ten on the sister-sister relationship; nineteen on the brother-brother relationship.

BETSY HEARNE

Booking the Brothers Grimm: Art, Adaptations, and Economics

DOING RESEARCH in juvenile publishing bears more resemblance to eavesdropping than to quantitative analysis. Publishers are loath to give out figures on the sales of a book, the percentages that are sold to institutional or trade markets, the advance and royalty fees to author, illustrator, or translator. One finds out these figures by listening carefully through many years of conversations with those who create, edit, and publish children's books. The ideas expressed here, based on more than a decade of eavesdropping as a book review editor, are exploratory and suggest several areas where statistical substantiation is revealing when it can be had.

My hypothesis is this, that while fairy tales, especially the Grimms', have been analyzed as recurrent for their aesthetic, psychological, cultural, and historical importance, there is a further reason for their perpetuation and popularity: the economics of publishing. I would like to point out four general time periods in England and the United States where this is particularly apparent and examine the last closely, considering some of the artistic and textural effects of recent economic shifts in juvenile publishing. Bear with me while I back up a bit before the Grimms, for a few obvious points, just to set the stage.

In the eighteenth and early nineteenth centuries, when juvenile publishing was beginning in England, chapbooks depended on folklore—then considered the lowest common denominator of public taste—for text. Fairy tales were short, readable, flexible to illustrate, easy to pirate and adapt, acceptable to lower-class families if not to educators, and accessibly numerous. In fact, not much else was available yet. Publishers had not invested time and money in developing writers for children. Aside from the odd lady poet or preacher, no one was interested in crafting stories for children. It's extremely important to remember that John Newbery's early publishing efforts were seen as an extension and booster of toy sales, not a new literary vision. Fairy tales populated chapbook texts by default.

The second half of the nineteenth century did see the growth and enrichment of children's literature by works of artistic and literary genius, but the growth of the children's book industry easily outstripped the amount of original work available. Furthermore, folklore was swinging into educational vogue, toward the end of the century, after years of disgrace. Through the work of folklore societies and educational philosophers, fairy tales were getting a seal of approval just at a time when childhood was becoming enough of a well-defined state to bear the weight of marketing strategies. And practically speaking, the Grimms' tales, widely circulated after the 1823 Edgar Taylor translation, offered the most numerous group from which to choose.

Andrew Lang's fairy-tale collections, which were published between 1889 and 1910 and drew heavily on Grimms' tales, represented a revolutionary packaging device. Many of the stories themselves were generally available to the public, but Lang's twelve uniform volumes, each entitled by a different color, had a neat, encyclopedic appearance. Their success derived partly from what we now call brand name identity. The Home Treasury, Aunt Mavor's Toy Books, the Richardson Chapbook series, Little Plays for Little People, Aunt Mary's Series, Walter Crane's Toy Books, and Gordon Browne's series of Old Fairy Tales were all examples of successful series. None, however, had the impact of Lang's authoritative editorial reputation (Felix Summerly notwithstanding) combined with the consistent packaging and wide distribution of Lang's books. His publishing enterprise was of enormous importance in extending an interest in fairy-tale reading for children, which had been temporarily obscured by the "child's story of real life," according to Mrs. E. M. Field's 1892 survey, quoted by Brian Alderson in his appendix to the new Lang editions.[1] Alderson also points out that the contemporary *Bookseller* called *The Blue Fairy Tale Book* "amongst the most popular juvenile gifts of the time," and its stories were excerpted for a series of school editions, Longman's Supplementary Readers, which spurred many imitative collections.[2] Its success immediately generated a commission for further volumes in red, green, yellow, pink, violet, and so on, a sales gimmick that assured a market among parents looking for the stamp of familiar value and among children, who love to collect anything, from bugs to books in a series.

Although Lang did fear that his work as a scholar in the Folk-Lore Society might be overshadowed by the famous series, his reduction of so many fairy tales to a similarity of style did not seem to dismay contemporaries, who included Joseph Jacobs and E. S. Hartland. His adaptations were smooth and witty enough to entertain parents as well as children. Indeed, Tolkien reproaches him for condescension: "I will not accuse Andrew Lang of sniggering, but certainly he smiled to himself, and certainly too often he had an eye on the faces of other clever people over the heads of his child audience."³

The black-and-white pen drawings by H. J. Ford in Lang's books were also standardized, competent in drafting but unremarkable in artistic impact. The Lang series represented an escalation in the commercializing of fairy tales. The textual modifications and graphic elaborations may seem slight compared to some examples I will give from current editions, but the potential financial value of fairy tales was not lost on juvenile publishers and would have far-reaching effects on the frequency with which, and the form in which, fairy tales would be published.

It is not insignificant that the first children's book department to be established in the United States, Macmillan's, began in 1918, the year World War I ended. In the two decades between World Wars I and II, two important facts coalesced: (1) numerous children's book departments were established, with editors drawn from, or well connected with, a professional pool of children's librarians trained in storytelling and knowledgeable about tales from the oral tradition; and (2) as in the previous two periods mentioned, there were not enough good children's book writers to keep up with the growth spurt in juvenile trade departments, but there was an influx of artists and illustrators immigrating from Europe with close cultural ties to their old country folklore and art. Ann Pellowski cites this as the major "internationalizing" force of U.S. publishing up to 1960.⁴ The single-edition fairy tale emerged as a financially rewarding showcase for their talents and a more commercially viable product for younger children—newly identified as an important market—than previous illustrated collections of fairy tales had been.

The year after the Caldecott Medal was established (1938), Wanda Gág's illustrated edition of *Snow White and the Seven Dwarves* (Coward McCann, 1938) was cited as an Honor Book. During this period, artists steeped in the Grimm tradition or Grimm stories that had resurfaced in Scandanavian, French, Italian, or East European and Russian areas included Wanda Gág, Boris Artzybasheff, Feodor Rojankovsky, Ingri and Edgar D'Aulaire, Fritz Eichenberg, Nicolas Mordvinoff, Kurt Weise, and Nicolas Sidjakov. Although not all of these artists illustrated Grimm stories, they set the precedent for single-edition fairy-tale picture books and created a climate for folkloristic or popularized styles that represented a distinct break in tradition from the fine-art illustration of previous fairy-tale collections illustrated by Walter Crane, Arthur Rackham, Edmund Dulac, and their contemporaries.

Until 1970, single-edition folk and fairy tales made a steady appearance in Caldecott Award and Honor Book citations, but after 1970 there was a dramatic jump toward predominance of folk/fairy-tale materials, culminating in the 1985 selection, when the winner and three out of four Honor Books, "Hansel and Gretel" among them, were single-edition folk or fairy tales. This selection of titles is indicative of a general economic trend, in the decade between 1975 and 1985, that has rejuvenated the place of fairy tales in children's literature more vigorously than ever before.

In the mid-1970s, federal funding to schools and libraries dropped sharply, resulting in institutional book-budget cutting all over the country. Moreover, a deepening recession made the public increasingly loath to vote tax support for libraries. Traditionally, publishers estimated that 85 percent of juvenile books were sold to libraries. That figure subsequently dropped to as low as 25 percent for some publishers. In an attempt to replace institutional sales, publishers turned to the bookstore trade and tried to catch the parental eye with art in all shapes and sizes.

Graphics carry the day when adults select on sight, with limited time in the store and limited personal knowledge of children's literature. Fairy tales are a favorite subject for stunning pictures. They make attractive, low-risk gifts—it's always safe to give fairy tales, especially Grimms', especially now that their developmental value has been endorsed by Bruno Bettelheim.

There is, then, a decrease in publishers' development of new writers whose original stories would not sell reliably to the general public and an increase in folk/fairy tales, which are in the public domain and therefore available at no expense. The publisher gets a more marketable product, the illustrator gets the whole 10–12 percent royalty fee (a steady figure over the last several decades) instead of splitting it fifty-fifty with an author. Most illustrators can't write, and they're just as greedy as the rest of us. Not to be too cynical, the best artists are indeed drawn to the depth and scope of fairy-tale material, and their established reputations allow them the choice of doing "their own" Sleeping Beauty, Cinderella, Snow White, or whatever story retains the grandeur of their childhood impressions. Many spend more than a year on every book, sometimes twelve-hour days, and they want a worthy focus, a dream come true, so to speak. They'll let the neophytes spend energy on cozy, domestic, run-of-the-mill, contemporary, or untried tales.

Three other factors are as important as U.S. national economic forces in enabling publishers to push lavish editions of fairy tales: first, new and dramatically cheaper technologies of full-color art reproduction (along with cost-cutting Far Eastern printing establishments); second, the publishers' escalation and public's enthusiastic acceptance of paperback editions; and third and most important, the movement toward co-production between American and British or European publishers, which can result in doubling print runs per book by 10,000–15,000 copies, thus allowing publishers on both sides of the ocean to keep costs at a minimum. And of course, what picture books cross the seas better than fairy tales, the literary coin of both realms? Contemporary domestic stories often present problems of cultural difference. The pictures may translate well, but the story may present too many unfamiliar elements of everyday life that would confuse young children. Often the fairy-tale texts don't require translation expense, either, since so many versions are already available in so many languages.

In addition to single-edition fairy-tale illustration by artists such as Trina Schart Hyman, Paul Galdone, Michael Hague, Mercer Mayer, Linda Bryan Cauley, Susan Jeffers, and Lisbeth Zwerger, all of whom have achieved nearly brand name sales status, there has been in the last two years an increase in the number of illustrated collections. While old favorites like Wanda Gág's *Grimm Tales* and *More Grimm Tales* (Coward McCann, 1936), Lore Segal and Maurice Sendak's *The Juniper Tree and Other Tales from Grimm* (Farrar, Straus, and Giroux, 1973), and Grosset and Dunlap's generic Illustrated Classics series volume are still going strong, new rivals are multiplying like rabbits. Within the last publishing season alone, several major collections have hit the market and are selling heavily in bookstores.

It is sometimes difficult to quantify the pervasive appearance of Grimm stories in such collections without actually counting them in the books. Since there are rarely any source notes, the Grimms do not appear in cataloguing cards, tracings, or bibliographies. The Grimms' version of "Little Red Riding Hood," for instance, appears in *The Baby's Story Book*, a collection of fifteen tales cited simply as "classics" in the book jacket, illustrated by Kay Chorao and published in fall of 1985 for $11.95 by Dutton, which recommends it for ages one to six (a sign of fairy tales edging into the toddler market). Another fall 1985 collection, *Helen Oxenbury's Nursery Story Book*, published by Knopf for $12.95, includes "Little Red Riding Hood" and "The Elves and the Shoemaker," also with no indication of source for any of the ten tales.

Even where title pages acknowledge the Grimms as the source, the Library of Congress, according to revised cataloguing rules, enters single-edition fairy tales and even many collections under adapter or illustrator. A 1985 book entitled *The Glass Mountain*, for instance, does have the following information on the title page: "Retold from the tale by the Brothers Grimm (originally entitled 'The Raven') and illustrated by Nonny Hogrogian." However, the CIP (cataloguing in publication), followed by most librarians and bibliographers, has Nonny Hogrogian as the main entry, with no reference to the Grimms even in the story's description.

The big new *Random House Book of Fairy Tales*, adapted by Amy Ehrlich, illustrated by Diane Goode, and introduced by Bruno Bettelheim (who seems to have forgotten his injunction against illustration in fairy tales), features more than twice as many stories from Grimm as from any other source. This collection, which does mention whether stories are from Grimm, Perrault, Andersen, or others, is nevertheless entered under the adapter, Amy Ehrlich. Its cover and illustrations are dominated by a reassuring sweet pink for popularized family gift-giving. In fact, Random House is leading many publishers in the exploration of fairy-tale markets beyond the institutional and trade store sales to mass market merchandizing.

In addition to the several general collections that include Grimm stories, others in the same season have concentrated on the Grimms entirely. *About Wise Men and Simpletons*, a beautiful edition of twelve Grimm tales translated by Elizabeth Shub with etchings by Nonny Hogrogian (Macmillan, 1971) has been reissued. Kevin Crossley-Holland's eleven selections for *The Fox and the Cat* (Lothrop, Lee, and

Shepard) suit a young age group, since most of the animal tales are brief and action-packed. These are also smoothly translated, with a fillip of humor in the diction ("You shabby whisker-licker, you spotted idiot, you poor scrounger and mouse-hunter, have you gone out of your mind?"). The watercolor paintings, some full-page and others smaller oval insets that relieve the text, are full of vitality and fine-line wit. The picture of a horse dragging a lion along by its back legs, which are firmly tied by the horse's tail, is typically lively.

The fourteen stories in *The Twelve Dancing Princesses,* edited by Naomi Lewis, illustrated by Lidia Postma, and published by Dial Press, are longer and more sophisticated, but they represent an appealing mix of old favorites like "Cinderella" and less common ones, such as "The Nixie of the Mill Pond." These have been slightly adapted, but not seriously tampered with. "Cinderella" alters the rhymes, for instance, but with full respect for literal meanings. Most extraordinary are Postma's haunting illustrations, which range in style from surreal to impressionistic to precise without seeming to break continuity. Most often, the muted colors and eerie compositions are meant to suggest rather than define, a provocative quality that is well matched with the imaginative depth of the tales.

Packaging, most bookstore dealers maintain, is crucial to how well these collections—all published in the space of a few months—will compete with each other. The combination of shiny covers, appealing art and format (popular rather than sophisticated), a sturdy binding— the look of the book is all. A generous number of favorite selections, mostly or perhaps entirely from the Grimms, with a few unknown variations for spice, sometimes a big-name introduction (as in Bettelheim's introduction to the 1985 Random House edition or Richard Adams's for the 1982 Routledge edition illustrated by Pauline Ellison), and of course a manageable price tag are important though often somewhat secondary considerations. Only the discriminating buyer has the background to consider real artistic and textual differences among the myriad fairy-tale versions available in both collections and single editions, which brings us to a crucial question: what are the aesthetic results of the economic forces and commercial pressures stimulating such a renaissance in the production of fairy-tale editions? How are the artistic and textual aspects modified, if at all, in the competition for broader markets?

I would summarize the general impact of adaptation in popularized picture-book editions of Grimm tales as one of toning down effects, of softening the bone-hard elements of plot, character, theme, symbolic imagery, and style—of eliminating the tales' sharp edges. A recent edition of "The Cat and the Mouse Set up Housekeeping" offers a good example. This has always been a troubling tale, with its stark warning of what happens to gullible mice who are foolish enough to set up housekeeping with a cat. However, that monition is its power as well. In *Godfather Cat and Mouse* (Macmillan, 1986), adapter Doris Orgel has offered an alternative to the mouse's being peremptorily gobbled up, by providing two possible endings ("some people say . . . " but "I say . . . "). In the first, Mousie is eaten; but in the second, she escapes through a hole she has gnawed in hunger, finds a new home with her rodent relatives, and leaves the cat forever watching shame-faced beside that mousehole. To this end, the story itself has been slightly altered to foreshadow the escape, but otherwise the abridg-ment does maintain close ties to the Grimms' version. Illustrator Ann Schweninger's earth-tone colors are subtly blended with simply defined linework, graceful shapes, and artfully framed compositions. There's a real world established in the art, serene on the surface, slightly menac-ing underneath, but ultimately orderly and controlled. This is a carefully—but nonetheless strategically—reshaped version, more attrac-tive to most parents, less forceful as folklore.

As early childhood development studies and baby-boom buyers expand the demand for literature for the youngest child, fairy tales are extended to an ever younger audience. "The Cat and Mouse Set up Housekeeping" is an extremely simple story, as easy in its action as "The Three Billy Goats Gruff" for children three to six years old to grasp. Thus it's a logical choice for a book for the very young. Yet its theme—that the aggressive gobble the gullible—is not for very young children. Therefore Doris Orgel, an excellent, experienced, Viennese-born writer, and Ann Schweninger, a meticulous artist, have drasti-cally altered the impact of this Grimm tale because of a basic shift in the market.

For a more consistent idea of what happens to a tale in its picture-book metamorphoses, I examined several editions of "Sleeping Beauty" that have been published in the past decade of drastic market shifts. The six versions I studied are representative of editions sent to the Center for Children's Books, a University of Chicago library which has received almost all of the juvenile trade books published annually since 1947 for review in a professional journal, *The Bulletin of the Center for Children's Books.* Three of the picture books are typical of expensive, lavish editions created by illustrators both widely acclaimed and prolific of single-edition fairy tales: Trina Schart Hyman (Little, Brown, 1977), Warwick Hutton (Margaret K. McElderry Books, 1979), and Mercer Mayer (Macmillan, 1984). According to title page statements, all three artists "retold" the stories themselves (Hyman's previous *Snow White* had been translated by Paul Heins). In other words, none shared royalties with a translator or adapter. At the time of publication, the books cost $7.95, $9.95, and $14.95 respectively, an increase of almost 100 percent in seven years for basically the same quality product. This increase was, according to the publishers, less profit margin than a reflection of escalating costs for paper and production.

The other three books are typical of a different kind of publishing entirely, the mass market. The first, *Sleeping Beauty with Benjy and Bubbles* (Holt, Rinehart, and Winston, 1979), is part of a "Read to Me" series, adapted by Ruth Perle and illustrated by Giulio Maestro, a prolific but uneven illustrator who does a large variety of children's books. The second, *How to Wake a Sleeping Beauty,* is part of a series called "The Magic Road" books (Grosset and Dunlap, 1984). It is a choose-your-own-ending oversize paperback written and illustrated by Kevin Scally. The third is *Sleeping Beauty* (Silver Burdett, 1985), part of the "Tell Me a Story" series, retold by M. Eulalia Valeri, translated by Leland Northam, and illustrated by Fina Rifa. This last version, and Hyman's, are the only two of the six which attribute the story to the Grimms, reflecting the problem, pointed out previously, of tracking down Grimm editions for an accurate count since titles can vary widely and adapters have become the main entry form. At the time of their publication, these books were $2.95, $3.95, and $3.75, respectively, representing a rise of slightly less than 30 percent over a six-year period. Mass-market print runs (usually 20,000 to 50,000 for juvenile books) would keep the prices low in relation to prices of trade counterparts (5,000 to 10,000 copies of most titles).

Both the adaptations and the art vary enormously among the six versions. The retellings range from a close rendition of the Grimms' "Briar Rose" to a version retaining only a few elements from it; the illustration ranges from fine art to cartoons, with very little of the folk-art influence seen in the 1930s to 1950s editions, nor of the less-is-more simplicity of style evident in Felix Hoffmann's vigorously spare *Sleeping Beauty,* published by Margaret K. McElderry at Harcourt, Brace, and Jovanovich in 1960. The unanimous choice of the Grimm version (though with no titular mention of Briar Rose) over the Perrault—i.e., the elimination of the Ogress/Queen Mother sequence in the second half of the story—is itself an indication of the "softening" trend mentioned earlier. In most cases of choice between Grimm and Perrault—"Cinderella," for instance—the Perrault is selected because it is the less harsh.

Hyman's *Sleeping Beauty* is an experience in narrative art, with twenty-five scenes framing the text and encompassing the viewer. Rich from the standpoint of design details and composition, the paintings are powerfully drafted and lush with deep hues. Each human is a portrait in action, rather than a stock figure, even in crowd scenes, and the main characters are developed graphically as well as descriptively.

The text itself is graceful, and here, too, the characters, while not overdrawn, are slightly extended: the redhaired princess, for example, is mischievous and clever as well as standardly beautiful, gracious, merry, and kind. There are slight touches of logic added, as in the excluded fairy's being "the oldest and most difficult," along with bits of elegance, such as the description of a hundred years passing: "The sky gathered up the seasons, and time went on" (unpaged).

Although Hyman's book is romantic, it is darkly so; there is stark realism in would-be rescuers' skeletal remains twisted among the thorns. The drama is fully enacted without either sacrifice or over-embellishment of basic elements. Whatever one thinks of Hyman's interpretation, her attention to craft shows deep respect for the story.

Hutton's *Sleeping Beauty* is a more restrained treatment in fifteen scenes, each a full-page painting opposite a page of text—a more formal layout than Hyman's tucking away of texts into curvaceous compositions. The art is elegantly stylized, its verdant hues empha-sized with Hutton's signature effects of sun and shadow in landscape. The text is plainer, shorter, less elaborately phrased, but fully inclusive of plot, character, and symbolic elements. The total effect is less filmic than Hyman's and more conducive to slow-paced absorption—indeed, two wordless double-page spreads bring the reader to a complete halt for thoughtful viewing: one is a sweeping, sunlit panoramic view, from above, of woods and castle during the burning of the spindles; the second is the same view, shadowed, after the woods have taken over the castle. This graphic subtlety indicating the passage of time is typical of Hutton's understatement in matching full-color productions to the spare fairy-tale texts with which he works.

Mercer Mayer, who illustrated a Grimm collection of twenty tales adapted by Nancy Garden in 1982, has taken considerable liberties with Sleeping Beauty. Several of the single-edition fairy tales he has adapted have introduced far-ranging if not bizarre features into traditional tales, a giant salamander and a unicorn into *East of the Sun and West of the Moon* (Four Winds Press, 1980), for instance. The text here introduces new elements of plot and character in addition to motivations for the old. The lonely king initially marries a stable girl and celebrates the wedding with twelve gold goblets for the twelve faeries in his kingdom. But a household manager deep in debt has substituted a gold-coated lead goblet, which falls to the Blue Faerie, who responds angrily: "Never shall you children bear, / For this insult will not repair!"

The good Star Faerie counteracts her: "Never shall you children bear / Until the silver owl appear." The standard green frog is here replaced by a silver owl, which the jealous king slays, leaving his newborn daughter protected only by a blanket the queen has woven from its feathers.

At the christening, the multicolored faeries reappear, but the Blue Faerie has not been invited. She appears, doubly enraged, because the silver owl had been her brother, and makes her second curse. The Star Faerie again softens it. Yet when the Blue Faerie shows up as the old woman and the princess falls asleep, the Star Faerie takes her time about enchanting the others until they have mourned the girl a full year.

To the surrounding thorn hedge Mercer Mayer adds a swamp with adders and vipers, a griffin, and a dwarf, the latter to warn off strangers. The Blue Faerie meanwhile marries a king and has a son, who eventually petitions his father to find the Sleeping Beauty and receives a sword to aid him. After the dwarf asks a test question about whether the prince is willing to forfeit his life for the unseen princess, there follow tests by an ogre, a griffin with the capacity to shrink, and treacherous visions through the swamp.

At the celebration of the prince and princess's wedding, the Blue Faerie shows up angrier than ever for a mother-son confrontation:

> "My blessing here can never be,
> For I shall take my son with me.

> Ashes to ashes and dust to dust,
> All mortals die and so they must.
> A curse I place upon this spot:
> All those with mortal blood shall rot."

The Star Faerie counters her:

> "If one faerie is by another faerie cursed,
> Then all the evil is reversed.
> It will haunt you down and be your own,
> For you must reap what you have sown."

The Blue Faerie is either destroyed, forgiven, or consigned to a convent, according to three suggested alternatives. The multicolored faeries withdraw from mortal company, the prince and princess fade into a somewhat mystically religious ending: "In the vaults of time they are buried together, but beyond time they live in eternity as we all shall do."

This text is sharply reminiscent of some of the eighteenth-century French court elaborations of fairy tales. Evil must be accounted for rather than stated; destiny alterable rather than inevitable; magic elaborated rather than assumed.

The illustrations are Celtic in motif, Gothic in tone, medieval in costume and setting. The rendering of persona varies from realistic in the main characters to cartoonlike in special effects, as in the neon-eyed skeletons that rise to claim the Blue Faerie. Actually, most of the faeries are quite voluptuous, and the dominant flesh tones throughout contrast sharply with intense patterns of color. The effects of both art and text make this almost a completely different story from that presented by Hyman and Hutton.

The cartoon versions also vary widely. The Benjy and Bubbles version alternates a page of rhyming jingles with an illustration, which is captioned by an alternative summary of the verse text in choppy, so-called easy-to-read prose:

> Year after year, their great sadness grew
> And none in the Kingdom knew what to do.
> And when Benjy the bunny tried to cheer them,
> They just wept when he came near them.
>
> . . .
>
> A King and Queen were sad.
> They did not have a child.

The artistic tone is comic slapstick, with figures awkwardly posed, colors jarringly bright, and expressions vapid. The white bunny Benjy, representing the good principle, and the brown cat Bubbles, representing the wicked, crop up disconcertingly as plot indicators. They also serve to thin any harshness of theme in this and other tales in the series. The verse is metrically poor and awkwardly rhymed, the prose devoid of depth.

However, the devastation wreaked on Sleeping Beauty by this version is superseded generously by the next, *How to Wake a Sleeping Beauty,* which claims: "The Magic Road brings a new dimension to traditional children's stories and hours of extra pleasure to their readers."

Although this version bears little resemblance to the Grimms', it is not without some semblance of absurd humor:

> "If you wish to wake Sleeping Beauty, you will need some of my special potion. . . . I know it looks bad, . . . eye of newt, toe of beetle and all that, but it works."

> You let a few drops of the red liquid fall on Sleeping Beauty's face. There is a flash and a puff of smoke. Your potion has had a strange effect. Instead of the Sleeping Beauty, you are now looking at the Sleeping Toad! Well, you've been a lot of help! Go back to page yellow 1 and start again!

If it were not for the grotesquely ugly illustrations, one might construe this as a spoof, but alas, intentional wit is missing, a fact which does not alter the book's popularity among choose-your-own-ending adventure fans who enjoy the you-are-there gimmick: "After one brief sound of the horn, Prince Oscar appears in the room. He kisses Sleeping Beauty and she wakes. From the noise outside, it is clear that everyone in the palace is waking up. Outside the princess's room, they are all waiting to thank you, especially the king." Even as a game, however, the book seems more confusing than most in its genre. Nevertheless, the "choose-your-own-ending" syndrome obviously represents more than a fad, since several of the trade editions offer alternative resolutions. This may be an effort to adapt the tales to current needs in the way oral tradition did so freely, to render flexible those versions long frozen in print.

The last book in this group is a wordless picture book, eight thick-papered pages long, with a paragraph-long text on the back cover and a two-paragraph explanation to parents about the importance of fairy tales and how to use the book: "Intonation and inflection should be inserted to bring the surprise, fear, and happiness to life for the child. Gestures will further intensify the words, and any stock phrases or rhymes should be said with emphasis."

The watercolor art, representing a few major scenes from the plot, isn't lurid but is static, with a delicate avoidance of any skeletons in the hedge and a heavy reliance on nursery-decor pink.

It is clear from even this brief an overview of representative samples that at least three, perhaps four, of the six versions have so altered the basic elements and tone of the tale that the motivation for their publication must have been marketing potential rather than aesthetic or psychological appreciation of the story's value. This is not to challenge the tale's impact on the reading public. The effect of six editions is wider-reaching than the effect of two or three, cumulatively strengthening the place of the story in the canon of children's literature and, as a metaphor, in children's minds. Yet we must pose the question of whether these multiplied effects are not inspired as much or more by financial motivation as by folkloristic, Freudian, chauvinistic, artistic, literary, or historical reasons. I would suggest, at the very least, that the Grimms have always been good business, a practical asset in a tenuous trade, and that fairy tales as a barometer of juvenile publishing economics bear further investigation.

Notes

This article was originally published in *Book Research Quarterly* (2:4, Winter 1986-87), published by Transaction Periodicals Consortium. Copyright Transaction, Inc., 1987.

1. Brian Alderson, "Postscript to the 1975 edition" of Andrew Lang's *The Blue Fairy Book* (New York: Viking, 1978), p. 359.

2. Ibid.

3. J. R. R. Tolkien, "Tree and Leaf," *The Tolkien Reader* (New York: Ballantine Books, 1966), p. 65.

4. Ann Pellowski, "Internationalism in Children's Literature," in Zena Sutherland (ed.), *Children and Books*, 7th ed. (Glenview, Ill.: Scott, Foresman, 1986), p. 657.

Selected Bibliography

Editor's Note: This list represents a selection of items from the notes to the individual essays, together with additional references included to enhance its usefulness as a guide to further reading on the subject of the Grimms and folktale.

I. TRANSLATIONS

David, Alfred, and Mary Elizabeth David. *The Frog King and Other Tales of the Brothers Grimm.* New York: Signet Classics, New American Library of World Literature, 1964.

Delarue, Paul (ed.). *The Borzoi Book of French Folk Tales.* Translated by Austin E. Fife. New York: Knopf, 1956.

Grimm, Jacob, and Wilhelm Grimm. *Grimm's Fairy Tales: Complete Edition.* Translated by Margaret Hunt and [revised by] James Stern. Introduction by Padraic Colum. Afterword by Joseph Campbell. New York: Pantheon, 1944. (Paperback ed., New York: Random House, Pantheon Books, c. 1972.)

——. *The Grimms' German Folk Tales.* Translated by Francis P. Magoun, Jr. and Alexander H. Krappe. Carbondale: Southern Illinois University Press, 1960.

——. *The Complete Fairy Tales of the Brothers Grimm.* Translated by Jack Zipes. New York: Bantam, 1987.

Perrault, Charles. *Perrault's Complete Fairy Tales.* Translated by A. E. Johnson et al. New York: Dodd, Mead, 1961.

II. EDITIONS

Grimm, Jacob, and Wilhelm Grimm. *Die älteste Märchensammlung der Brüder Grimm: Synopse der handschriftlichen Urfassung von 1810 und der Erstdrucke von 1812.* Edited by Heinz Rölleke. Cologny-Genève: Fondation Martin Bodmer, 1975.

——. *Kinder- und Hausmärchen der Brüder Grimm in ihrer Urgestalt: Vollständige Ausgabe in der Urfassung [1812/1815].* Edited by Friedrich Panzer. Wiesbaden: Emil Vollmer, [1955].

——. *Kinder- und Hausmärchen: Gesammelt durch die Brüder Grimm. Vergrößerter Nachdruck der zweibändigen Erstausgabe von 1812 und 1815 nach dem Handexemplar des Brüder Grimm-Museums Kassel mit sämtlichen handschriftlichen Korrekturen und*

Nachträgen der Brüder Grimm sowie einem Ergänzungsheft, Transskriptionen und Kommentare. Edited by Heinz Rölleke with Ulrike Marquardt. 3 vols. Göttingen: Vandenhoeck & Ruprecht, 1986.

———. *Brüder Grimm: Kinder- und Hausmärchen, nach der zweiten vermehrten und verbesserten Auflage von 1819, textkritisch revidiert und mit einer Biographie der Grimmschen Märchen versehen.* Edited by Heinz Rölleke. Cologne: Eugen Diederichs, 1982.

———. *Kinder- und Hausmärchen: Kleine Ausgabe.* Berlin: Reimer, 1825.

———. *Kinder- und Hausmärchen: Ausgabe letzter Hand mit den Originalanmerkungen der Brüder Grimm, mit einem Anhang sämtlicher, nicht in allen Auflagen veröffentlichter Märchen.* Edited by Heinz Rölleke. 3 vols. Reclams Universal-Bibliothek, 3191–93. Stuttgart: Reclam, 1980.

———. *Märchen aus dem Nachlaß der Brüder Grimm.* Edited by Heinz Rölleke. Wuppertaler Schriftenreihe Literatur, 6. 3d rev. ed. Bonn: Bouvier, 1983.

III. GENERAL

Aarne, Antti, and Stith Thompson. *The Types of the Folktale: A Classification and Bibliography.* (See Thompson, Stith)

Beit, Hedwig von. *Symbolik des Märchens: Versuch einer Deutung.* 3 vols. 2d rev. ed. Berne: Francke, 1960.

Bettelheim, Bruno. *The Uses of Enchantment: The Meaning and Importance of Fairy Tales.* New York: Alfred A. Knopf, 1976; New York: Random House, Vintage Books, 1977.

Bottigheimer, Ruth B. (ed.). *Fairy Tales and Society: Illusion, Allusion and Paradigm.* Philadelphia: University of Pennsylvania Press, 1986.

Brackert, Helmut (ed.). *Und wenn sie nicht gestorben sind . . . : Perspektiven auf das Märchen.* edition suhrkamp, 973. Frankfurt a.M.: Suhrkamp, 1980.

Campbell, Joseph. *The Hero with a Thousand Faces.* 1949; New York: Meridian, 1956.

Carloni, Glauco. "La fiaba al lume della psicoanalisis." *Rivista di psicoanalisi,* 9 (1963), 169–86.

Christiansen, Reidar Thoralf. *European Folklore in America.* Oslo: Universitetsforlaget, 1962.

Cooper, J. C. *Fairy Tales: Allegories of the Inner Life.* Wellingborough, Northhamptonshire: Aquarian Press, 1983.

Darnton, Robert. *The Great Cat Massacre and Other Episodes in French Cultural History.* New York: Basic Books, 1984.

Dégh, Linda. *Folktales and Society: Storytelling in a Hungarian Peasant Community.* Bloomington: Indiana University Press, 1969.

Delarue, Paul. "Les contes merveilleux de Perrault et la tradition populaire." *Bulletin folklorique d'île-de-France,* 14 (1953), 511–17.

Doderer, Klaus (ed.). *Über Märchen für Kinder von heute.* Weinheim and Basel: Beltz, 1983.

Dorson, Richard M. "Folklore and Fakelore." *American Mercury,* 70 (1950), 335–43.

———. "Fakelore." *Zeitschrift für Volkskunde,* 65 (1969), 56–64.

Dundes, Alan (ed.). *The Study of Folklore.* Englewood Cliffs, N.J.: Prentice-Hall, 1965.

Dundes, Alan. "The Study of Folklore in Literature and Culture: Identification and Interpretation." *Journal of American Folklore,* 78 (1965), 136–42.

——. *Interpreting Folklore.* Bloomington: Indiana University Press, 1980.

——. "Nationalistic Inferiority Complexes and the Fabrication of Fakelore: A Reconsideration of Ossian, the *Kinder- und Hausmärchen,* the *Kalevala,* and Paul Bunyan." *Journal of Folklore Research,* 22 (1985), 5–18.

Fink, Gonthier-Louis. *Naissance et apogée du conte merveilleux en Allemagne.* Annales littéraires de l'Université de Besançon, 80. Paris: Les belles lettres, 1966.

Franz, Marie-Louise von. *An Introduction to the Interpretation of Fairy Tales.* New York: Spring, 1970.

——. *Problems of the Feminine in Fairy Tales.* Rev. ed. New York: Spring, 1976.

Fromm, Erich. *The Forgotten Language: An Introduction to the Understanding of Dreams, Fairy Tales and Myths.* New York: Rinehart, 1951.

Göttner-Abendroth, Heide. *Die Göttin und ihr Heros: Die matriarchalen Religionen in Mythos, Märchen und Dichtung.* 3d ed. Munich: Verlag Frauenoffensive, 1983.

Henssen, Gottfried. "Deutsche Schreckmärchen und ihre europäischen Anverwandten." *Zeitschrift für Volkskunde,* 50 (1953), 84–97.

Heuscher, Julius E. *A Psychiatric Study of Fairy Tales: Their Origin, Meaning and Usefulness.* 2d rev. ed. Springfield, Il.: Charles C. Thomas, 1974.

Holbek, Bengt. *Interpretation of Fairy Tales.* FFC 229. Helsinki: Academia scientiarum fennica, 1987.

Karlinger, Felix (ed.). *Wege der Märchenforschung.* Wege der Forschung, 255. Darmstadt: Wissenschaftliche Buchgesellschaft, 1973.

Krappe, Alexander Haggerty. *The Science of Folklore.* New York: Dial, 1930.

Laiblin, Wilhelm (ed.). *Märchenforschung und Tiefenpsychologie.* Wege der Forschung, 102. Darmstadt: Wissenschaftliche Buchgesellschaft, 1969.

Liebermann, Marcia R. " 'Some Day My Prince Will Come': Female Acculturation through the Fairy Tale." *College English,* 34 (1972–73), 383–95.

Lüthi, Max. *Volksmärchen und Volkssage: Zwei Grundformen erzählender Dichtung.* Berne and Munich: Francke, 1961.

——. *Märchen.* 2d rev. ed. Sammlung Metzler, 16. Stuttgart: J. B. Metzler, 1964.

——. *Es war einmal . . . : Vom Wesen des Volksmärchens.* Kleine Vandenhoeckreihe, 136–37. 3d ed. Göttingen: Vandenhoeck & Ruprecht, 1968.

——. *Das Volksmärchen als Dichtung: Ästhetik und Anthropologie.* Studien zur Volkserzählung, 1. Cologne: Eugen Diederichs, 1975.

——. *The European Folktale: Form and Nature.* Translated by John D. Niles. Philadelphia: Institute for the Study of Human Issucs, 1982.

Mallet, Carl-Heinz. *Kennen Sie Kinder?* Hamburg: Hoffmann und Campe, 1981. Translated by Joachim Neugroschel as *Fairy Tales and Children.* New York: Schocken, 1984.

——. *Kopf ab! Gewalt im Märchen.* Hamburg: Rasch und Rohring, 1985.

Metzger, Michael M., and Katharina Mommsen (eds.). *Fairy Tales as Ways of Knowing.* Berne: Peter Lang, 1981.

Nitschke, August. *Soziale Ordnungen im Spiegel der Märchen.* 2 vols. Stuttgart-Bad Cannstadt: Frommann-Holzboog, 1976–77.

Propp, Vladimir. *Morphology of the Folktale.* Translated by Laurence Scott. 2d rev. ed. Edited by Louis A. Wagner. Austin: University of Texas Press, 1968. (Orig. publ. in Russian, 1928.)

———. *Theory and History of Folklore.* Minneapolis: University of Minnesota Press, 1984.

Ranke, Kurt (ed.). *Enzyklopädie des Märchens: Handwörterbuch zur historischen und vergleichenden Erzählforschung.* 12 vols. (planned). Berlin: Walter de Gruyter, 1975-.

Ranke, Kurt. *Die Welt der einfachen Formen.* Berlin: Walter de Gruyter, 1978.

Röhrich, Lutz. *Märchen und Wirklichkeit.* Wiesbaden: Franz Steiner, 1956.

———. "Sprichwörtliche Redensarten aus Volkserzählungen." In Karl Bischoff and Lutz Röhrich (eds.), *Volk, Sprache, Dichtung: Festgabe für Kurt Wagner.* Gießen: Wilhelm Schmitz, 1960, pp. 267–69.

———. *Sage und Märchen: Erzählforschung heute.* Freiburg im Breisgau: Herder, 1976.

Rowe, Karen E. "Feminism and Fairy Tales." *Women's Studies: An Interdisciplinary Journal,* 6 (1979), 237-57.

Rumpf, Marianne. *Ursprung und Entstehung von Warn- und Schreckmärchen.* Folklore Fellows' Communications, 160. Helsinki: Suomalainen Tiedeakatemia, 1955.

Scherf, Walter. *Lexikon der Zaubermärchen.* 2d ed. Kröners Taschenausgabe, 472. Stuttgart: Alfred Kröner, 1986.

Stone, Kay F. "Things Walt Disney Never Told Us." *Women and Folklore* (special issue of *American Folklore*), 88, (1975), 42–50. (This issue also appeared as Claire R. Farrer [ed.], *Women and Folklore.* Austin: University of Texas Press, 1975.)

———. "The Misuses of Enchantment: Controversies on the Significance of Fairy Tales." In Rosan A. Jordan and Susan J. Kalcik (eds.), *Women's Folklore, Women's Culture.* Publications of the American Folklore Society, 8. Philadelphia: University of Pennsylvania Press, 1985.

Thompson, Stith. *Motif-Index of Folk-Literature: A Classification of Narrative Elements in Folktale, Ballads, Myths, Fables, Mediaeval Romances, Exempla, Jest Books, and Local Legends.* 6 vols. Folklore Fellows' Communications, 106–11. 2d ed. Copenhagen: Rosenkilde and Bagger, 1955-58.

———. *The Folktale.* New York: Holt, Rinehart and Winston, 1946; rpt. Berkeley: University of California Press, 1977.

———. "Fifty Years of Folktale Indexing." In Wayland D. Hand and G. O. Arlt (eds.), *Humaniora Essays in Literature, Folklore, Bibliography Honoring Archer Taylor on His Seventieth Birthday.* New York: Augustin, 1960, pp. 49–57.

———. *The Types of the Folktale: A Classification and Bibliography. Antti Aarne's Verzeichnis der Märchentypen Translated and Enlarged by Stith Thompson.* Helsinki: Suomalainen Tiedeakatemia, 1961.

Waelti-Walters, Jennifer. *Fairy Tales and the Female Imagination.* Montreal: Eden, 1982.

Wesselski, Albert. *Versuch einer Theorie des Märchens.* Prager deutsche Studien, 15. Reichenberg: Sudetendeutscher Verlag Franz Kraus, 1931.

Winterstein, Alfred. "Die Pubertätsriten der Mädchen und ihre Spuren im Märchen." *Imago,* 14 (1928), 199-274.

Zipes, Jack. *Breaking the Magic Spell: Radical Theories of Folk and Fairy Tales.* Austin: University of Texas Press, 1979.

——. *Fairy Tales and the Art of Subversion: The Classical Genre and the Process of Civilization.* New York: Wildman, 1983.

——. *Don't Bet on the Prince: Contemporary Feminist Fairy Tales in North America and England.* New York: Methuen, 1986.

IV. The Grimms and Folktale

Bastian, Ulrike. *Die Kinder- und Hausmärchen der Brüder Grimm in der literatur-pädagogischen Diskussion des 19. und 20. Jahrhunderts.* Frankfurt a.M.: Haag & Herelsen, 1981.

Berendsohn, Walter A. *Grundformen volkstümlicher Erzählerkunst in den Kinder- und Hausmärchen der Brüder Grimm.* 2d rev. ed. Wiesbaden: D. Martin Sändig, 1968.

Bolte, Johannes, and Georg Polívka. *Anmerkungen zu den Kinder- und Hausmärchen der Brüder Grimm.* 5 vols. Leipzig: Dieterich, 1913–32; rpt. Hildesheim: Georg Olms, 1963.

Bottigheimer, Ruth B. *Grimms' Bad Girls and Bold Boys: The Moral and Social Vision of the Tales.* New Haven: Yale University Press, 1987.

Dégh, Linda. "*Grimm's Household Tales* and Its Place in the Household: The Social Relevance of a Controversial Classic." *Western Folklore,* 38 (April, 1979), 83–103.

Ellis, John M. *One Fairy Story Too Many: The Brothers Grimm and Their Tales.* Chicago: University of Chicago Press, 1983.

Hagen, Rolf. "Perraults Märchen und die Brüder Grimm." *Zeitschrift für Deutsche Philologie,* 74 (1955), 392–410.

Hand, Wayland D. "Die Märchen der Brüder Grimm in den Vereinigten Staaten." *Hessische Blätter,* 54 (1963), 525–44.

Hennig, Dieter, and Bernhard Lauer (eds.). *Die Brüder Grimm: Dokumente ihres Lebens und Wirkens.* Kassel: Weber & Weidemeyer, 1985.

Mieder, Wolfgang. " 'Das muß ich über den grünen Klee loben': Wilhelm Grimms Sprichwörter und Redensarten in den Märchen." In Wolfgang Mieder, *"Findet, so werdet ihr suchen!": Die Brüder Grimm und das Sprichwort.* Berne: Peter Lang, 1986.

——. *Grimms Märchen-modern: Prosa, Gedichte, Karikaturen.* Stuttgart: Reclam, 1979.

Nissen, Walter. *Die Brüder Grimm und ihre Märchen.* Göttingen: Vandenhoeck & Ruprecht, 1984.

Rölleke, Heinz. "Die 'stockhessischen' Märchen der 'alten Marie': Das Ende eines Mythos um die frühesten KHM-Aufzeichnungen der Brüder Grimm." *Germanisch-Romanische Monatsschrift,* n.s. 25 (1975), 74–86.

——. "John M. Ellis: One Fairy Story Too Many." *Fabula,* 25 (1984), 330–32.

——. *Die Märchen der Brüder Grimm.* Artemis Einführungen, 18. Munich: Artemis, 1985.

——. *Wo das Wünschen noch geholfen hat: Gesammelte Aufsätze zu den Kinder- und Hausmärchen der Brüder Grimm.* Wuppertaler Schriftenreihe Literatur, 23. Bonn: Bouvier, 1985.

Schindehütte, Albert (ed.). *Krauses Grimm'sche Märchen.* Kassel: Johannes Staude, 1985.

Schmidt, Kurt. *Die Entwicklung der Grimmschen Kinder- und Hausmärchen seit der Urhandschrift nebst einem kritischen Texte der in die Drucke übergegangenen Stücke.* Hermaea, 30. Halle: Max Niemeyer, 1932; rpt. Walluf-Wiesbaden: Martin Sändig, 1973.

Schoof, Wilhelm. *Zur Entstehungsgeschichte der Grimmschen Märchen: Bearbeitet unter Benutzung des Nachlasses der Brüder Grimm.* Hamburg: Ernst Hauswedell, 1959.

Spörk, Ingrid. *Studien zu ausgewählten Märchen der Brüder Grimm: Frauenproblematik-Struktur-Rollentheorie-Psychoanalyse-Überlieferung-Rezeption.* Diss. Graz, 1983. Hochschulschriften Literaturwissenschaft, 66. Königstein/Taunus: Anton Hain, 1985.

Tatar, Maria M. *The Hard Facts of the Grimms' Fairy Tales.* Princeton: Princeton University Press, 1987.

V. INDIVIDUAL TALES

Belgrader, Michael. *Das Märchen von dem Machandelbaum.* Frankfurt a.M.: Peter Lang, 1980.

Bricout, Bernadette. "Les deux chemins du petit chaperon rouge." In James C. Austin et al. (eds.), *Frontières du Conte.* Paris: Éditions du Centre national de la recherche scientifique, 1982.

Calvetti, Anselmo. "Una versione romagnola di Cappuccetto Rosso." *In Rumâgna,* 2 (1975), 85–95.

——. "Tracce di Riti di Iniziazione nelle Fiabe di Cappuccetto Rosso e delle Tre Ochine." *Lares,* 46 (1980), 487–96.

Christiansen, Reidar Thoralf. *The Tale of the Two Travellers or the Blinded Man.* Helsinki: Suomalainen Tiedeakatemia, 1916.

Cox, Marian Roalfe. *Cinderella: Three Hundred and Forty-Five Variants of Cinderella, Catskin, and Cap o'Rushes.* Publications of the Folklore Society, 31. 1893; rpt. Nendeln/Liechtenstein: Kraus 1967.

Delarue, Paul. "Le Petit Chaperon Rouge." *Bulletin folklorique d'île-de-France,* N.S. 12 (1951), 221–28, 251–60, 283–91.

Dollerup, Cay; Iven Reventlow; and Carsten Rosenberg. "A Case Study of Editorial Filters in Folktales: A Discussion of the Allerleirauh Tales in Grimm." *Fabula,* 27, nos. 1–2 (1986), 12–30.

Drewermann, Eugen. *Schneeweißchen und Rosenrot.* Olten and Freiburg im Breisgau: Walter, 1980.

Dundes, Alan. *Cinderella: A Folklore Casebook.* New York: Wildman, 1983.

Fink, Gonthier-Louis. "Les Avatars de Rumpelstilzchen: La Vie d'un Conte Populaire." In Ernst Kracht (ed.), *Deutsch-französische Gespräche im Lichte der Märchen.* Münster: Aschendorff, 1964, pp. 46–72.

Girardot, N. J. "Initiation and Meaning in the Tale of Snow White and the Seven Dwarfs." *Journal of American Folklore,* 90 (1977), 274–300.

Hanks, Carole, and D. T. Hanks, Jr. "Perrault's 'Little Red Riding Hood': Victim of the Revisers." *Children's Literature,* 7 (1978), 68–77.

Jäger, Hans-Wolf. "Trägt Rotkäppchen eine Jakobiner-Mütze? Über mutmaßliche

Konnotate bei Tieck und Grimm." In Joachim Bark (ed.), *Literatursoziologie.* Vol. 2. Stuttgart: W. Kohlhammer, 1974, pp. 159–80.

Jones, Steven Swann. "The Structure of Snow White." *Fabula,* 24 (1983), 56–71.

Karlinger, Felix. " 'Schneeweißchen und Rosenrot in Sardinien: Zur Übernahme eines Buchmärchens in die volkstümliche Erzähltradition." *Hessische Blätter,* 54 (1973), 585–93.

Lüthi, Max. "Die Herkunft des Grimmschen Rapunzelmärchens (AaTh 310)." *Fabula,* 3 (1959), 95–118.

Mieder, Wolfgang. "Survival Forms of 'Little Red Riding Hood' in Modern Society." *International Folklore Review,* 2 (1982), 23–40.

Pancritius, M. "Aus mütterrechtlicher Zeit: Rotkäppchen." *Anthropos,* 27 (1932), 743–78.

Ritz, Hans. *Die Geschichte vom Rotkäppchen.* Emstal: Muriverlag, 1981.

Roberts, Warren E. *The Tale of the Kind and Unkind Girls: AA–TH 480 and Related Tales.* Berlin: Walter de Gruyter, 1958.

Róheim, Géza. "The Wolf and the Seven Kids." *Psychoanalytic Quarterly,* 22 (1953), 253–56.

Röhrich, Lutz. "Der Froschkönig und ihre Wandlungen." *Fabula,* 20 (1979), 170–92.

Rooth, Anna Birgitta. *The Cinderella Cycle.* Lund: C. W. K. Gleerup, 1951.

Rumpf, Marianne. "Rotkäppchen: Eine vergleichende Märchenuntersuchung." Diss., Göttingen, 1951.

Soriano, Marc. "Le petit chaperon rouge." *Nouvelle Revue Française,* 16 (1968), 429–43.

Verdier, Yvonne. "Le petit Chaperon Rouge dans la tradition orale." *le débat,* no. 3 (juillet-août, 1980), 31–61. Orig. as "Grands-mères, si vous saviez: le Petit Chaperon dans la tradition orale," *Cahiers de Littérature Orale,* 4 (1978), 17–55.

Veszy-Wagner, Lilla. "Little Red Riding Hood on the Couch." *Psychoanalytic Forum,* 1 (1966), 400–415.

Zipes, Jack. *The Trials and Tribulations of Little Red Riding Hood.* South Hadley, Mass.: Bergin and Garvey, 1983.

——. "A Second Gaze at 'Little Red Riding Hood's Tribulations,' " *The Lion and the Unicorn,* 7-8 (1983-84), 78–109.

Notes on the Contributors

RUTH B. BOTTIGHEIMER, adjunct assistant professor at the State University of New York, Stony Brook, organized the 1984 conference on folktale at Princeton, and edited essays from that conference as *Fairy Tales and Society: Illusion, Allusion and Paradigm* (1986). She is author of *Grimms' Bad Girls and Bold Boys: The Moral and Social Vision of the Tales* (1987).

LINDA DÉGH, distinguished professor of folklore at the Folklore Institute, Indiana University, is a past president of the American Folklore Society. Her books include *Folktales of Hungary* (1965) and *Folktales and Society: Storytelling in a Hungarian Peasant Community* (1969); and she edited *Studies in East European Folk Narrative* (1978).

ALAN DUNDES is professor of anthropology and folklore at the University of California, Berkeley, and a past president of the American Folklore Society. He is author of *Interpreting Folklore* (1980) and *Life Is like a Chicken-Coop Ladder: A Portrait of German Culture through Folklore* (1984), and edited *The Study of Folklore* (1965).

GONTHIER-LOUIS FINK, professor at the Institut d'Études Allemandes, University of Strasbourg (France), wrote *Naissance et apogée du conte merveilleux en Allemagne 1740-1800* (Birth and Apogee of Wondrous Tales in Germany, 1966).

BETSY HEARNE, assistant professor, Graduate Library School, University of Chicago, wrote *Choosing Books for Children: A Commonsense Guide* (1981), and edited *Celebrating Children's Books: Essays on Children's Literature in Honor of Zena Sutherland* (1981). She was editor of the Children's Books Section *Booklist* of the American Library Association from 1973 to 1985, and is editor of the *Bulletin of the Center for Children's Books*.

WOLFGANG MIEDER, professor of German at the University of Vermont, has written especially on proverbs. Among his books are *Das Sprichwort in der deutschen Prosaliteratur des 19. Jahrhunderts* (Proverbs in German Fiction of the 19th Century, 1975), *Das Sprichwort in unserer Zeit* (Proverbs in Our Time, 1975), *Proverbs in Literature: An International Bibliography* (1978), *"Findet, so werdet ihr suchen!": Die Brüder Grimm und das Sprichwort* ("Find, then you will seek": The Brothers Grimm and Proverbs, 1986).

AUGUST NITSCHKE, professor of German at the Institut für Sozialforschung, University of Stuttgart (West Germany), authored the two-volume study *Soziale Ordnungen im Spiegel der Märchen* (Social Order as Reflected in Fairy Tale, 1976–77).

LUTZ RÖHRICH is director of the Folklore Institute, University of Freiburg (West Germany). His books include *Märchen und Wirklichkeit* (Fairy Tale and Reality, 1956) and *Sage und Märchen: Erzählforschung heute* (Legend and Fairy Tale: Narrative Research Today, 1976). He is an editor of the multivolume *Enzyklopädie des Märchens* (Encyclopedia of Fairy Tale).

HEINZ RÖLLEKE, professor of language and literature at the Bergische Universität/Gesamthochschule Wuppertal (West Germany), has reported his findings on the Grimms and their tales chiefly in articles, twenty of which he collected and published as *"Wo das Wünschen noch geholfen hat": Gesammelte Aufsätze zu den Kinder- und Hausmärchen der Brüder Grimm* ("When Wishing Still Helped": Collected Essays about *Grimms' Fairy Tales*, 1985). He is also editor of several important scholarly editions of the Grimms' stories, including *Die älteste Märchensammlung der Brüder Grimm* (The Grimm Brothers' Oldest Fairy Tale Collection, 1975).

WALTER SCHERF served as director of the Internationale Jugendbibliothek (International Youth Library) for almost thirty years and teaches at the University of Munich. His books include *Lexikon der Zaubermärchen* (Encyclopedia of Magic Tales, 1982; 2d ed. 1986) and *Die Herausforderung des Dämons: Form und Funktion grausiger Kindermärchen* (The Demon's Challenge: The Form and Function of Terrifying Children's Fairy Tales, 1987).

KAY STONE, associate professor of folklore, University of Winnipeg (Canada), is author of articles on reception of the Grimms' tales in North America, especially as adapted by the Disney films and as received by women. She is also a professional storyteller.

MARIA M. TATAR, professor of German, Harvard University, wrote *Spellbound: Studies on Mesmerism in Literature* (1978) and *The Hard Facts of the Grimms' Fairy Tales* (1987).

DONALD WARD, professor of German and Folklore, University of California, Los Angeles, won second place in the Chicago Folklore Prize competition for his book *The Divine Twins* (1968), and edited and translated *The*

German Legends of the Brothers Grimm (1981). He is an associate editor of *Fabula: International Journal of Folktale Studies.*

JACK ZIPES, professor of German, University of Florida, is an editor of *New German Critique.* Among his books are *Breaking the Magic Spell: Radical Theories of Folk and Fairy Tale* (1979), *The Trials and Tribulations of Red Riding Hood* (1983), and *Fairy Tales and the Art of Subversion: The Classical Genre for Children and the Process of Civilization* (1983).

Index